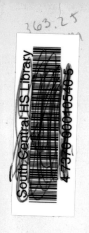

THE FORENSIC SCIENCE OF C.S.I.

Also by Katherine Ramsland

THE
FORENSIC SCIENCE OF
C.S.I.

Katherine Ramsland

BERKLEY BOULEVARD BOOKS, NEW YORK

A Berkley Boulevard Book
Published by The Berkley Publishing Group
A division of Penguin Putnam Inc.
375 Hudson Street
New York, New York 10014

This book was not authorized, prepared, licensed, or endorsed by any entity involved in creating or producing the *C.S.I.* television series.

PRINTING HISTORY
Berkley Boulevard trade paperback edition / September 2001

Visit our website at www.penguinputnam.com

Library of Congress Cataloging-in-Publication Data

Ramsland, Katherine M., 1953–
The forensic science of C.S.I. / Katherine Ramsland.
p.   cm.
ISBN 0-425-18359-9
1. Crime scene searches.   2. Forensic sciences.   3. CSI: crime scene investigation.   I. Title: Forensic science of CSI.   II. Title.

HV8073 .R325 2001
363.25—dc21
2001035327

PRINTED IN THE UNITED STATES OF AMERICA

10 9 8 7 6 5 4 3 2 1

For Ruth Osborne,
because she shared the experience

CONTENTS

Acknowledgments

Many people helped with different parts of this project, and I wish to thank each of the professionals noted or quoted in the book as well as those below who are otherwise unacknowledged:

The New Jersey State Police Forensic Science Bureau personnel went out of their way to explain how various things work in a crime lab, in particular, Lieutenant John Hook and Linda Jankowski.

Thanks to Josh Behar, who'd already sent me off to learn about autopsies and medical examiners, and to Tee, who gave me a lead in that same direction.

Many thanks to Ruth Osborne, who helped circumvent my ineptness with a VCR, and to Sally Craggs, from the *C.S.I.* chat list, who taped the early episodes. Also from the list, Justin gave me the lead on the scent pads. Diane Alington provided a patient ear as I worked my way through the book.

I'm also grateful to Elyse for her *C.S.I.* website, and for keeping all of us informed about upcoming episodes and articles.

I may be most grateful to Marilyn Bardsley, who got me started writing about forensic science and who keeps me immersed in every facet of crime. That interest probably started with Dean Koontz, whose own immersion in criminal psychology was inspiring. Thanks, Dean. And thanks to my professors at John Jay College of Criminal Justice.

Lastly, it was fun working with Kim Waltemyer, who followed the course of various crimes and was genuinely eager to know more about these procedures.

Introduction

C.S.I.: Crime Scene Investigation features a team of passionate crime scene investigators led by unit supervisor Gil Grissom on the night shift in the city of Las Vegas, Nevada. Using the latest techniques of forensic science, Gil, Catherine, Nick, Warrick, and Sara work under pressure to collect and analyze evidence for solving a gamut of criminal acts from theft to rape to murder. Even the tiniest piece of glass or fiber can make all the difference. And while their analyses often help to solve a mystery, a lot of the technology and methodology they use *remains* a mystery to watchers. The following pages will offer all the evidence needed to demystify the jargon and unravel the science.

Crime scene investigators are not freelance detectives à la Sherlock Holmes. They work for the state, or more precisely, the court, and everything they do has a legal goal: find provable evidence of who did this, how they did it, and why. Thus, the court system and its rules of admissibility are always in the background, influencing the evidence collection process.

A primary concern is evidence handling. In "Sex, Lies, and Larvae," Warrick grumbles about having the boring job of testifying on the chain of custody of some piece of evidence, and Grissom warns him not to view such testimony lightly. Juries need to feel confident about the evidential process. In fact, evidence handled badly can be successfully challenged, letting a dangerous killer or rapist walk free. That means that all their hard work might be done for nothing. Before they even get to a crime scene, they need to know the legal demands, and while there, they must stick to the rules.

Everything that a crime investigator does may be held up for display in a courtroom. It's likely that Grissom and his band of C.S.I.s are in court fairly often. In fact, many crime labs and crime investigation units run moot courts to expose their personnel to legal interrogation. Since their work is aimed toward finding evidence that proves motive and convicts (or exonerates) a suspect in a crime, it's instructive to understand how the court receives it.

First, C.S.I.s need to know about prior cases, since unusual new evidence faces resistance. When Warrick discovers that a thief left an earprint, Catherine questions its feasibility for a case. He reminds her of a 1999 case in Washington state that successfully convicted a man based on earprint evidence. However, he doesn't seem to know that the appeals court threw out the verdict because earprint technology was not yet proven as a scientific method.

What does this mean? If they follow scientific procedure, how can the legal world say it isn't so?

That's the second thing the C.S.I.s need to realize.

Courts are notoriously conservative, but it's also true that many "experts" hawk their theories as "scientific," and judges don't have time to thoroughly examine each and every one. Claiming expertise does not make one an expert in the eyes of the law, and just because some technique of collection or analysis is "scientific" does not make it automatically admissible. For example, the new technique of "brain fingerprinting" is being proposed as science, but it will get the same extensive legal scrutiny that DNA and fingerprinting got before they were finally accepted. And even fingerprinting has been questioned lately by the courts.

So what must the C.S.I.s keep in mind for expert testimony about evidence analysis? Two court rulings: *Frye* and *Daubert*.

In 1923, the District of Columbia Court of Appeals issued a guideline for the admissibility of scientific evidence. In a case known as *Frye* v. *United States*, the defense counsel tried to enter evidence about a device that measured blood pressure during deception (a forerunner to the polygraph). The court decided that the claim or theory on which testimony is based must be "sufficiently established to have gained general acceptance in the particular field in which it belongs." That is, it had to be accepted by the relevant scientific community. This *Frye* Standard became general practice for many years.

Critics, however, claimed that it excluded theories that were novel but supported by evidence. For some types of evidence—specifically from behavioral science—the *Frye* test was more effectively replaced in many states by a standard cited in 1993 in the Supreme Court's landmark decision in *Daubert* v. *Merrill Dow Pharmaceuticals, Inc.* The court decided that the *Frye* Standard was not a necessary prerequisite and conferred on the trial judge the responsibility for deciding if evidence is sufficiently reliable to be admitted. Thus, "scientific" has come to mean being grounded in the methods and procedures of science, and "knowledge" must be stronger than subjective belief or speculation. The judge has only to focus on the methodology, not on the conclusion, and must determine:

- whether the theory can be tested

- whether the potential error rate is known

- whether it was reviewed by peers and has attracted widespread acceptance within a relevant scientific community

- whether the opinion is relevant to the issue in dispute

- whether there are standards that control the technique's operation

In other words, the court wants to avoid pseudoscience, so entering evidence on something like an earprint must pass these standards. While that did not happen in the case that Warrick cites, it can still happen in the future as increasingly more scientists support the reliability of the earprint. New techniques can be admitted for special circumstances, but only if they are based on scientifically valid principles.

Not all cases are equal, however. The same treatment does not apply in family court, and since plenty of gang violence occurs in Vegas among kids, the team must also be aware of juvenile proceedings. While juveniles have the right to due process and to a lawyer, they generally get lesser sentences—even if they commit the same crimes that adults are committing. This kind of leniency can frustrate investigators, as it does Sara when a teenager rapes and shoots a woman in "Too Tough to Die."

Unfortunately, they're bound by the system. The problem is that it's a system that evolved from nineteenth-century beliefs about children, formed without awareness of the brutality and violence that kids today can exhibit. Family court, where juvenile cases are heard, developed under the doctrine that children under seventeen were too immature to form criminal intent and the court was to act as a benign, rehabilitating parent.

Courts became like social service agencies. Punishment was lenient and court personnel were informal. The "courtroom" was a family conference around a table. The first crime was generally dismissed and probation officers were assigned to give judges progress reports, with a maximum sentence of eighteen months.

Although an increase in violent juvenile crime in the 1980s precipitated some reforms, including the waiver of children into adult courts, the leniency problems still exist. Kids can shrug off their crimes. That means that the C.S.I.s can work as hard on evidence for a juvenile case as they do for an adult case, but the end result can be much less satisfying.

In any event, they do work for the courts and must remain aware of what the system both demands and disallows. With that in mind, let's go right to the crime scenes and follow the evidence.

ONE

Scene of the Crime

CRIME SCENE ANALYSIS

A crime scene is a location where an illegal act took place, from assault to burglary to murder, and it comprises the area from which most of the physical evidence is retrieved. Crime scenes can be anywhere. In the desert. Beneath a house. Inside a long-distance truck. Even a body can be a crime scene (as with a man who apparently jumped to his death). A single crime might join two or more places, as in "Cool Change," when a man is pushed off a hotel balcony (the hotel room and the sidewalk are the crime scenes). Conversely, the same place may be the scene of multiple crimes, as in "Table Stakes," when the C.S.I.s suspect a second murder took place on a property where another body is found. No matter the crime scene, however, Grissom urges the team to "read the room," or "listen" to the body before doing anything, a Zen-like approach of assessing the whole before looking at its parts.

Indeed, crime scene analysis is a combination of criminalistics and criminology. Criminalistics is the application of science to the physical evidence, such as bloodstains, DNA, and bullet trajectories. Criminology includes the psychological angle, which involves studying crime scenes for motives, traits, and behavior that will help to interpret the evidence. For example, when the paint from the dented fender of a man's car matches the paint found on the body of a hit-and-run victim, criminalistics links him to the crime. However, when his confession rings false, ideas about deception on the part of an ordinary person involved in a crime come from criminology, and the investigator then takes the case further to see what the man is hiding. While a crime scene unit tends to focus on the physical evidence, some psychology is always at play, and at times the team must consider this before drawing conclusions.

When some area becomes a crime scene, the primary concern is to preserve it for evidence. How the evidence gets handled depends on what it is. Investigators come in with different types of kits to ensure that everything is properly documented and collected. That means the crime scene itself is key to any criminal investigation.

With that in mind, let's look at how a crime scene is defined, who manages it, what equipment they use, and how they collect and transport evidence.

THE INITIAL CALL

When a crime is initially discovered, a call goes out to authorities—generally via 911. A dispatcher then notifies patrol units in the neighborhood to check it out. Uniformed police arrive and make a decision as to whether they need other personnel (the homicide or arson unit, for example). They note the time and write down or record any other pertinent observations, such as whether doors or windows were open, but refrain from touching or moving anything. Evidence can be found anywhere, including on doorknobs and light switches. Officers should note whether there are any distinct odors, the lights are on or off, the blinds are drawn, mail or newspapers have piled up, or food is spoiled. If someone at the scene is attempting to clean it up (a frequent occurrence), that person must be stopped. It may be that some of the scene can be restored, as when Grissom discovers that a supermarket employee has cleaned mustard from the spot from which a woman disappeared and replicates the evidence by smashing a jar of mustard on the floor. Re-creations such as this can help investigators make further discoveries.

Investigators must assume that whoever was at the scene has left something there or taken something away, and probably both. As Grissom points out to Nick, this is Locard's Exchange Principle.

Dr. Edmond Locard believed that "every contact leaves a trace," and he relied on this principle when he began his forensic laboratory in Lyons, France, in 1910—one of the first in the world. In other words, there's a cross-transference of small traces between a perpetrator and a victim or the crime scene. Locard proved it when he looked into the case of Émile Gourbin, a man accused of strangling his mistress. Gourbin had an alibi, but Locard scraped beneath the man's fingernails and found flakes of skin coated with the dead woman's face powder. Gourbin subsequently confessed.

Some of the most compelling evidence that convicted serial killer Ted Bundy of the murder of his last victim were ninety-eight cross-transfers of fiber, some found on her from his vehicle, some on him from her clothing.

Whether the suspect left something or took something, it's up to the C.S.I.s (also called crime scene analysts or Ident technicians) to make the connection. To preserve all traces, officers must take care to avoid contamination and they must also restrict access to all non-principal personnel, including curious officers. Too many feet coming into a crime scene can obliterate evidence on the floor or ground. (In the famous case of Dr. Sam Sheppard, who served ten years for the murder of his wife, an officer casually flushed a toilet containing a cigarette. That lost evidence may have been significant, since no one in the home smoked.) Also, if an officer moves something (like a gun used for suicide) or leaves something behind, it can deflect the direction of the investigation. Grissom constantly reminds police officers and rescue personnel to be careful at the scene. If they leave footprints or fingerprints, it can confuse the case; if they step on something or touch something, it can obliterate evidence.

In the event that there is a seriously injured person at the scene, such as with the Jane Doe in "Too Tough to Die," the first priority is first aid and transport to the hospital, even if that damages evidence. The officer should note the person's position when found and record a description of wounds or injuries.

If the perpetrator is present, the officer makes an arrest. Any and all suspects are detained. Otherwise, the officers control the scene by marking the perimeter with tape or an obvious barrier, and by keeping everyone clear of the defined area. This prevents the destruction of evidence. For example, if someone is found hanging who clearly is dead, he needs to remain hanged until the crime scene unit arrives. If the rope looks like it might break, the officer must try to support the body. If for any reason the body must be moved, then the officer needs to take accurate notes, sketch the pose of the corpse when found, and transport it in that same pose, if possible. If found facedown, it must remain facedown.

One of the primary criticisms in the investigation into the death of JonBenet Ramsey, the six-year-old beauty queen who was found murdered in the basement of her family home, is that she was moved by her father from where she was found. There was no possibility of getting trace materials from the surface of her body because he covered her with a blanket and carried her upstairs. Then he and his wife both held her and hugged her while a dismayed cop looked on.

AN ASIDE ABOUT SIN CITY

The locale of a crime often establishes a frame of reference for the investigation. In *C.S.I.*, the setting is Las Vegas, named by the early Spanish explorers "the Meadow."

The general area is a broad desert valley of hot, dry terrain with little vegetation, but the city is built on what had been a charming oasis. At first it was used as a service stop for the transcontinental railroad, but now it's home to skyscraper hotels, nonstop entertainment, and opulent gambling casinos. Racketeers from all over came to set up shop and flex their muscles, and for a while the place was dominated by the Italian-Jewish crime syndicate. Huge hotels went up, crowned by an entire strip of flashy neon signs, and inside the showgirls wore increasingly less clothing. Then Howard Hughes's multiple investments gave the place respectability and corporations moved in. They rebuilt many of the casinos into fabulous hotels that included activities for the entire family, making millions for their efforts. During the past two decades, the race has been on to see who could build the hotel/casino with the most rooms, the most imaginative decor, the most slots, and the best shows.

These days thirty million visitors arrive annually to lose some $8 billion in the casinos, stay in the 125,000 hotel rooms, see shows, or get married in some wedding chapel with an Elvis Presley look-alike. To go to the City of Sin means to let loose. Rules that guide behavior back home don't count there. "I'm in Vegas" is often the excuse heard by the C.S.I.s when they catch someone committing a crime, and people gamble, have sex, eat, and drink in ways that transform them into strangers even to themselves. This is glamorous hedonism at its height and people are there to forget themselves.

The city has its own jargon, much of it tied to the casinos, and that shows up in episodes that involve gambling-related crimes, such as a "hit" on a "runner."

Las Vegas appears to be the nation's suicide capital—many of the victims from out of town and mostly men—and this must be kept in mind for every death investigation that is not clearly a homicide. People have died from guns, overdoses, hanging, and carbon monoxide poisoning. Only a small percentage of suicides jump off buildings.

Consistent with the city's history, the show often gives the feeling of a sinister mob presence, when some murders get investigated as professional hits. In "Table Stakes," Warrick finds no clues to solve the death of a man in an elevator, shot with a stolen gun and decorated with a symbol known to organized crime. In another episode, Nick and Catherine scour a restaurant where five people died, including the former owner of a casino and his bodyguard.

Even Liberace gets into the picture in "Table Stakes." A pianist "boy wonder" who grew up to become one of the highest-paid performers in the world, Liberace's flamboyant style embodied the essence of Sin City, and he outdid himself with one extravagant costume after another. Even one of his cars was covered in rhinestones. Apart from the casinos, the Liberace Museum is the most popular attraction in Vegas, so it's no surprise that it served as the backdrop for one scene.

At any rate, Las Vegas is a macrocosm that significantly colors the microcosm of a crime scene.

PROCESSING THE SCENE

In the case of a major crime, like a bombing or a homicide, detectives are called in. (On *C.S.I.*, that generally means Detective Jim Brass.) They're in charge of the investigation, and rule over the crime scene. One of the most difficult aspects of controlling a scene is defining its boundaries. It might be a single room in a building, such as with an equivocal death that turns out to have been a suicide. However, if there's been a murder, the crime scene could extend to other rooms where the killer left traces of his or her presence, out into a hallway, and even into a neighborhood. If someone was raped in one place and then transported elsewhere, the crime scene extends from the point of abduction to the vehicle of transport and to the other location where he or she was left.

For example, in "To Halve and to Hold," a dog finds a human tibia bone in the desert and since the rest of the 205 bones are not readily present, a rather wide area becomes the potential crime scene. In cases such as this C.S.I.s perform a "grid search": that is, they walk the approximate area, shoulder to shoulder, stopping only when someone in the line signals that something appears to be evidence. A flag is set down in the place where it was found, and this procedure continues until everything is collected. Of course, the crime scene "visual" covers a large area and potentially stretches out even farther. C.S.I.s have to determine how much of the scene they actually need to search—how much is enough? It's rare that C.S.I.s get the chance to return to a scene while it's still fresh, so they have to stay with it as long as possible and pick up everything they can find that might be construed as evidence.

That's why an area gets marked off as the spot for taking breaks, storing equipment, and briefing the various personnel who come in. Sometimes a mobile crime lab is set up there for quick processing of certain types of evidence. An outer barrier may also be established around the defined scene in order to keep onlookers at a distance.

The first twenty-four-hour period after a crime is considered the most crucial because the evidence is relatively undisturbed and witnesses have better memories. The suspect's trail is still fresh and reporters have generally not alerted him or her to what the police know. Roadblocks can be set up and descriptions posted. It's also possible to persuade a friend or relative of the suspect to help. Sometimes a K-9 unit is brought in to track the perpetrator before the trail gets contaminated.

Before anything is done, the investigators must decide whether a search warrant is needed. If a search or seizure of evidence is made without protecting the rights of the people involved, then the evidence can be thrown out in court—along with anything deduced from the evidence. Grissom warns Nick about this before ordering a K-9 unit to track a suspect. No matter how successful, if they don't follow procedure, whatever they find is worthless. (He does get around this obstacle by having the dogs track the scent to the house where the suspect lives. They don't need a warrant for this, as long as they stay outside.)

If the person who controls the property offers permission to search, then the search is legal. If not, the warrant must be obtained from a judge. To get a warrant from a judge, investigators must prepare an affidavit that details exactly what they are looking for, where they need to search, and why they think the item(s) are in that location. In other words, they must supply probable cause. A "no-knock" warrant is issued only if there is compelling reason to suppose that the evidence may be destroyed if any warning is given, or that the officer may be in danger. Any search must be confined to the location and items listed on the warrant. In the case of an obvious crime scene, searchers may look for all evidence associated with the crime. If they want to return to a scene, they need to post an officer there to indicate that the search based on that warrant is still in progress, or else get a new warrant.

TYPES OF EVIDENCE

There are two kinds of evidence: testimonial and physical. Testimonial comes from anyone who was near the scene and saw something, such as the young men in the Alpha Phi frat house in "Pledging Mr. Johnson" after an alleged suicide. Such witnesses are separated, detained, and interviewed. Some are transported to headquarters to make formal written statements. However, eyewitnesses are often unreliable and some of what they say may be taken with a grain of salt. Still, detectives can use it to help obtain whatever search warrants they may need, and they then coordinate their movements with the prosecutor.

Physical evidence is grouped into one of five categories:

1. Temporary (may change or be lost)

2. Conditional (associated with specific conditions at the crime scene)

3. Associative (links a suspect or victim to a scene)

4. Pattern (blood, impressions, tire treads, residue or evidence of the *modus operandi*)

5. Trace/transfer (produced by physical contact with some surface)

In jurisdictions that have funding for full facilities, physical evidence is reserved for the crime scene technicians who are trained in how to collect it, and for the criminalists, identification technicians, or forensic scientists who do the analyses. Forensic science—also known as just forensics—is the application of the scientific method to legal proceedings. Forensic methods may be employed in various aspects of both civil or criminal cases, but criminalistics is most often noted for its use in crime scene processing.

The people trained to do this are looking for things that should not be there—foreign elements that seem out of place. They know that people routinely shed hairs and fibers and that many things can be used as weapons. They will have various duties, including taking notes, evaluating the scene, sketching it, photographing it, finding and collecting physical evidence for analysis, using different types of equipment, and preparing detailed reports. Sometimes they will take portable processing equipment to the scene, where they will work with the evidence. They must also be prepared to testify in court about what they write in those evidence reports. Essentially they're looking for:

- Fingerprints

- Impressions from tools, shoes, car tires, fabric, and teeth

- Body fluids like semen, blood, and saliva

- Other biological evidence such as hair, fingernail scrapings, and body tissue

- Trace evidence such as glass, plant spoors, fibers, paint chips, gunshot residue, and accelerants

- Weapons or the evidence of them, such as shell casings

- Questioned documents, which include forged checks, fake suicide notes, and ransom notes

- Special evidence in cases of arson or explosions

C.S.I.s who live in a populated area with a high rate of violent crimes may spend most of their time collecting and documenting evidence, whereas a technician in a place where the crime rate (or law enforcement budget) is low may have a number of duties, from evidence collection to photography to lab analysis. The duties and assignments will differ from one place to another. In the C.S.I. lab in Vegas, there appear to be numerous lab technicians who put the evidence under a microscope or through some other type of instrumental processing and present the analysis results.

However, it should be noted that while the *C.S.I.* team spends a lot of time chasing down suspects, informing families about a death, and interrogating people, these activities are generally reserved for the detectives. The show takes some license for the sake of increased drama and character development, but C.S.I.s do not replace detectives. As noted earlier, the detectives are always in charge of the investigation. In the real world C.S.I.s would never be given the liberties that Gil and his team enjoy.

The Las Vegas C.S.I. team is on the night shift, serving in what Detective Brass claims is the number-two crime lab in the nation.

When not on duty, they may be on call, which means coming in if the workload demands it. Some evidence is time-sensitive.

Evidence collected at the scene may serve several purposes:

1. Prove that a crime has been committed

2. Indicate key aspects of the crime

3. Establish the identities of the victim or suspect, or determine what kind of investigation must be done to identify them and see how they interacted

4. Corroborate (or not) any testimony given by witnesses

5. Help to exonerate a suspect who is innocent

6. Provide leads for further investigation

7. Pressure suspects into giving confessions

As C.S.I.s enter a crime scene, they need to be skilled at "reading" the scene to form an idea of what may have happened. However, they must also stay open to other possibilities. When Grissom decides to investigate the innocence of a man charged with arson and murder, Nick and Sara stick to their belief that he's guilty. Yet Grissom persists, knowing that new leads can change evidence interpretations, and in the end his persistence pays off. Having some idea up front helps guide the collection of evidence, but that idea needs to be flexible.

Crime scene investigators have the authority to decide the nature and extent of other services needed at the scene, such as calling in an artist or anthropologist. They can bring out special equipment or lighting, or ask for police personnel to assist. In many places, they have the power to make an arrest and even to carry a weapon.

To qualify as crime scene investigators, potential candidates must complete a minimum number of hours of training in crime scene processing (as determined by the jurisdiction), some of which must be devoted to latent fingerprint processing, and some to major death investigations, photography, and blood spatter pattern analysis. In some low-level technical jobs, it's not necessary to have a college degree, but the more sophisticated the analysis, the more education is required. They may need training in arson investigation, police procedure, and pathology—and in fact they ought to have some exposure to a morgue. (It's unlikely that rookie Holly Gribbs would be as unfamiliar with an autopsy as she appeared to be.) Before taking on such a job, they should see what can happen to bodies in various circumstances, such as a drowning or burning. Although criminalistics is not criminology (which focuses on motive and behavior), some exposure to forensic psychology (especially deception detection) and criminal profiling is helpful. There may be special certifications required for C.S.I.s as well, such as by the International Association for Identification, Crime Scene Certification Board. In general, a C.S.I. should have background in chemistry, biology, computer programs, anthropology, and police and court procedure.

CRIME SCENE KITS

Often we'll see one of the C.S.I.s bring a kit to a scene, such as Grissom's serology collection kit for making tests where a body may have been cut up. Another kit they always have on hand contains tools like a hammer, pliers, a saw, and a screwdriver for removing evidence that may be on part of a structure, and many investigators who anticipate long hours bring water, snacks, and a change of clothing. In the trunk of their vehicle or in a C.S.I. van, they will keep boxes, jars, cans, and paper bags of all sizes for evidence collection.

Crime kits come in different sizes and contain instruments and implements for different purposes, from collecting latent fingerprints to vacuuming trace evidence. They can be purchased commercially or investigators can put together their own version.

Basically, a fishing tackle box can serve as a receptacle for the many items needed for crime scene preservation and initial analysis:

- crime scene tape and a box of chalk

- handheld magnifying glass

- flashlight

- tweezers and a box of swabs

- pen, sketchpad, and logbooks

- camera with extra film, a cassette recorder, and blank tapes

- paper sacks and envelopes

- disposable clothing, gloves, and masks

- string

- measuring implements

- orange evidence flags or markers

- lint pick-up adhesive roller

- portable alternative light source (ALS), which means infrared, ultraviolet, or laser

Preparation for long hours at a crime scene is key, so whatever is used up must be replaced immediately.

The specific-use kits for processing the scene have standard contents as well.

1. A basic fingerprinting kit might contain the following:

- fingerprint powder (in different colors to contrast with different color surfaces and to apply to different types of sur-

faces; also comes in a fluorescent version for use with alternative light sources)
- fiberglass dusting brushes
- camel-hair brushes to clean dust from prints
- clear lifting tape and dispenser, and/or lift tabs
- latent print cards and elimination print forms, with markers
- fingerprint card container, to keep them separate
- ink pad for taking prints on the spot
- magnifying lens, scissors, tweezers, and scalpel
- towelettes for removing ink
- evidence rulers of different lengths or measuring tape
- evidence seals, tags, bags, and boxes of different sizes
- disposable gloves

A more comprehensive (and larger) fingerprinting kit may have magnetic powders of different colors, applicator brushes, a feather brush for fluorescent powders, a UV lamp for illuminating powders, filter goggles, fuming glue (Super Glue) for lifting prints from rough surfaces, Cobex sheeting for handprint and footprints, photographic scales, a postmortem kit for taking prints off deceased victims, retabs to allow rerolling a smeared print, and a palm print roller (which can also be used on feet).

2. A casting kit for tire and footprint (from foot or shoe) impressions would include casting powder, casting compound (dental stone), a water container and mixing bowl, mixing implements, casting frames of different sizes, rubber lifters, a fixative, and snowprint wax spray, which helps to take castings from snow.

3. Another type of casting kit is designed to take impressions from tool marks. It may include an extruder gun that allows a mix of casting material (polyviylsiloxane) to be squeezed into awkward places to get clean impressions. In the case where the

serial number may have been scraped off of a tool, a serial number restoration fluid is available for different types of metals.

4. For shootings, an investigator might use a laser trajectory kit, which helps to assess projectile paths at a crime scene. The kit includes a laser pointer, an angle finder, a centering cone, penetration rods, and a tripod mount.

5. Trace evidence collection requires different procedures for different types. To collect broken glass, for example, the C.S.I. may need only tweezers with sharp points and an evidence container. For soil samples, fiber, and hair too small to see clearly, they may use tape lifts or a trace evidence vacuum that comes equipped with special filters. Each kit comes with a knife for scraping dried evidence, and a wide variety of containers for different types of evidence, such as metal cans for paint chips or glass. For lifting prints from dust, a special electrostatic print lifter sends an electric charge through a piece of film that will make the dust adhere in the right pattern (which Grissom used at the Collins house massacre).

6. Gunshot residue kits are developed for labs that use either atomic absorption (AA) analysis or the scanning electron microscope (SEM). For AA, kits have evidence containers with seals, a nitric acid dispenser, and directions for testing on different parts of both hands. The SEM kit contains aluminum mounts for the hands and uses adhesive carbon material. To find out if a suspect has recently handled a gun or metal weapon, a trace metal detection reagent, mixed with alcohol, makes the contact patterns visible under ultraviolet light.

7. Equipment for detecting the presence of blood that may have been wiped clean or washed away includes sterile swabs, phenolphthalein reagent, leucomalachite, and luminol spray. These come in disposable chemical applicators for field kits and include distilled water and contact test paper. The kit comes with a color

chart and a way to determine positive reactions. Luminol may also come in a spray bottle.

8. A serology kit for the collection of any type of bodily fluid features sterile water, swabs, gauze, tweezers, a blade, gloves, pipettes, vials for collection, and absorption papers. A portable ultraviolet lamp may be included.

9. A special kit for collecting entomology specimens would need to have specimen jars, waxed containers, vials, labels, aluminum foil, ethyl alcohol, a magnifier, and spatulas. It may include a guidebook and a net, tweezers, gloves, ruler, maggot screen, maggot motels, and labels. For keeping track, most kits include a pencil and a checklist.

10. A hazmat kit aids in assessing potentially hazardous situations, such as with chemical leaks, fires, and any other situation involving toxic gases. This kit helps to determine what types of dangerous vapors might be in the air.

11. A sexual assault kit contains evidence envelopes for such things as fingernail scrapings and foreign substances; a sexual assault incident form; authorization form; swabs; smear slides with appropriately labeled mailers; blood collection tubes; instructions for both male and female victims; pubic hair combs and mailers; bags for pulled head hair and pubic hair; scissors; and evidence seals with biohazard labels.

Portable workstations may be brought to the crime scene so technicians can safely work with the chemicals to process such things as latent prints. These stations may also be used to air-dry bloody clothing. Portable equipment includes gas chromatography, ground-penetrating radar, and night vision capabilities.

In cases of extreme decomposition of a corpse, modified gas masks (antiputrefaction masks) may be needed. These are generally kept in the vehicle rather than in a kit.

FORENSIC SPECIALTIES

Sometimes criminalists with special education and training get involved as well, either at the crime scene or later at the lab, to help with identification and analysis. These will be treated more in depth in later chapters, but in a nutshell, they include:

Anthropologist: examines bones to help determine identity and may also get involved in time-of-death issues as well as forensic art (computer enhancement, facial sculpture).

Artist/sculptor: provides sketches of the offender, uses computer enhancement to come up with a rendition of someone, or uses two- and three-dimensional facial reconstruction on decomposed remains.

Accountant: does financial investigations for deducing motive and identifying suspects.

Ballistics expert: has knowledge about the functioning of firearms and bullet projectiles.

Botanist: studies plant growth at a crime scene and analyzes plant spores.

Chemist/trace expert: studies the molecular component of pieces of evidence like glass, paint chips, fibers, and dyes. Also does toxicology.

Dactyloscopist: analyzes fingerprints.

Entomologist: studies the developmental stages of insects to help establish time of death or body dump sites.

Geologist: analyzes soil content to provide information about where a body may have been.

Geographical profiler: uses computer models to help establish where a serial offender may reside.

Linguist: analyzes the spoken or written word to match separate messages with a single individual, probe underlying intent, and tell something about the person's educational level and reading sources.

Mental health expert/criminologist/profiler: helps to determine how the evidence is to be interpreted by analyzing potential motives and criminal behavior from a crime scene. They can also predict what a serial offender might do, narrow down identifying characteristics, and explain puzzling aspects of a crime.

Odontologist/dentist: studies teeth, which means they can examine teeth impressions, bite marks, and dental formation for identification.

Serologist: analyzes body serums like blood, semen, and saliva, and may offer information about DNA and blood pattern analysis.

THE CORONER

If there's a body, the coroner/medical examiner commands the scene. The scope of his or her abilities and authority is different from state to state.

The coroner system originated in England and the office was originally set up as a "crowner," or someone who collected taxes for the king. One's manner of death had implications for taxes, because in certain types of deaths the king confiscated the property. Thus, for a fee the crowner could "define" the cause of death in a way that benefited the relatives. Eventually the office evolved into that of a death investigator, and that system was brought over to the States. Each state has its own way of doing things, and in some places the coroner is an elected official with no medical training. He or she hires a medical examiner to do autopsies and other medicolegal investigation procedures. In other states, medical examiners with degrees in medicine and training in pathology (knowledge about changes in the body after injury) have replaced the coroner, and in still others, the coroner is also a medical examiner.

When the coroner is called in Las Vegas, that means someone from the Clark County Coroner/Medical Examiner's Office. This coroner is appointed and has training in medicine and pathology. According to the description for that office, he or she

- investigates all deaths by violence, criminal means, suicide, or any unattended death

- orders autopsies

- provides identification of victims

- conducts inquests

- holds unidentified remains in the morgue

- keeps violent death statistics

At the crime scene, the coroner decides whether there is reason for an autopsy. He may then do some rudimentary examinations, such as looking at the eyes and taking the body's temperature via the liver. He also directs the photographer to take specific photos from different angles. The corpse's hands—and sometimes feet, if bare—get carefully bagged to preserve anything that may be found under the nails. If the body has been dead long enough and left out in the open, it will be covered with maggots, and those, too, are collected and bagged. Before the body gets moved, it may be out-lined where it lies for later reference.

This begins the death investigation, which is covered in the next chapter.

PHOTOGRAPHING THE SCENE

Once detectives have determined the crime scene boundaries and taken whatever notes they need, the photographer documents the scene. Depending on the size of the lab and the number of crimes to be covered, there may be a designated photographer. Otherwise, taking photos may be one task among many for busy C.S.I.s. When a woman was found raped, shot, and left for dead in "Too Tough to Die," Nick took the photographs. Sara was the photographer for a dead male stripper found in the Lucky Seven Hotel. Although we do not get to see their technique, crime scene photographers tend to follow certain protocols:

1. They use both black-and-white and various types of color print film (some may use digital cameras for ready access to computer enhancement).

2. They use cameras with different types of lenses, both normal and wide angle, as well as lenses for close-up work; they may also need a telephoto lens for distances.

3. They bring separate extension flashes or other types of sup-plementary lighting to "paint" a crime scene with light for better detail and depth photography.

4. They bring a tripod to keep shots steady.

5. They use a photograph log to keep track of each shot.

6. They bring filters for better depth.

7. They include different types of scales in the photos for ac-

curately measuring things like shoe imprints (as Catherine did with the bloody sock imprint in "Evaluation Day").

8. They take at least two photos of each shot, in case one is blurred. (Nick and Sara both take a risk when breezing through this task with a one-shot method.)

If a digital camera is used, the photos can be quickly developed with portable equipment that plugs into a cigarette lighter.

The procedure for crime scene photographers is to first walk through the scene to get perspective (taking care not to move, touch, or step on anything). They then discuss with the investigating officers (or other technicians) what should be photographed in greater detail because photographs need to be taken before evidence is moved or collected.

The first photographs should provide an overview of as much of the scene as possible, from several different angles, to show the scene as the photographers saw it when they first entered. That means they "pan" the camera to take overlapping shots (or use a video camera). This makes it possible for those who were not present to get a good sense of the scene. In a room, for example, photographers should take pictures from each corner. Notes that link important details with each photograph should be made as it is taken. They also take photos of the entire building, if the crime occurred within, and of any entrance into the scene. The overview photos need to include the position of any items considered to be evidence, such as weapons, bodies, or discarded clothing.

Then mid-range photos are taken, focusing on the position of items considered as evidence. This simply provides a closer image of these items in context.

Finally, each item of evidence is photographed in close-up detail, such as gunpowder residue on a hand, blood spatter patterns, or anything that seems out of place. Also, photos should be taken of anything with a serial or identification number. Records are especially important at this stage, and if the scene is videotaped, then the photographer can describe things for the audio. In all cases, other investigators or equipment should be kept out of the photos or videos.

To get good photographs that will show a lot of detail, photographers have to keep four things in mind:

1. Set the camera for the correct exposure, with a way to record any evidence that may be in shadows (such as inside cars).

2. Get the maximum depth of field possible, which is achieved with smaller rather than larger lens openings and with shorter focal length lenses.

3. Get good perspective that contains no distortions.

4. Keep a sharp focus for best detail.

At the autopsy of Present John F. Kennedy, the FBI photographer failed to document which photos were exit and which were entry wounds. No scale was provided to note their size and the photos of the internal organs were fuzzy. As a result, it was difficult to make determinations about the shooting after the body was no longer available.

Flash illumination is sometimes needed, even in daylight, to expose whatever may be in the shadows. Supplementary light sources, such as a flashlight or stand-alone overhead lights may help. Surfaces that may reflect light and thus affect automatic flash have to be treated differently, such as angling the flash away from the surface or using a larger lens opening. Some photographers bring along a light refraction shield.

Each crime scene has a unique character, which will determine the type of photographs needed for analysis and possible use in a courtroom. Color film is best, except for evidence that needs the best contrast to show detail. In that case, black-and-white film is used.

Bodies are photographed from five angles:

1. Head to feet

2. Right side

3. Feet to head

4. Left side

5. Straight down from above

Then close-ups are taken of any wounds, ligature marks, bite marks, or bruises. Most are taken with a scale for accurate measurement. If weapons are present, photos must show them in relation to the body. Once the body is moved, the area underneath it is also photographed, as well as parts of the scene without the body.

In the case of living victims, photographs must be taken of all injuries, as well as a photo of the person's face for identification purposes.

Other photos at the scene will include tire treads, trace evidence, fingerprints, blood, and footprints. Impressions may have to be photographed with flash or light sources placed at an angle to get the best detail effect. Signs of activity in the room, such as cigarette butts in an ashtray, destruction of property, or a glass of wine, have to be photographed as well, with notes made. If there's evidence of a struggle, it's documented. Dusted fingerprints must also be photographed before they're lifted, and black-and-white film (sometimes with color filters) is best.

Suspected arson, such as in "Fahrenheit 932," requires photography of any potential entrance points into a building and all areas of fire damage, especially where it was most intense. Also, photographs of burn patterns on walls, windows, or doorframes, show the fire's direction of movement. In this episode, a burn pattern on the doorframe of a room where the accused claimed the door had remained close contradicted him: if the door had been closed, the fire would not have burned the doorjamb.

In the case of a death that appears to be a suicide, such as the two men found in bathtubs in the pilot episode and "Anonymous," the scene is classified as an equivocal death, which means it's investigated as a homicide until it's conclusively shown to be a suicide. In such cases, whatever was used to bring about death is photographed: a rope with the knot, a gun, the victim's hands, a kicked-over chair, or a note. Any wounds are documented, both entrance and exit. If there is any discoloration on the body or articles grasped in its hand, this must be carefully photographed.

Bloodstain photography is done with color film, unless high contrast is needed. First, the bloodstain or spatter must be shown in the context of the scene, and then close-ups are made with an oblique light angle. If luminol (a chemical agent used to bring out bloodstains not readily apparent) is needed, then a certain procedure must be followed, because luminol requires darkness to show up. First, spray the luminol in darkness to locate the area. Then turn on lights and take a normal photo of the area. Then set the camera to underexpose the next photos, darken the room, spray a light coating of luminol, and take photographs of the fluorescent pattern, spraying every twenty seconds as needed. (Luminol also reacts to other substances such as bleach, so spraying in places that smell like bleach should be avoided.)

Besides photos, sketches are made for an accurate depiction of the scene. This is especially valuable if the scene is larger than a photograph can capture. It also leaves out nonessential clutter. The entire scene is also measured, and the measurements are added to the sketch. If there is a body, it is measured from two fixed points. (Some computer programs provide professional-quality diagrams from a few simple measurements.)

Photographs are meant to refresh the memory of the investigators and to show placement of physical evidence. They can also indicate traits of the offender and aid in the classification of the crime, so the value of doing this procedure correctly cannot be over-estimated.

COLLECTING AND PRESERVING EVIDENCE

Once the scene has been photographed and documented, the search for evidence begins. First, a plan of operation is formed in order to minimize the potential contamination of evidence. Initially, infor-mation is limited so C.S.I.s take a walk-through to see the scene from several angles. If certain evidence looks fragile, it gets collected right after it's photographed. If there appears to be a hazard, such as biohazards from decomposing bodies, special equipment and clothing are used. All evidence gets a numbered flag or marker to show where it was found, which will later be added to a diagram of the crime scene. A notebook keeps track of what each numbered marker stands for.

Then certain people are designated to search specific areas. At the Richmond mansion in "Table Stakes," Grissom sends Warrick and Catherine to different locations near the pool, while Nick goes with him to the fishpond. In fact, each investigation begins with specific assignments, in part to limit the number of people involved. They are charged with carefully documenting anything they see or find. If several people are at work on a single scene, their collective reports will be used to reconstruct the crime. All notes should be taken in chronological order and only the facts should be recorded.

The type of terrain determines the search pattern used. If the crime scene is inside a car, such as when Warrick and Sara investi-gate an equivocal death that appeared to be either a suicide or a shooting by a cop, the scene is pretty contained. Nevertheless, they know that the car may have to be dismantled to make a thorough investigation. If the scene is in the desert, it potentially stretches beyond the obvious and may require a number of searchers.

C.S.I.s are aware that the initial collection and preservation of evidence, as well as the chain of custody, will be scrutinized by defense lawyers for weaknesses. Proper protocol must be followed to the letter. Chain of custody means that each person who handles evidence signs off on it, records what is done with it on what dates, and replaces it in its secure storage location. The evidence that is submitted to court must be the same evidence that was collected, and the DA must be able to prove this.

The poor handling of evidence in the O. J. Simpson trial in 1994 turned the case. The potential corruption of blood samples for DNA evidence provided reasonable doubt about the handling of everything else and about the claims of the prosecution, resulting in a verdict of not guilty.

To ensure its integrity, evidence is kept in a container with labels for recording the case number, the victim or suspect's name, and all signatures of people who have handled it. Even so, some evidence gets lost, as was the case in "Too Tough to Die" when a screwdriver used as a weapon in an allegedly justifiable homicide was lost.

To collect evidence at a scene, C.S.I.s need to have tweezers, rubber gloves, and an assortment of envelopes and containers for bagging it. Plastic bags or containers should be avoided for organic matter because they accelerate the deterioration of biological specimens and evaporate accelerants, although if blood-soaked articles cannot be air-dried at the scene and must be transported without leakage, plastic is allowable for hasty transport.

Gathering all of the trace evidence may involve a "fingertip search," starting at a central point and spiraling around until the scene is covered. Investigators may also divide the search area into zones. Whatever method is used, the goal is to systematically cover the area. Trace evidence must all be kept separate and documented in the order in which it was found. Even two different samples of the same paint are kept separate so that the lab techs will know where at the scene they were discovered. Pairs of things, like socks and shoes, also go into different bags.

Vacuums equipped with special filters may pick up fiber, dirt, glass fragments, and hair, although these will also mix evidence together. Another technique is to pick up a blanket or clothing and shake it onto a sheet of paper, or use tape to pick up fibers or dirt. Sometimes a metal detector works best. The lab itself may have a preferred method and should be consulted.

Impressions such as footprints or tire tracks require casting in plaster or dental stone, but they must first be measured and photographed—especially if there is any sign of wear—in case the casting damages the patterns. They're also sprayed with fixative. Where there may be a series of shoeprints, the distances between them must be measured.

Fingerprints, shell casings, firearms, bodily fluids, bite marks left on food, and tool impressions all have specific methods of removal and preservation, which will be covered in later chapters. Items with prints on them, such as a glass or cigarette lighter, are carefully packaged to send to the lab.

Soil samples can also prove useful if soil from the crime scene can be matched to soil on the shoes or clothing of a suspect, or in a transport vehicle. Grissom hoped to do this in "Cool Change" when he found dirt from the roof of a building on a suspect's pants.

If a car is the crime scene, it must be checked for scratches, missing paint, and evidence wedged into the upholstery. In one case, a tooth found embedded in the steering wheel clinched it.

Documents are collected for many different reasons, such as a psychological autopsy, a victim analysis, a check for forgeries, and acquiring samples of the victim's handwriting.

Questioned specimens must also be paired with known specimens for an analysis to be meaningful. Bringing in a tooth believed to have belonged to a missing woman offers nothing for DNA analysis unless they can also provide a known specimen of her tissue or hair. A paint chip doesn't fly unless there's a car with paint chipped off for comparison, and the same goes for the fibers that Nick found on the watch of a homicide victim. He needed a swatch of the carpet.

In cases like arson, a control sample of the type of material that was burned is brought in for comparison with the burned sample. The fire's heat may have altered the material, so finding a piece in its original state helps to make an accurate analysis.

Some evidence is unique to a person or crime, such as DNA samples and spent bullets. Other material like fibers, glass, and paint are identifiable for close matches, but not for uniqueness. They help build a case, but fail to offer the same weight of proof that unique evidence does. Thus, the more unique evidence they can find, the better.

Once the C.S.I.s have photographed, cataloged, collected, and preserved the evidence, they transport it to the lab. Evidence clerks there log it in and continue to ensure its preservation until it can be properly analyzed. The scene itself may remain secured so that it may be revisited.

Evidence goes in one of two directions: bodies end up in the morgue for autopsy while physical evidence goes to the lab. We'll look first at how the bodies are handled and what happens during a death investigation.

TWO

Handling Bodies

The death investigator is a medical examiner or coroner. In rare circumstances, a certified layperson with strong medical background may team up with a forensic pathologist. Some hire out for private investigations in wrongful death or insurance cases, and some work for a government office. To keep things simple, we'll call this person the DI, although on *C.S.I.* it's always someone from the coroner's office.

To be certified by the American Board of Forensic Pathology entails a five-year residency, with at least another year of training in a medical examiner's office. All DIs must be familiar with forensic pathology or work with someone who is, because they have to know the difference between a murder and death from a contagious disease, or between an accidental erotic fatality and a real suicide. They must also know the protocol of body removal and be able to decide which deaths actually need to be investigated.

Death investigation involves determining several things about a death, such as how it occurred, when it happened, and what caused it. The cause of death is whatever led to it, such as a lethal knifing, a bullet to the head, or asphyxiation by strangling. Pathologists are concerned with both proximate cause (chain of events leading up to the death) and the immediate cause (the injury or disease that killed the person). The mechanism of death is about the specific physiological alterations that made death occur.

The manner of death falls into one of five categories:

1. Natural (died in an environment not considered hostile)

2. Accidental (fell victim to a hostile environment)

3. Suicide (the person caused his own death)

4. Homicide (someone else caused the death)

5. Undetermined

Not all homicides are criminal, but those that are include death by auto, manslaughter (recklessly causing a death), and murder (knowingly causing a death or bodily injury leading to death). A noncriminal homicide might be a killing justified as self-defense.

The first officer at the scene notifies the DI of a suspicious death and he or she arrives as quickly as possible. The faster they get there, the more accurate will be the first assessment of the postmortem interval (PMI), and no one should move the body until the DI arrives. Certain initial examinations may be performed at the scene to acquire information that might otherwise be lost.

On the day after Christmas in 1996, around six in the morning, Patsy Ramsey placed a 911 call. Her daughter, JonBenet, had been kidnapped and there was a ransom note. Around 1:20 that afternoon, John Ramsey discovered his daughter's body in the wine cellar. She lay on her back, her bound arms over her head, and her mouth closed with duct tape. Ramsey ripped it off and carried her upstairs. He laid her on the floor and covered her with a blanket, thus interfering with the dropping body temperature. She was in a state of rigor mortis, but no one there could give an expert assessment.

The coroner arrived almost seven hours after the discovery of the body. It was now between fourteen and twenty-two hours since the girl had been murdered. He spent about ten minutes examining the wounds, but did not take the body's temperature. He pronounced her dead and sent her to the morgue. The next morning he autopsied her but was unable to establish a time of death.

Any deaths not the result of natural causes, such as disease or expiring in bed from old age, should be investigated. Even natural deaths may be investigated if caused by a contagious disease that could harm the community. All childhood deaths are investigated, as are deaths of people in the public eye. Generally, the laws of the jurisdiction in which the body was discovered govern the methods and means of investigation, some being more minimal (due to budget) than others.

Many deaths are categorized as "unattended deaths." In other words, the person died in a place other than a hospital, hospice, or long-term care facility, and no physician had recently examined him or her for some illness. If a physician does not feel comfortable signing the death certificate without examination, then a death investigation ensues. If a death was expected and there is no threat to anyone from it, then the investigator may let it go. They'll get a look at the body later in the morgue, funeral home, or hospital.

All aspects of a death investigation are confidential. Catherine was out of line when she told the husband of a deceased woman that his wife had been having an affair, and, as can often happen, her precipitous breach had serious consequences.

Body discovery scenes outside are categorized by how the body is found: buried, exposed, or submerged in water. If the body is buried, soil samples are tested for the presence of added substances, such as quicklime. Bodies lying exposed may have parts missing, due to scavengers attacking the corpse. Bodies found in water where boats are present may have injuries from propellers. In any event, corpses outside may have undergone changes unrelated to their demise.

With body discovery scenes inside, the crime scene is generally more preserved, although the corpse may have been dismembered and stored someplace for a long period of time.

Going into a crime scene, DIs must wait until it's secured and then take care not to interfere with the investigation, but must also be prepared to exercise authority. They are responsible for the body, and they work best when they work *with* the team of detectives and C.S.I.s. The detectives at the scene decide whether it's a homicide, but they're guided by the DI's findings. They make their own non-intrusive examination of the body and do sketches before it gets removed.

At the scene, the DI briefly examines the body and makes some preliminary notes and diagrams. Above all, he must avoid disturbing any trace evidence that might linger on the corpse. He may also direct the photographer for specific photographs or take some of his own. If the wound is visible, he'll try to determine whether it was made by a knife, gun, or blunt instrument. At the least, he should examine the eyes, and note the presence of blood at the scene and whether it approximates the amount of bleeding that would ensue from a specific type of wound. (If not, that may mean the body has been moved from another locale.) Only the coroner authorizes body transport.

The DI also decides if there is to be an autopsy, which generally occurs for any unattended death and always for a homicide. (The assumption of homicide may be mistaken, but it's better to operate that way than in the reverse.) If insects are present, the DI works with an entomologist. If the corpse has deteriorated to skeletal form, he may call in a forensic anthropologist.

The crime scene technicians generally search for evidence in a way that clears a path to the body. The officer in charge then directs the coroner through the scene and to the body. He should be vigilant, looking over the entire scene, especially if it appears to be close to a place with easy transportation access. He may then suggest some theories and ask if certain things have been considered, such as whether a body was merely dumped at the scene.

The body gets removed by lifting and wrapping it in a clean white sheet to preserve all evidence but taking care to avoid contact with any body fluids. (Investigators may wear disposable gowns and gloves to do this.) The body is then placed into a body bag for transport. Some MEs feel that the body temperature should be taken at least twice at the scene before a body is removed, via the liver, ear, or rectum. Once the body gets refrigerated at the morgue, the decomposition is considerably retarded.

TIME OF DEATH

At the crime scene, the DI makes an informed guess at the approximate time when the individual expired, because it will then be subject to photographs, transportation, and other delays, and over that period of time there will be changes in the corpse.

Time of death is difficult to say with certainty, unless there was a witness who looked at a watch, because there are too many individual variables. Someone may be on a drug that decreases the flow of blood to her fingers and toes, and that interferes with the usual progress of postmortem cooling. Someone else might have been chased up steps or for a long distance before being killed, and the antemortem activity could cause immediate rigor. Elderly women and children can go in and out of rigor so minimally that it can be difficult to feel it. As one coroner said, "It's an inaccurate science."

None of the following factors is wholly reliable, since all are affected by diverse conditions, but taken together they can provide a fairly reasonable estimate. Specifically, these include:

1. Body temperature (*algor mortis*)

After death, bodies stop breathing, so without oxygen, they cannot maintain the normal temperature of 98.6 degrees Fahrenheit. Typically a body cools at the rate of approximately one to one and one-half degrees per hour until it takes on the temperature of its surroundings. However, if the weather is cold, the temperature may drop more quickly. And conversely, an obese person tends to cool more slowly than someone with little body fat. Heavy layers of clothing can insulate a corpse, and exercise prior to death, as well as certain drugs, can raise the temperature.

2. Discoloration (*livor mortis*)

Also known as postmortem lividity or hypostasis, this refers to the dark purple color of the body that is found closest to the ground where it's lying. It appears about one to two hours after death and becomes fixed within eight to ten hours. Lividity is caused by the cessation of the heart's pumping action, which allows the red and white blood cells to separate. The red cells then settle into the lowest parts. A dead man found lying on his back will exhibit lividity on his back. If it appears elsewhere, that means the corpse has been moved since death. Discolored skin that blanches when touched indicates that lividity is not yet permanent—the death was more than two hours earlier but probably not as long as ten. (Some deaths will have a different appearance because substances such as carbon monoxide keep the blood a bright red color, and bodies that have lost a lot of blood will not discolor.)

3. *Rigor mortis*

Immediately after death, bodies go limp, but within fifteen minutes to fifteen hours (average time, two to three hours), accumulating waste products stiffen the muscles. This first shows in the face, lower jaw, and neck, and over the next twelve to eighteen hours spreads throughout the body, lasting as long as thirty-six hours. Beginning again in the head and neck area, the body loosens up. This process may take as long as ten hours from start to finish.

Factors that affect the onset and release of rigor include the presence of heat, which speeds it up, and differences in musculature. It's often the case that obese people fail to develop this stiffness at all. Additionally, not all muscle rigidity is actually from rigor. A suicide gripping a revolver, for example, is not necessarily in rigor. This could be "cadaveric spasm," which is an immediate stiffening of the hands and arms just before death.

4. Ocular indicators

If the eyes remain open after death, a thin film forms on the surface. The potassium content from the breakdown of red blood cells enters the eyes, and within two to three hours, they look cloudy. (Grissom examines this in the case of a head found in a truck.) Eyes that are closed develop the same conditions, but it takes much longer: cloudiness may not occur for an entire day. Since the ambient temperature does not affect this process, some pathologists view it as a more reliable PMI measure than the first three.

5. Food digestion

This is based on an assumption that the stomach digests food and empties into the intestines at a predictable rate, but many things can influence this process. The type of food, the body's metabolizing rate, the presence of drugs or medication, and the person's emotional condition prior to death may all have some effect on how fast food is processed. Even exercise right before death can slow it down. The amount of food consumed can do the same. A light meal may remain about two hours, a heavy meal four to six hours. Examination of the small intestine is also done to trace the path of the food.

6. Personal factors

Aside from indicators in the corpse, other factors during the investigation may play a part. If a witness can place the person alive at a specific time in a specific place, then obviously that person was not dead at that time. If she had an appointment and failed to show up, that means she was not where she was expected.

7. Decay/decomposition rates

Because bodies may be found at any time from seconds after death to years later, DIs quickly get familiar with the stages of decomposition. The rate at which these stages occur depends on certain environmental factors, such as air temperature, whether the body was buried in earth or left in water, whether it was exposed to the sun or wrapped in a blanket, or whether it was placed in a cool cellar. Injured areas decompose more quickly than other parts, especially if there's insect activity. Because of these disfiguring changes, it's best to make a thorough examination as quickly as possible. If the smell is really bad, investigators can use specially scented masks or cream under their noses, but some coroners feel that if you go into the smell and breathe it in, it soon diminishes.

Aside from those mentioned above, decomposition takes place in the following stages:

- When the heart stops beating, the skin pales and starts to look waxy.

- The part of the body where the blood has settled discolors into a purplish red. The eyes flatten and the extremities turn blue.

- Desiccation, or the appearance of burning, shows up on drying mucous membranes.

- The body then putrefies, signaled by a greenish discoloration in the skin, starting in about two or three days in the lower abdomen and caused by the proliferation of bacteria. Soon this will spread over the rest of the abdomen and into the thighs and chest, and the face will swell and become unrecognizable.

- As rot spreads, a foul odor develops. Bacteria in the intestines produce gases that bloat the body and eventually turn the skin black. Bloating by the second week after death also makes the tongue, breasts, scrotum, and eyes protrude, and it pushes the intestines out through the rectum.

- Soon the skin blisters from these gases, detaches from the muscles, and bursts. The top layers start peeling off. Then the internal organs break open and liquefy. At this point, the body starts purging fluids from the orifices, and teeth, hair, and nails loosen.

- Under certain conditions, such as bodies submerged in water, a cheesy substance called "adipocere" forms as fatty tissues harden and keep the body preserved.

Left alone in a warm and moist climate, a body can decompose to a skeleton within a few weeks, while in other conditions it can take months, even years. In a hot, dry climate, some bodies merely mummify. Water preserves twice as long as open air, and burial extends that time frame by several weeks. While the PMI gets increasingly difficult to ascertain, decomposed bodies that have tissue left can still be subjected to toxicology analysis for potential cause of death.

The forensic anthropology department at the University of Tennessee at Knoxville (UT-K), has a special facility for analyzing PMI. This protected two-and-a-half-acre field is dedicated to the study of decomposing human remains, and there's no other place like it in the world. Outsiders call it "the Body Farm," but those who work there know it simply as the research facility.

The facility's founder, Dr. William M. Bass III, is an acclaimed expert on skeletal identification and entomology. He acquired this latter skill because many of the discovered bodies on which police consulted him were covered with maggots. To his surprise, the literature on the subject was sparse, so Bass requested property from the university for studying cadavers. He soon acquired a plot of land and the unclaimed corpses of several homeless men. As they lay exposed to the elements, they provided crucial medicolegal information about what happens to bodies under such conditions.

"Before our work, no one had ever established a time line," Bass points out. "There are a lot of factors that can affect how a body decomposes, but we found that the major two are climate and insects. When a person dies, the body begins to decay immediately and the enzymes in the digestive system begin to eat the tissue. You putrefy and this gives off a smell. The first of the critters to be attracted to a decaying body are the blowflies. They come along and lay their eggs, which hatch into maggots. The maggots then eat the decaying tissue in a fairly predictable way." Measuring and recording this information gave the facility its raison d'être.

Entomologists agree that there are four main direct relationships between insects and corpses:

1. The necrophagous species (flies and beetles) that feed directly on the corpse, and their stages of development over about two weeks helps to indicate how long the person has been dead.
2. Predators and parasites of the flies and beetles (other types of beetles that prey on eggs and maggots). Wasps are also para-

sitic on the maggots, and since each species tends to specialize, it's easy to tell what kinds of flies have been on a body.

3. Wasps, ants, and beetles that feed on both the body and the maggots. (Wasps that capture too many flies can actually delay decomposition).

4. Spiders that use the body as a habitat to prey on other insects.

As each stage of decomposition is analyzed, it's added to the growing data bank available to law enforcement. Thus far, almost three hundred corpses have been used in the studies. They have been placed in a car trunk, left in direct sun, placed under canvas and plastic, buried in mud, hung from a scaffold, locked into coffins, refrigerated in the dark, zipped into body bags, or submerged in water. Some are even embalmed.

When there's an ongoing project, the person assigned to it makes a precise digital record at regular intervals of various aspects of the disintegration process. He or she may also use an electronic nose with thirty-two sensors to record changes in the various odors. The hope is to develop sprays that can be used to train cadaver dogs. Scientists are also trying to isolate specific biochemical markers that will provide precise measurements of the PMI.

In "Sex, Lies, and Larvae," Grissom collects insect specimens so that he can grow them into adults and use "linear regression" to estimate the age of bugs found on a corpse. That means he can then estimate the PMI based on the predictable stages of larval development of the types of insects present. What he doesn't realize is that insect development can be affected by unexpected factors, and his painstaking work will have to be revised with this in mind. Even so, he finds out that sometimes there's little respect for the entomologist from the officers in charge, in part because so few people really understand the science.

M. Lee Goff is head of the forensic sciences program at the Chaminade University of Honolulu and author of *A Fly for the Pros-*

ecution. He describes the many ways that entomologists can contribute to a forensic investigation.

"Most frequently the forensic entomologist is asked to estimate the postmortem interval based on insect activity," Goff points out. "In some instances, there may be factors that serve to delay the onset of insect activity, and these must be considered."

Insects and their activity can also help in:

1. Showing that a body may have been moved

2. Serving as specimens for toxicological or drug analysis

3. Providing DNA materials from insect ingestion contents

4. Supporting or contradicting an alibi

5. Assessing when wounds were made to a body

In one case, Goff recalls that three different species of maggots were found on a female corpse. He put the evidence from their larval development into a computer program, and it came back with the result that no such corpse could exist. That meant that he had to reevaluate his data. He discovered that the way in which the body had been positioned, and the fact that it had been partially submerged in water, had altered the stages of insect activity. While it is generally the case that two of those species would not have been on a corpse in the specific stages in which they were found, there was something unique about this crime scene that made it possible. This experience made him reconsider unique characteristics of crime scenes that can throw off the formulas.

In general, the field of forensic entomology has supplied important information about how bugs come and go from a corpse. As Sara learns from Grissom, insects arrive in stages. As each feeds on the body, it changes the body for the next group, which is attracted to those particular changes. The job of the forensic entomologist is to interpret these relationships so that they can offer leads to law enforcement officers. "At present," says Goff, "entomology is relatively well accepted by crime scene investigators."

To revise his results, Grissom gets the carcass of a pig, because its stages of decomposition are closest to that of humans. He wraps it in a blanket as tightly as the victim's body was wrapped and then sets up cameras to record the PMI changes in the larval stages.

While such a method may seem farfetched to armchair observers, Goff confirms that he does indeed use pigs for research. "For each study, I use three pigs. One is placed directly on the ground or on whatever substrate I'm investigating. This pig is left undisturbed. A second pig is placed onto a welded wire-mesh weight platform. This pig is used to determine the rate of biomass removal by weight and will be weighed each time the site is visited. It's also equipped with thermocouple probes inserted into the mouth, abdomen, and anus to determine changes in internal temperatures related to decomposition. The third pig is also put on a welded wire-mesh platform placed directly on the substrate. This pig serves for sampling of insects and other arthropods."

As Goff points out, examining the gut contents of insects also helps to establish what a person ingested. This proved to be valuable in another case, when Grissom directs Warrick to cut open the maggots found on a dead young man, and finds a substance called jimsonweed, which turns out to be an important lead.

THE AUTOPSY

In many cases, the autopsy provides the most crucial pieces of evidence, as when it contradicts a story concocted by three women in "To Halve and to Hold" who rented a hotel room where a dead stripper is found. Let's have a look at one in more detail.

On C.S.I., victims of homicide get transported to the morgue, which has a refrigerated holding area for corpses while their fate is decided. Here they are tagged with a name or the case number for quick identification. They can stay in the drawers for about four days or so without suffering the effects of decomposition.

An autopsy is a postmortem examination of a corpse to determine manner and cause of death for an official report. Around 25 percent of all deaths are subject to it, including homicides, cases of sudden infant death syndrome, overdoses, industrial accidents, hit-and-run victims, deaths in prison, deaths that may involve a public hazard, and sudden unexpected deaths that have no clear explanation. Suicides sometimes get autopsied, as do some victims of motor vehicle accidents. If funds (and personnel) are available, unidentified bodies generally get autopsied.

Autopsy means "to see for oneself." One of the first on record was performed on Julius Caesar in 44 B.C., to determine the cause of his death. He had been stabbed twenty-three times, including a fatal wound to the chest.

On occasion, autopsies may be ordered after a body has already been buried. For example, a photograph of a bruise appears to have been a bite mark, but it's not sufficiently clear, so the body might be exhumed to obtain a more definitive impression to compare against the teeth impressions of a suspect. It may also happen that an autopsy was performed badly or facts were misstated. In the case of a Pennsylvania resident murdered by her husband, the coroner indicated that she had an intact appendix. The imprisoned man sued for a new trial, claiming that his wife had had an appendectomy and thus the corpse could not be hers. The body was exhumed and it turned out that the coroner had been mistaken: evidence of an appendectomy was present, and DNA tests also proved that the murdered woman was in fact the man's former wife. His conviction stood. (He obviously didn't count on an exhumation, since he knew whose body was buried in the basement of his expensive new home.)

The autopsy is part of the death investigation process, particularly if the death is suspected to have been part of a crime. A good understanding of the circumstances surrounding the death aids in the procedure. A broken lamp next to the dead stripper told the coroner to look for head injuries. In the case of a child who died from a hit-and-run, the ME looked for impressions on the body that would identify the runaway car—and among the bruises she found two numbers from the license plate.

The C.S.I.s often attend the autopsies for their specific cases, as do the homicide detectives. That way, they can discuss the case and assist one another with finding evidence. The investigators ought to have a list of objectives for the ME and requests for additional procedures beyond routine. Being present, they can answer questions that arise during the autopsy, and they can assist in the safe transfer of evidence.

An autopsy may be partial, selective, or complete, but most are partial. This means that only part of the body is examined for cause of death (for example, because there was an injury only to the head), while a selective autopsy may involve only one specific organ, such as the heart or brain. Sometimes only a head comes in, as happened in "Final Evaluation," and the flesh was boiled off the skull to get at the wound patterns for a precise identification of the weapon. (Anthropologists use this method when decomposed remains are found that still have flesh clinging to them. They use a detergent-based solution and strip the bones with great care.)

Family members should always be alerted about an autopsy (but not asked for permission) because some religions prohibit this procedure. Whether or not it goes forward depends on the higher public good and the local statutes that govern suspicious deaths. Some cases are always autopsied, no matter what objections there may be.

The MEs record all circumstances surrounding the death, along with any information they have about the deceased person. On the same form, they will record the results of the external examination, which means listing all physical characteristics. When the examination is complete, they will also state the cause of death and sign the form. This is presented as their official statement to families and to the court.

Over the steel autopsy table, which is equipped for draining away liquids, is a smaller dissection table for cutting up and examining organs, like the heart and liver. Near this is a hanging scale for weighing the organs as they're removed. A large tank on the floor collects fluids.

Before anything is done to it, the body gets photographed, both clothed (if it was clothed when found) and unclothed, or both dirty and cleaned up, or trussed and untrussed. (Kaye Shelton's corpse, for example, yielded evidence linking her wound to the bullets used only after she was cleaned up.) Then the body is X-rayed, weighed, fingerprinted, and measured, and any identifying marks are recorded. Sometimes an attempt may be made to lift latent prints from the skin, but they disappear quickly. Old and new injuries are noted, along with tattoos and scars. Trace evidence, such as hair and fibers, is collected off the body and from under the fingernails. Even the nails are clipped. The wrapping sheet, along with clothing and trace evidence, is stored to be sent for analysis. Anything that is wet from blood is air-dried first. In cases of suspected suicide by gunshot, hands are swabbed for gunpowder residue.

Once the body is clean and free of all hindrances (clothing, ligatures, jewelry), it is laid out on its back on the steel table. Often a block is placed under the head to stabilize the body. The surgeon then makes what is known as a Y incision, which is a cut into the body from shoulder to shoulder, meeting at the sternum and then going straight down the abdomen into the groin. That exposes the internal organs and provides easy access. A saw or tree branch cutter is used to cut through the ribs and collarbone so that the rib cage can be lifted from the soft internal organs as one piece.

If there's an X ray of an injury or a lodged bullet, the coroner uses this as a guide, because he might have to trace a trajectory path or avoid cutting into a knife wound. The next step is to take a blood sample from the heart to determine blood type, and then start taking the organs out, one by one, to weigh them. If there's fluid in an organ, it gets drained for a sample, and then the stomach and intestines are slit open to examine the contents. Samples are taken for testing.

Injuries are generally categorized as blunt-force trauma, gunshot, and sharp-force trauma. In all cases, the number of wounds is recorded and each wound is carefully measured and its characteristics described. A detailed examination must be made because wounds that are small can be hidden under folds of skin or in the mouth.

1. A blunt-force injury comes from impact with a blunt object, or something with no sharp edges. MEs determine the direction of impact, the type of object that caused it, and how often the contact was made. A suspect weapon may or may not be available, but if it is, then wound patterns can be matched to the weapon.

Sometimes lacerations result, which is a tearing injury from impact and has ragged or abraded edges, often with bruising. There may also be abrasions, which are friction injuries that remove superficial layers of skin. Contusions are ruptures of small blood vessels.

Wound examination is done with care. Crushing wounds result from blunt violence where the skin is close to bone, and these wounds tend to bleed into the tissues. Often they're made by blows from a hammer or an ax head. Bite marks are also a form of crushing wounds and can be crucial evidence.

2. With gunshot wounds, the coroner looks for tattooing and stippling (burns from gas and powder residue) or fouling (soot) around the wound (neither of which is present with weapons shot from a distance of more than three and a half feet). A shotgun blast makes its own distinct pattern. He also measures the size of the exit and entry wounds and extracts any bullets left in the body in order

to determine the type of gun they came from. Photos are taken to help make an estimate of how close the shooter was to the victim. The broader the area of stippling, for example, the farther away the gun was held. Contact wounds, in which the gun was held against the skin, often leave an imprint from the muzzle, and more powerful guns cause gaping wounds with powder residue and "blowback"— hot gases from the gun that fail to penetrate the body and blow back to the exterior, ripping the skin.

"Rifled" weapons (rifles and many handguns) fire single bullets, stabilizing their trajectory with grooves in the barrel. Unless they're too damaged, bullets will show some characteristics of the grooves, and the weapon may also eject identifying shell casings. If no casings are found at the scene, it may be an indication that the shooter used a revolver, which retains spent cartridges until manually reloaded. "Smoothbore" weapons like shotguns have no grooves and often fire multiple pellets.

Entrance wounds are generally round and surrounded by some abrasion. Exit wounds are irregular, bruised, without stippling, and larger than the entrance wound. They can also show protruding skin. However, there are cases where the two types of wounds look too similar to differentiate, and detailed work on the trajectory path inside the body may be needed.

3. With knife or "incised" wounds, the coroner must make a distinction between cut and stab or puncture wounds, and among different types of piercing implements such as an ice pick and a small knife. A cut is longer than it is deep, while a stab wound is deeper than it is long. Most knives have a flat edge and a sharp edge, which can be seen in the wound angles. Some wounds are defensive, such as cuts made on the palms or fingers of a victim's hands. Cuts associated with suicidal gestures are known as "hesitation wounds," as the person attempts to inflict self-damage.

Aside from wounds, victims may have been asphyxiated in some manner. Asphyxiation results from cutting off oxygen to the brain. Before a homicide can be ascertained in such cases, another possibility must be eliminated: autoerotic hypoxia, otherwise known as "terminal sex." This occurs when people—generally males—engage in masturbation while restricting oxygen to the brain. They may tie a ligature around their neck, or use plastic bags, electrocution, aerosol propellants, and mood-heightening drugs. One clue to this form of accidental death is that the victim could be wearing fetish clothing, ranging from a horse bridle to cross-gender underwear to cowboy outfits—or perhaps nothing at all. Many use bondage equipment, and often the victims are adolescents or people in their early twenties. In an actual case, one man was found dead at home, lying on his stomach and trussed up with numerous ropes and straps. He'd been dead for several days, the result of asphyxiation from a black plastic bag placed over his head. His feet were tied together and raised up behind him by a rope that was attached to a metal hook in the ceiling. His arms were bound behind him with a series of belts. Apparently he'd managed to extricate himself on other occasions, but not this time.

Asphyxia can be caused by hanging, obstruction of airways with some object, smothering, or strangulation, and each has specific manifestations, such as a crushed hyoid bone in the throat. Carbon monoxide poisoning can also cause asphyxiation, and this can be from suicide, an accident, or a homicide staged to look like a suicide.

All bruises should likewise be photographed, especially any that appear to be bite marks. A clear photo must be taken of them in order to compare later to teeth impressions from suspects. Otherwise the body may have to be exhumed.

Bodies that were discovered in water are checked for water in the lungs, as was the case with the showgirl Lacey Duvall in "Table Stakes," which indicates whether death occurred from drowning or before the body was placed in the water.

After examining wounds and injuries, pieces are cut from the organs to place on slides for further analysis in ballistics, toxicology, histology, and trace. (Contrary to what happens on *C.S.I.*, this process can take several weeks . . . even months.) If any organs are needed for evidence, they must be preserved. Otherwise, they all go into a bag and get put back into the body before it's sent for burial.

The last thing examined is the head and brain. The eyes are probed for hemorrhages that reveal strangulation. After that, an incision is made in the scalp behind the head and the skin is carefully peeled forward over the face to expose the skull. Using a high-speed oscillating power saw, the skull is opened and a chisel is used to pry off the skullcap. Then the brain can be lifted out and weighed.

A crime scene photographer may also take photographs during the autopsy. Generally, the pathologist doing the technique will direct the photographer as to what photos are needed, and color film is always used. Close-ups are made of all wounds, tattoos, scars, or bruises, and these are made with a scale laid next to the wound or mark. Photos are taken again after a wound is washed or a body part shaved. All of this may be done with a special medical lens or close-up accessory. Notes must be made, especially if there are numerous wounds.

There are many cases where bodies (or skeletons) are found without identifying information. While they're put through an autopsy, another search gets under way to establish their identities. This, too, involves a specific protocol.

THREE

ID Unknown

When bodies are found, the first priority is to determine who they are. Sometimes they have ID in a pocket or purse, or they're wearing something like jewelry or a badge that provides a quick lead, but other times there are no obvious clues. They become either "Jane" or "John Doe" and that's whose life after death we'll follow here. Identification of an unknown person may involve anything from databases to anthropology to forensic art.

In a place like Las Vegas, through which millions of tourists pass every year and where there is still occasional evidence of organized hits (as Warrick discovered on a case he couldn't solve), an unidentified body could be almost anyone. The task of identification is therefore magnified, especially if the death is a murder that someone is trying to hide. Yet since most homicides involve someone whom the victim knew, it's important to quickly establish identity to minimize chances of the perpetrator's escape. The *C.S.I.* team faces this with an unconscious rape victim, a female floater, and several bodies found just outside town.

JANE DOE

In "Too Tough to Die," Nick, Grissom, and Sara investigate the rape and attempted murder of an unidentified, comatose black woman found on the side of the road with two bullets in her head. To find a matching description and ID the victim, Sara first narrows the possibilities with available clues (type of clothing, presence or absence of a wedding ring), and then spends several hours checking through a missing-person database. There are several resources she could've been using.

A missing person is someone who has been gone for more than twenty-four hours without apparent reason, or a mentally deficient person or child under eighteen who has been reported by a concerned party. To assist law enforcement officers in the search, data about missing people gets entered into files by someone who knows them. A John or Jane Doe is also considered a missing person, on the grounds of simply having no identity, and data from the corpse is also entered into the records. The hope is that there will be a sufficient amount of overlapping information between a lost relative and a found body to make a match.

Many children are runaways and some adults just decide to get up and leave without telling anyone, but the Missing Persons Bureau is most concerned with cases where 1. someone involuntarily disappeared, and 2. they have an unknown body. The crimes generally associated with missing persons who did not leave on their own or wander off are homicide, suicide, and kidnapping.

People who report someone to the Missing Persons Bureau must supply:

- A full description of what the person looks like

- A photo, if possible

- A description of what the person was wearing when last seen

- A description of any objects that the person might have had with him or her

- Some sense of where the person was last seen or had intended to go before disappearing

- All possible information about the person's hobbies, habits, educational background, distinguishing marks (tattoos or scars), type of car, addictions, medical history, family history, business associations, and romantic involvement(s)

- Information about where the person frequently went

While many identifications are straightforward, whenever a J. Doe is discovered, the first procedure for later comparison is to make a file of the following information:

- gender

- age

- height

- weight

- dental features

- blood-type factors and DNA

- scars or other unusual marks

- evidence of medical procedures

- fingerprints

- types of personal effects found with the body

- full description of the body and facial features

If there's more than one body at a scene, such as with a car accident, the possibility of commingled personal effects must be considered before making an identification. (Just because a wallet is lying next to a body does not mean it belonged to that person, although police have mistakenly made such assumptions, resulting in a funeral for the wrong person—it happens!)

Where a sufficient number of items appear to match, the reporting family or friend is brought together with those in possession of the corpse. They're asked to make what's called a visual identification, as Bobby did with Eric in "Friends and Lovers" and Tammy Felton did with her father. The body is stored in a morgue drawer, and it's pulled out and uncovered for a close examination. If the face is unrecognizable, the friend or relative might look for some other identifying feature. (When the gangster John Dillinger was killed in 1934, he'd recently had cosmetic surgery to change his appearance. His sister did not believe the corpse was his until she saw a scar on the back of his thigh.)

If there's a chance that some evidence still exists on the body, however, and that any type of viewing could disturb it, then relatives are asked to wait. It can also happen that relatives come in to make an identification while intoxicated, and such a state might distort their perceptions sufficiently to undermine its accuracy.

Sometimes a forensic artist will make a postmortem drawing from photos of a corpse, because the corpse is in such bad condition that a visual ID would probably be useless and also quite horrifying. Investigators may also need a drawing to publish in a newspaper. The advantage to having a drawing over a morgue photo is that the artist can give the person the look of life. Sometimes death so distorts someone's features that even his close relatives don't know him.

If visual identifications fail to pay off, then detectives continue to check various missing-person databases, available through state agencies, the FBI, and even the Internet. When trying to identify Jane Doe, Sara might have checked the following sources:

- Missing-person records

- Fingerprint databases, such as AFIS (Automated Fingerprint Identification System, containing data for most jurisdictions)

- CODIS (Combined DNA Index System)

- International Association for Identification (which has state divisions)

- Local newspapers that might list a person as missing, with a photo

- Physician records, if there was a recent surgery or X ray

- Dental Society database using teeth impressions

- National Crime Information Center (NCIC)

- Autopsy results about last food ingested, which could indicate where it was purchased or eaten

There are numerous databases for missing children as well, such as the National Center for Missing and Exploited Children. If someone is suspected to be in another country, the Missing Persons Bureau informs Interpol to request assistance. To help, they ask for a set of fingerprints and a recent photo. (In one case, Grissom even suggested reading the serial number off the breast implant of a strangled woman and tracing her identity through the manufacturer.) Yet even with all of this, there is no standard processing protocol for missing persons, and many reports remain filed away in local jurisdictions rather than included in a centralized data bank.

These databases are used for solving crimes as well as for identifying missing persons, so much of the information below is relevant to other aspects of criminal investigation, such as finding a biological match. To utilize the databases most effectively, investigators need to know about the following facts and procedures:

IDENTIFIERS

Fingerprints

In "Pledging Mr. Johnson," a body surfaces, with fingers too shriveled to get accurate prints. Grissom asks Catherine to put her own hand inside the skin of the dead woman's hand so it will fill out and provide a surface for a print. This is because bodies found in water are generally in such condition that identification can be difficult. They may bloat and blacken, and often creatures have nibbled at them. Fingerprints are the best way to establish who they are, although the epidermis of the skin may be missing, loose, granulated, or coarsened. If loose, it can be cut and examined on slides. If wrinkled, water or paraffin can be injected to make the surface firm (or a finger inserted, as Catherine so unwillingly did).

In Florida in 1997, an indigent man died, and when no one claimed his body, it was taken to a funeral home to be buried in a pauper's grave. No one seemed to notice that his left hand was missing, but when it washed up onto the banks of the Manatee River, the skin was not fit to print, so the investigator put his hand inside the skin of the finger in order to get the impression. The hand was traced back to its body and buried.

Still other difficulties may be encountered when trying to take a print from a corpse. If it's mummified or decomposed into a dehydrated state, the skin may be too hard to work with. Some methods of hydrating the skin have been effective (injection with water or glycerin), but the investigator may actually have to read the print from the finger rather than from a print card. In some cases, the print can be cast with dental casting material or photographed. It's also possible to cut the fingers off at one of the middle joints to soften the skin with hand or fabric softener.

If the body is in a state of rigor, then the joints need to be massaged or bent back to loosen them for taking the prints. (If the fingers are rigidly bent toward the palm, it's sometimes necessary to cut some tendons to bend the hand backward as far as possible.) Then the fingers may be braced together with a device called a spoon so that the papillary patterns of the tips can be inked and pressed against thin fingerprint cards. (The cards are rolled against the finger rather than the other way around.) Several prints should be taken of the same finger to avoid ending up with only one that may be smudged. When all of the fingers are done, the best set of prints is selected and placed in J. Doe's file.

One way to take prints without using ink is with a technology called "Livescan." The finger is inserted into a machine that has a sensor pad that scans it as a digital image, which can be sent to an AFIS database. However, only some morgues have access to this.

Three-dimensional print technology is now available for clearer images than an inked print produces. These are thought to be superior to computer scans of print cards because interpreting prints into digital imagery involves a binary system of black and white that can darken gray areas. Unfortunately, this technology may require an entirely new database.

Positive identification via databases is made from an accurate comparison between fingerprints in the files and those taken from the corpse. In "Sex, Lies, and Larvae," Brass identifies a woman found in the wilderness via AFIS as Kaye Shelton, and because of a "preschool printing initiative" in the case of four-year-old Melissa Marlowe, her prints can be matched to her twenty-one years later. A match requires exemplars (original samples) already in the database, such as from a job or crime.

Fingerprints are matched according to the pattern of ridges and valleys present on the fingertip. Ridges start, stop, divide, and swirl around in ways unique to each person. To make a comparison, the print expert picks out several identifying ridges and makes sure that every point between the two prints being compared is the same. If one print pattern bifurcates, the other one had better. If one swirls to the right, so must the other. Experts examine thickness and location of pores, breaks in ridges, and changes in direction. Once two points of identity are located, the ridges between them are counted. The number must be the same for both exemplar and questioned print. While there are no minimum number of points of comparison needed to declare a match, a comparison expert will try for as many as possible. They know that only one point of dissimilarity is sufficient to say that the prints from the file are not consistent with the prints from the person.

AFIS was a significant advance in fingerprint identification. Whereas a search for similar prints once took weeks of tedious work, now it takes only about ten minutes. Most jurisdictions have access to statewide AFIS banks. However, with several incompatible AFIS technologies in use (because different vendors produce them), prints stored in one system cannot be searched by another. That means that the prints may have to be sent to several different places—at least until computer software overcomes the differences.

Even without AFIS, a match can be made. If a relative thinks the corpse might be a certain person, but the corpse is in bad shape, then fingerprints taken from the missing person's home or workplace can serve for comparison purposes. No prints are taken from the dead, however, until all possible trace evidence is removed from the hands and from under the fingernails.

Depictions

Certain photographs are taken of the deceased to keep in a file. Full-face and side-profile views are taken (but not when the corpse is bloated), along with photos of any identifying marks, such as scars or tattoos. Special attention is paid to the ears. Clothing and teeth may also be photographed, and even badly decomposed bodies may yield significant marks. (It's a good idea to go over the body with an infrared light to find marks that otherwise may not be visible, as Sara did in one case of child abuse.)

In addition to a photograph, a thorough description of the body is kept in the file. It will include the basics of height, weight, and general physical condition (without confusing decomposition effects such as bloating with body build), as well as color and style of hair, presence of facial hair, the shape of the head and face, and anything about the person that stands out. Since reddish hair may indicate only the effects from lying outside in a dry or hot area, care is taken to note conditions that might affect the color. Eye color, too, may be altered from its original condition, and noses and lips usually swell up and change their shape. People familiar with postmortem changes will know best how to take down descriptions.

Every article of clothing needs to be described in detail, including missing buttons, rips, stains, and discoloration. If shoes are available, the size is noted. Watches may be traced back to watchmakers or identified via the American Watchmakers Institute. Eyeglasses, too, might be traced to an optometrist, who would have records of clients. Some jewelry may have initials or other identifying marks. Many rings indicate membership in an organization or graduation from a specific educational institution.

Handwriting

If there's a handwritten document available on a J. Doe, it's possible to compare it to an exemplar found in the residence of a missing person who police suspect may be the victim. (However, those documents may have been planted on the corpse or may belong to someone else.) Experts compare for stylistic and personal characteristics. The writing style is the general manner of writing taught in a certain culture, but people generally reshape the style in some way idiosyncratic to them.

Document examiners look at the slope of the writing, whether the person was right- or left-handed, the size of the letters relative to one another, the way the letters are formed, the length of spaces between words or letters, and the repetition of mistakes in spelling or grammar.

Teeth and Bones

Teeth are the hardest substance in the body and tend to last the longest. They also exhibit such individual characteristics that identification via dental impressions is as reliable as identification with fingerprints. Even if a corpse is badly mutilated or decomposed, the teeth generally retain their characteristics. They even resist most fires.

Descriptions of teeth indicate:

- How many are present and which ones are missing (if any)

- Recent injuries or extensive dental work

- Whether any of the dental work is unusual (such as a filling that looks like batwings)

- Evidence of partial or full dentures

- Enamel coloration

- Crowding and spacing characteristics, as well as buckteeth

- Tobacco stains (if any)

- Type of occlusion

- Age (from worn areas, loose teeth, root transparency, closing of root openings)

- Chips, breakage, or other damage

X rays are made if necessary, and forensic dentists are often consulted. Impressions of a corpse's teeth can be sent to various types of dental data banks, as Nick did with the teeth of the older man whose bones were found scattered in the desert. He got a hit from a local dentist whose patient had the right dental characteristics. In cases where people are beyond recognition by visual inspection, dental work may be the only way to identify them. If they've decomposed to skeletons, then anthropological methods are used.

From bone structure, an expert can determine gender, height, injuries during life, ethnicity, and age. (In the case of Kaye Shelton in "Sex, Lies, and Larvae," an X ray revealed to Grissom and Sara that the female murder victim had multiple healed fractures, which indicated a history of spousal abuse. Had she not been identified through AFIS, they could have checked at various hospitals.) Personal identification comes from comparing X rays of fractures or evidence of illness that can be matched to a person's medical records.

If part of the face is missing, as with accidents, explosions or gunshots, some reconstruction may be required to get an accurate appearance for photos. Mortuary supplies are ideal for this purpose, and an expert embalmer can consult or assist with such a procedure. However, they need to be instructed not to hide scars or other facial features that may help with identification. This work is less about creating a "memory picture" than about linking a body with a name.

Blood Type and DNA

Blood is grouped by type—A, B, AB, and O—and by Rh factors. It's drawn from the heart or major vessel of the J. Doe for typing and comparison against medical or military charts of missing persons. While a match is not conclusive, because many people share the same blood type, the lack of a match does eliminate possibilities. If John Doe has Type A negative blood, and the missing Jack Daniels has Type O positive, then John Doe is not Jack Daniels.

More precise than blood typing is DNA profiling (sometimes referred to as DNA fingerprinting), which is based on our genetic makeup. Keith Inman works in the California Department of Justice

DNA laboratory, and with Dr. Norah Rudin, he wrote *An Introduction to Forensic DNA Analysis.*

He explains that the term "DNA fingerprinting" is a misnomer because it does not distinguish between identical twins the way fingerprinting does. Comparing the method with fingerprinting raises the wrong expectations.

What DNA profiling does, he points out, is examine small sections of human DNA known to vary among people. Like blood-group typing, different people have different types, but DNA is far more discriminating.

Let's have a closer look at what it is and how it's analyzed.

DNA, or deoxyribonucleic acid, is the genetic blueprint that gives us our distinguishing characteristics. It's found in the nucleus of the cell. We inherit half of our DNA from our mother and half from our father. The DNA molecule resembles a twisted ladder, called a double helix, which consists of four chemical subunits, or bases (adenine, guanine, cytosine, and thymine). These bases pair together in predictable ways. When strung together in paired chromosomal strands (double-stranded helix), A always aligns with T, and G with C, etc., to form cellular protein and enzymes.

DNA is coiled quite tightly inside the cell nucleus, but unrolled, a molecule of DNA is approximately six feet long. Although some parts of our DNA are universally human—two arms, ten fingers, two legs, etc.—certain sections contain the codes that give us our individual uniqueness, a fact that holds true for all the cells throughout the body. Thus, by looking at the unique DNA parts—called polymorphisms—experts can determine whether a particular strand of DNA found in a specimen is "indistinguishable from" the DNA of a particular person.

Nuclear DNA exists only in cells that contain nuclei, so it's not in red blood cells, the hair shaft, or the outer layer of the skin, but is found in cells mixed in body fluids, and in hair follicles, tooth pulp, bone marrow, and all muscle and organ tissue. Thus, a DNA sample can be taken from almost any part of J. Doe's body and compared against DNA databases.

Since the DNA repeats in every nucleate cell, so do the polymorphic regions. These base pairs are called Variable Number of Tandem Repeats, or VNTRs, because the exact number of repeated sequences varies from person to person, which means its length also varies. It's the VNTRs that offer genetic identification.

To find the polymorphisms, one must first separate out—or "extract"—the DNA from the cell environment. The first method developed for this is known as Restriction Fragment Length Polymorphism, or RFLP. The way it works is that the extracted DNA is mixed with substances called restriction enzymes that "recognize" a particular sequence of DNA bases and "digest" or cut the DNA strand into fragments. The amount in each fragment varies from person to person. Those fragments are then placed at one end of a foot-wide container of gel and an electrical current is applied (a process called electrophoresis), causing them to move through the gel at different speeds and line up at the positive pole according to size. Then they're treated in such a way that the DNA double helix can be unzipped into single strands or bands.

The scientist then takes the pieces from the gel with a nylon membrane called a Southern Blot, and the DNA fragments are fixed to the membrane. The A, T, C, and G bases of the strand become exposed. They get treated with a chemical or radioactive synthetic single-strand genetic probe. The probe seeks out and binds to its complementary base, revealing a pattern.

The probe identifies some pieces of the DNA with dark bands, as revealed by an X ray (autoradiograph or autorad) of the membrane. This looks similar to the bar codes on food packages at the supermarket, except that unlike supermarket packages, it's different for each individual. Then a print is made of the polymorphic sequences, which can be compared (visually or by computer) to prints made from other specimens. The interpretation of a sample is based on statistical probability, and the estimate of any two people having the same DNA can be as high as one in several billion.

While this method was in use for over a decade, it had some drawbacks: it required a considerable amount of DNA material to work with (a semen stain the size of a quarter, for example), and it did not do well with degraded samples.

Then a method that worked with smaller samples was developed, specifically to replicate the DNA. This is called Polymerase Chain Reaction, or PCR. It mimics the cell's ability to replicate its own DNA, and can take a few cells and multiply them millions of times to get the size of the sample required—and do it in short order! In addition, PCR can work with degraded or aged specimens.

Also known as molecular Xeroxing, PCR begins with DNA extraction from the cell. This is heated in a thermocycler to make it split. The temperature is lowered and then raised again while a reaction mixture is added, which produces a copy (called amplification). The process is then repeated about thirty times. The reaction mixture consists of a pair of DNA segments that indicate the target segment and an enzyme that catalyzes the reaction, plus the four bases mentioned before. It can copy both parts of the separated DNA strand.

Once the DNA is copied, the analysis continues, and the results can be read as a series of colored dots. The intensity of the color represents the amount of the DNA amplified. This is called the "dot blot."

Linda B. Jankowski is the DNA technical director for the New Jersey State Police Forensic Science Bureau. She has a master's degree from Rutgers University in molecular biology and has been trained in DNA analysis at the FBI academy at Quantico. Keeping up with the trends in criminal investigations, she says that the method most commonly used these days is STR, which stands for Short Tandem Repeat. "PCR is a generic term for a method of replicating sections of DNA," she explains, "and depending on what sections of DNA you replicate, you do a further analysis to get the actual profile. The further analyses pursued now by labs all over the world are the STRs."

STRs are regions of a DNA molecule that have short segments of three to seven repeating base pairs that are less susceptible to degradation than the longer segments used for RFLP. How STR typing works is to amplify it via PCR, then separate it in an electrophoretic gel or a capillary device. There are hundreds of different types of STRs in human genes, which means that the lab tech can extract and amplify a number of different DNA markers in a single analysis (which is known as "multiplexing"). Generally, for specificity of identity, they work with thirteen core loci, or sites, as stipulated by the FBI.

This method is as discriminating as RFLP and reduces the time required for results. It also needs only a small sample.

Another DNA test that works on even smaller samples—as few as fifteen to twenty cells—is the LCN, or Low Copy Number test. It's time-consuming and expensive, and as of this writing has not yet been tested in a court case. While it may enable forensic scientists to do more with less, there's a problem.

"The technology to make LCN widely available and affordable for crime labs," says Jankowsi, "is several years in the future. The LCN procedure is being discussed quite a bit in law enforcement seminars, but the problem is that you have to tweak up the sensitivity of your analysis to a point where contamination is a real issue. You're starting with so few cells that to get a final result, you have to increase the sensitivity of your analysis, and any single cell that gets introduced at any step of the way can contaminate the results. We need a very sterile technique, but the problem is that the crime scene isn't sterile, so it's difficult to get a profile from a few cells with the LCN technique and not get contamination."

Although there are collection kits for DNA samples that include swabs and specific types of containers, at this point, it must all go from the crime scene to the lab for analysis. However, in the future, that may change. "What they're hoping to do," Jankowski reveals, "is get portable DNA analysis that can be taken right to the crime scene, and make it more automated and quick. Around the country, they're developing a technique with SNPs—Single Nucleotide Polymorphisms—which is very discriminating and fast. However, STRs are firmly entrenched, and whenever you change to a new technique, that means a new database, so STRs will be around for a while."

At times, a cell nucleus isn't available, so another method for missing-person identification is to extract and analyze mitochondrial DNA (mt-DNA). This substance is found in the cytoplasm of most cells, and it's different from that found in the nucleus. For one thing, it doesn't get lost through decomposition as the cell nucleus does, enduring in the bones for centuries. For another, it stays the same in a family for generations and it's only inherited through the maternal line. That means when a J. Doe is being identified, DNA can be extracted from living relatives on the mother's side. They will possess an identical mitochondrial DNA type.

"Mitochondrial DNA analysis is not done at a lot of labs in this country," Jankowski points out, "but the FBI lab and some private labs do it. It can be done with old or degraded samples. It can also be used on hair shafts and bones. You would try to get the STRs first if you can, because they give you greater discriminating power, but with the mitochondrial DNA, there are so many copies of it in each cell that you can get a result even when you can't get STRs. As part of the CODIS program, they're working on a mitochondrial database for missing persons. Relatives of someone reported missing would volunteer to give samples."

Mitochondrial DNA analysis was instrumental in identifying a group of skeletons dug up in Russia in 1979. Believed to be those of Czar Nicholas II and the Romanov family, who were executed in 1918, the skulls were too badly crushed for any type of reconstruction. In 1992, a group of American forensic experts was assembled to assist with identification. There were nine skeletons, rather than the expected

**eleven, and fourteen bullets recovered from the hidden grave. Tests
were done on the czarina's bones, and blood samples were taken from
a known relative on the maternal line of Britain's Queen Elizabeth II.
They matched. The same type of testing was also done on the deceased Anna Anderson, who had claimed for half a century that she
was the Romanov daughter Anastasia. She wasn't.**

Now what about the databases? The federal DNA Identification
Act of 1994 provided $40 million for the development of DNA tech-
nology in state and local crime laboratories and authorized the FBI
to create a National DNA Identification Index. The national system
is called CODIS, or the Combined DNA Index System, a database
of DNA samples taken from felons, as well as body fluid evidence
collected at crime scenes such as assaults, rapes, and homicides. Each
state has its own database (all states mandate the collection of DNA
samples from convicted offenders) and the FBI is in the processing
of connecting them all so that law enforcement agencies around the
country can establish links among cases and identify homicide victims. The state systems are called SDIS, and local systems within
states—the participating member forensic science agencies—are
LDIS. These may include those based in large cities as well as mobile
regional laboratories.

If identification cannot be made in a reasonable amount of time,
then local missing-person reports are monitored for several months,
and the material is resubmitted to national and statewide databases.
It may also help to publish the person's photo in the newspaper to
drum up leads.

When X rays, DNA, fingerprints, and other information fail to
find a match, then special procedures may be utilized. This is where
forensic consultants come in, such as forensic anthropologists (primarily for bones), forensic artists (sketch, reconstruct, or re-image a
face). Now let's see how different types of forensic artistry can assist
in the idenfication process.

IDENTITY AND ANTHROPOLOGY

In "Who Are You?" the C.S.I.s are faced with the task of identifying a skeleton embedded in the concrete beneath someone's home. Fortunately, the concrete holds a perfect impression of the victim's features, which means Grissom can bring in the services of a forensic sculptor. What Grissom encounters in the search for the victim's identity is similar to what happened in a real case.

In Los Angeles in 1987, the skeletal remains of a woman were found encased in the cement foundation of a home. She had been stabbed multiple times. The wet cement had formed an outline of her face before hardening. The police artist used this to make a death mask, from which she then made a sketch that was shown to the public. A man came forward with a possible name, and that meant they could match that woman's fingerprints from a workplace to prints left in the concrete. Rubber silicone was poured into the hand molds and allowed to dry. When removed, it showed a clear ridge pattern, which allowed an identification. Along with this, they were able to make out clear defensive stab wounds on her hands.

A forensic sculpture may be done by an anthropologist or an artist trained in science and pathology, so let's look first at the field of anthropology, or the study of humans. The discipline consists of four subfields:

1. Physical anthropology: the study of the primate order, past and present, such as primate biology, skeletal biology, and human adaptation

2. Linguistic anthropology: the study of the development of language in culture

3. Cultural anthropology: the study of human society, past and present

4. Archaeology: the study of past cultures through material remains and artifacts

Forensic anthropology generally utilizes methods from physical and archaeological studies, along with knowledge of osteology (the study of bones), under the auspices of the law. Some anthropologists may also specialize in body decomposition and entomology, but they tend to team up with pathologists, odontologists, and homicide investigators to identify remains, point out evidence of foul play, and help with estimates of the time of death.

"Forensic anthropologists identify bones," says Dr. Stanley Rhine, professor emeritus at the University of New Mexico, in his book *Bone Voyage*. "They also assist in the recovery of bodies and perform many other tasks having to do with human remains in that interesting intersection of medicine and the law. A well-thought-out plan for recovering a body should include a forensic anthropologist." Such experts, he points out, can distinguish among injuries to the bone that occurred before or after death—and even while the person was in the process of dying.

The medicolegal anthropological examination begins with evaluating the bones to make certain they're human. If so, a chain of custody is established in terms of who will be in charge of handling the bones and making determinations about identity. Then the bones can be transported to a lab for analysis.

It's possible that not all of the bones will be available for bodily reconstruction. As Grissom mentions to Catherine when they search for a disarticulated (separated) skeleton in the desert, the human body has 206 bones. If they can't all be found, several key bones can still reveal quite a bit.

Human bones taken together weigh about twelve pounds for the average male and ten for females. Often, the speculations about whether a skeleton is male or female is based on expectations, so a very small male could be mistaken for female, especially if the pelvis bone is unavailable. To the trained eye, bones "speak." They can indicate whether the person was right- or left-handed, was calcium deficient, had a debilitating illness, suffered fractures during life or after death, and sometimes can even reveal the occupation he or she had.

The basic identifying factors that investigators need to know, which can often be read from bones, are:

- Gender: the male pelvis is narrower than the female, and certain features of the skull (supraorbital ridge and nuchal crest) are larger in males.

- Age: read from calcifications, the stages at which bones are uniting, successive changes in the pelvis, evidence of bone diseases like arthritis, and the way teeth are worn down.

- Previous trauma: if a bone was broken or fractured and there are hospital records, this can help with identification.

- Race: one of three races can be determined from variations in the facial structure, especially the nose and eye sockets. In Negroids and Mongoloids, the nose ridge is broader than in Caucasians.

- Height: an intact corpse can be measured, but a disarticulated or incomplete skeleton has to be pieced together. Dr. Mildred Trotter devised a formula for determining height from the long bones of a skeleton, and Grissom uses this on the skeleton from the desert to determine that the man was about six feet tall. The formula, used on dry bones without cartilage and utilizing an osteometric calculation board, is generally as follows:

Length of femur multiplied by 2.38 + 61.41 cm = height

Length of tibia multiplied by 2.52 + 78.62 = height

Length of fibula multiplied by 2.68 + 71.78 = height

If all three bones are available, all three are measured and the results are used to get an average. Tables are also available for making estimates on whether the person was slender, of medium build, or heavy.

FORENSIC ART

According to Karen T. Taylor, author of *Forensic Art and Illustration,* there are four basic types of forensic art:

1. Composite imagery, such as a police sketch from eyewitness reports

2. Image modification and image identification: the enhancement and manipulation of photos, such as with age progression or fugitive updates

3. Reconstructive aids: methods to help identify postmortem remains, such as two- or three-dimensional facial reconstruction from skulls

4. Demonstrative aids: visual information for presenting cases in court, such as charts or crime scene reconstructions

Composite Drawing

Taylor is versed in all aspects of forensic art, so she understands how involved the skill can be. "The work that forensic artists do is complex," she says, "and it's easy to underestimate, particularly with composite drawing. Interviewing the victim of a traumatic event and trying to retrieve the memory that's encoded and associated with the trauma is quite difficult. It must be done with great care. You have to know how to handle a person who's been through something like that, so artists have to be trained in how to do this. A face gets encoded and stored in someone's mind, and ideally we perform the retrieval in a way that corresponds to the encoding process."

While there are software programs that purport to accurately duplicate the composite drawing process, Taylor is cautious about them. "It doesn't work well when software is designed to pull up a whole screen of isolated pairs of eyes, noses, or mouths to choose from. People don't relate to that. They need to see the features in the context of the rest of the face. One thing that's often underestimated is the importance of proportion. I know of a high profile case in which a computer system for facial composites was used and it was far off from the suspect's actual appearance because the system's user had no knowledge of facial anatomy and no understanding of the spatial arrangement of facial features. I refer to this as the gestalt of the face or the holistic grasp of the features. That's what gets encoded about a face in our minds, and that's what we want to retrieve to document that likeness. We have to ask the right questions to get the right proportions."

Superimposition

While composite drawings can be done for missing persons and with victims of trauma, or from eyewitness accounts, many bodies are found in such deteriorated condition that other methods must be used, particularly if there's no one around to offer a description of what the person looked like when alive. One of these, used for skeletal remains, is known as "superimposition," which means placing one image on top of another to make a close visual comparison.

In 1985, a team of forensic anthropologists went to São Paulo, Brazil to identify what were said to be the remains of the Nazi war criminal Josef Mengele, who'd run experiments in Auschwitz. The bones had been exhumed from a grave bearing the name Wolfgang Gerhard, and most were fractured and in disarray, including the skull.

For comparison purposes, they had few records of the living Mengele. There were no dental X rays, and only the number of fillings had been noted in his files. From extensive examination, the bones proved to be those of a right-handed Caucasian male between sixty and seventy. Estimates from bone measurements came within half a centimeter to Mengele's height. That was sufficient to continue.

The anthropologists decided on a technique called "video skull-face superimposition." Piecing together the shattered skull, they marked it with pins at thirty points of comparison. They did the same with photographs of Mengele and set the skull and photo side by side. On both, they trained cameras. If all thirty points lined up, then they could say they had a positive identification of the Nazi fiend.

The cameras recorded and then superimposed the images, and the experts carefully examined the matching areas. Finally, they pronounced the exhumed skull as that of war criminal Josef Mengele.

Sometime later, Mengele's dental X rays were located and compared with the skull's remaining teeth. They proved a match, supporting the video superimposition.

Forensic Sculpture

A forensic anthropologist or forensic artist might also be called in to do a facial reconstruction, known as a forensic sculpture. This skill dates back to 1895. Anatomist Wilhelm His created full-size models that looked remarkably similar to his subjects. On the skull that allegedly had belonged to composer Johann Sebastian Bach, he managed to reconstruct a face based on the bone structure that looked sufficiently like the composer to authenticate the skull. After this, forensic sculpture was developed in Russia for years before it became a more common instrument of law enforcement in America.

The skull must first be prepared. Since it may be evidence in a crime, it must be handled with care, i.e., not picked up by the eye sockets and always stabilized to prevent it from rolling. If teeth fall out, a dentist needs to replace them. It may be that some parts have deteriorated or been damaged, so they need to be restored. Cotton wadding works to support fragile bones, and sometimes certain parts of the skull, such as the eye sockets or a bullet hole, can be taped for protection. The actual "reconstruction" is a term used to describe the soft tissue projections outward from the bone, which will have different thicknesses in different areas. (Dr. Stanley Rhine was one of the experts who developed tissue depth tables, which take into account muscle formation, fatty deposits, connective tissue, and skin types.) Artists rely on certain established formulas to mold features like the nose and mouth.

Before the physical work begins, the artist or anthropologist gathers all of the information about the case to study it. When bones from the assassinated Russian royal family, the Romanovs, were found, for example, knowing that they'd been shot, bayoneted, and battered with gun butts helped to explain many of the injuries. Also, anthropologists will provide details about gender, age, race, and other features that help to determine how a face would probably look.

Artists study various parts of the skull, including the teeth, to determine how a person looked before death. Missing teeth are evaluated for whether they fell out before or after death. If they fell out after death, dentures or partial dentures may be used for the restoration.

Briefly, one technique involves:

1. Making a two-dimensional blueprint for a guide.

2. Making a cast of the skull (or just using the skull itself).

3. Drilling small holes in strategic places for inserting thin wooden or vinyl pegs that serve as measures of skin, tissue, and muscle depth (or sometimes they're glued on).

4. Using modeling clay, the muscles and features around the

nose, mouth, cheeks, and eyes are carefully built up along the bony structure and a thin layer of plastic or clay goes over the skull. The neck is developed and then ears are formed and attached to the sides of the skull.

5. Individual features, such as the width of the nose and mouth, are developed from combining formulas with educated guesses about idiosyncrasies; textures are added to humanize the face, along with eyebrows.

6. Then a wig and prosthetic eyes are put into place, and the eyelids are formed and perhaps makeup applied that is similar to what an embalmer might use for cosmetic enhancement. (If hair is found at the scene, it provides clues for the artist, from thickness and color to style.) Glasses, jewelry, or items of clothing discovered with the skeleton are arranged where appropriate on the finished reconstruction.

7. Photographs and/or drawings are made based on the sculpture for use on posters and in the newspaper.

By the anatomical method, muscles are created individually for making a face, while the tissue depth method relies on data about the depth of facial tissue on various types of faces, collected at twenty-one points for both genders and all three racial groups. Some approaches combine both. No matter which method is used, the artist needs to know a lot about facial anatomy.

Another technique is to set the skull on a turntable. As it turns, information is fed into a computer via a laser beam and assembled into a likeness, based on information from other faces with similar measurements and racial origins.

Forensic sculpture was used to try to identify seven of serial killer John Wayne Gacy's victims. In 1973, twenty-eight bodies in various stages of decomposition had been found beneath his house or in his

garden (with five more in the river). Because few parents of missing boys could believe that their sons would engage in the kind of homosexual activity that Gacy claimed happened, they offered little assistance. Detectives had to use dental records, fingerprints, and X rays to identify many of the corpses. When fewer than half of the bodies were identified after six weeks, they called in forensic anthropologist Clyde Snow.

Snow compiled measurements and a chart for each skull, based on thirty-five points of reference that could be compared with descriptions in missing-persons reports. For example, he determined that one skeleton had been five-feet-eleven, was left-handed, had sustained a head injury, and had broken his left arm. All of this matched the missing former marine, David Talsma.

After a year, there were still nine bodies left to identify, so Snow invited sculptress Betty Pat. Gatliff to work on seven of the skulls. Her first step was to establish the thickness of the skin, and to do this, she glued pencil erasers on it at various strategic points. Then she applied modeling clay in accordance with certain measurements. That gave her an idea of what the mouth and cheeks would have looked like. Then she made noses, inserted prosthetic eyes, and added a wig of the appropriate color. One victim was identified and five more were tentatively identified.

Two-Dimensional Reconstruction

Also used for the same purpose, but less time-consuming, is the method of two-dimensional reconstruction from the skull, pioneered by Karen Taylor. This involves all the same information as the three-dimensional approach, but after the markers are added, the technique diverges.

"I applied all the rubber markers to the skull as if I were going to do a three-dimensional reconstruction," Taylor explains, "and then photographed it. I developed prints of the frontal and lateral views that were life-size, one-to-one with the skull. I then did life-size drawings based on photos of the skull and incorporated the information from Betty Pat. Gatliff's method. To determine the width of the nose, we measure the nasal aperture—the pear-shaped opening of the nose—and add so many millimeters on each side if the individual is Caucasoid, and so many if they're Negroid, etc. So by doing it life-size, the same information applies."

Image Manipulation

In "Face Lift," Teri Miller works on a computer enhancement from photos of a young kidnapping victim to see what she might look like as a grown woman. Using a program based on what forensic artists know about facial development through stages of growth, as well as a photo of the victim's mother, Miller recalibrates the dimensions and creates a computerized composite that can help with identification. While she seems to manipulate the image quickly and easily, this can actually be a painstaking process.

Computer-generated or hand-drawn age progressions are utilized in most cases of reported missing children who have been gone for a considerable period of time. They also help to assist in the capture of fugitives from the law who have been on the run long enough to have changed, or who have a reputation for changing their identities via facial hair, weight gain or loss, disguise, and hair dye. The artist takes into account the way most humans age, with reference to specific family characteristics such as weight and wrinkle formation. If a photo isn't available, a sketch can serve the same purpose.

When family-killer John List left five dead bodies in his home in New Jersey in 1971, all leads dried up. Fifteen years later, an old photo was manipulated to add features like jowls, a double chin, and droop-

ing eyes that would have been characteristic of a man his age at the time. Someone recognized him from these photos, although it was not until a three-dimensional rendition was made and televised in 1989 that he was finally caught. The tip that was called in was from the same person who had identified him based on the enhanced photos.

When an age progression is done with a computer program, the features to be added can be painted directly into the computer image.

Mary H. Manhein, author of *The Bone Lady,* directs the Forensic Anthropology and Computer Enhancement Services Laboratory (FACES) at Louisiana State University. For the first decade of its existence, the laboratory offered the typical work of forensic anthropology. In 1990, the staff added another feature: "We have a computer enhancement component, where we do age progression on missing children and adults. My assistant was trained at the National Center for Missing and Exploited Children, yet we take it beyond what they do, because we also do computer enhancement on missing felons and missing adults. And we can clear up videotapes of robberies of convenience stores, and do the three-dimensional facial reconstructions that helps get people identified."

The work of Manhein and others indicates that there's more involved with image manipulation than Teri Miller implies. On the photo of a child, age progression involves:

- The use of a photo after the age of two

- Having access to photos of siblings the same age at which the child was when she disappeared

- Having access to full frontal facial photos of the parents, and even of grandparents or other relatives that the child resembles

- Photos of parents at the age to which the child will be progressed

- Information about medical conditions that can affect appearance

- Information about quantifiable growth data

Using a computer-generated age progression, the photo gets scanned into the software. The software then helps to predict the structural changes that the face would undergo during specific ages, and it morphs the photo into those changes. The child's face would broaden and lengthen, because faces grow downward and forward. Secondary teeth replace baby teeth, and the bridge of the nose rises. The cranium expands and the eyes become less rounded. The mouth widens to make room for more teeth and the nose lengthens. Light-colored hair tends to darken. By age twelve, the face is looking more adult, with the chin forming and the nose still growing. Eventually the cheekbones become more prominent and eyebrows fill in.

Then the child's photo, now at the appearance appropriate to the age, may be laid side by side against the photo of a parent or sibling, and the two are merged by degrees, according to the way the artist handles the controls.

Since the face has stopped growing in adulthood, aging an adult's photo, such as for a fugitive update, involves a different approach. Artists need to know how faces age, hairlines recede, and hair color changes. It helps to have access to photos of family members around the target age. Some knowledge of personal habits, such as smoking or eating, also helps, and as people age, they often wear glasses. The type of personality they have affects tension lines in the face, and something in their medical history may affect how they look.

Sometimes, to cover all bases, the artist will develop multiple appearances. General anatomical guidelines of how faces age through the decades, such as a sagging jawline, hair loss, and thinning lips, provide the most important clues.

No matter which method is used, there's no doubt that forensic art offers significant assistance in identifying those Jane and John Does whose identities cannot be determined with visual inspections, fingerprints, or morgue photos.

In the end, Sara discovered the identity of the unconscious rape victim in "Too Tough to Die" from a missing-person database. Had it turned up nothing, she might have used forensic art to publish a drawing, as Grissom did with the woman discovered in the house foundation.

While work goes on to establish a victim's identity, the lab technicians are busy with biological and trace materials. Let's see where the physical evidence collected at the crime scene ends up.

FOUR

Traces

One of the earliest documented uses of physical evidence was the 1784 case of John Toms, in England. Based on a torn wad of paper in his pocket that matched the newspaper used to pack gunpowder in his pistol, he was convicted of murder. As his case proves, there are times when a single piece of physical evidence establishes the essential link, but there are other times when an abundance of evidence just isn't enough.

All trace evidence ends up in some section of the crime lab, whether it's sand, cat hair, pollen, or fiber from a crime scene rug. Some items get compared with a database or held to compare later with other evidence, and others go through an extensive analysis on sophisticated machines. It's called trace evidence because it's so small it can easily be missed.

Trace evidence, though often insufficient on its own to make a case, may corroborate other evidence, narrow leads, or even prompt a confession. Because trace evidence can be any number of things, there are numerous ways to handle it. The main point is that some apparently foreign object or piece of material is present at a crime scene, and tracing its origin can assist in an arrest and conviction. Even something as tiny as a cubic zirconium can be useful, as when Warrick matches it to a suspect's ring. Similarly, finding some trace from the victim or crime scene—soil, hair, fiber—on a suspect can impact a case.

FOLLOWING THE EVIDENCE

One of the key issues in crime investigation is the need to individualize any piece of evidence. Things like shoeprints, fibers, and plant pods are generally known as "class evidence." That means the item can be grouped with a class of items like it, and its evidential value is less weighty than if it's clearly tied to an individual the way a fingerprint is. A plastic garbage bag used to wrap a dead baby is fairly useless as evidence unless it can be matched to others in the possession of a suspect that all have the same unique machine imprints. The paper used for a printed ransom note belongs to a large class of that type of paper until a mark made by a particular printer can be traced to the suspect's office. While that's not conclusive evidence, it can still be powerful. The more unique something is when tied to a suspect, the more likely that it will have value to the prosecution process.

Thus, in "Who Are You?" grains of sand found deep inside the skull of the victim are sent to the lab to determine mineralogy, one of the most time-consuming aspects of soil comparison. This generally involves the microscopic examination of several hundred minute grains of a given sample through their optical properties. However, new computer programs have been developed that categorize the spectra and simplify the sorting process. Greg appears to be using one of these when he quickly delivers the news that the sample is man-made quartz crystal, which the team ultimately links to the suspect's home fish tank.

Similarly, the fictional detective Sherlock Holmes took great care to look for the smallest clues, and his painstaking observations actually influenced modern criminal investigations. Anything was possible fodder for his deductive reasoning, and minute evidence could shift the case in a completely new direction. Nothing was too inconsequential, and anything might be part of the chain of reasoning that eventually led to resolution.

That means that every piece of physical evidence must be analyzed. Sometimes, the C.S.I.s do this work. Othertimes, greater specialization is needed. Whether scientist or technician, they work according to Einstein's three rules:

1. Out of clutter, find simplicity.

2. From discord, make harmony.

3. In the middle of difficulty, find opportunity.

THE CRIME LAB

The first police lab in the United States opened in 1924, directed by August Vollmer, the Los Angeles chief of police. In 1929, the Scientific Crime Detection Lab was founded in Evanston, Illinois. The success of this lab convinced the FBI they needed one, too, and this opened in 1932 with a single comparison microscope. The American Society of Crime Laboratory Directors (ASCLD) offers guidelines on how a crime lab should be managed and certification based on the highest standards.

In the first episode of *C.S.I.*, we see rookie Holly Gribbs in Grissom's office and parts of the lab (specifically the morgue). Although she's been through forensics training, her inexperience offers viewers the chance to see a crime lab through the eyes of a newcomer. We also see the lab instruments whenever an evidence technician is involved in an analysis.

Not all crime labs are as nicely equipped or spacious as this one, but it does give the appearance of sterility and professional efficiency. The crime lab is essentially a science lab, with various sterile workstations set up for different purposes, but it is not for experimentation. The task here is to help solve crimes or link suspects to a crime scene. Evidence that passes from one area to another must be carefully handled with a specific protocol to avoid contamination. A blood-soaked shirt may be sent first for trace analysis to remove any fibers or hairs, which can fall off quickly. Then it goes for serology analysis. If a technique is destructive to evidence, as is the case with some fingerprint technology, evidence is sent last to the lab technicians who use that technique. That means personnel in each section must know how the lab functions as a whole.

This is where police officers are trained about the proper handling of physical evidence, because in learning how it gets corrupted, they have a better idea of what they should do at a crime scene. They also get to know the lab technicians, with whom they will work as a team. If they all cooperate, the lab personnel can offer valuable information to help narrow down suspect possibilities. For example, when Greg gets a sample of semen from a murder victim, he compares it with the CODIS database and tells Nick that it matches a particular fugitive from Texas. Lab technicians can also tell investigators what else they need to make a proper analysis (more of a sample, or a known sample to match against a questioned sample).

A lab setup depends on the needs of the community, the governmental level at which it operates, and available funding. Many smaller labs are satellite stations that analyze only the most basic evidence and send anything that needs sophisticated analysis to a central lab. The FBI labs, which are the largest in the world, are obviously better equipped than a small municipal lab, and they can coordinate crime scenes and offender profiles because they have an extensive amount of computerized information. If the lab for the Las Vegas Crime Scene Unit is a full-service lab, which it appears to be, it would likely include the following divisions and personnel:

- Evidence clerks: they log in the evidence, assign a primary investigative unit, and the case is properly coordinated with the case.

- Drying area: temperature-controlled room for wet biological evidence, such as a bloodstained shirt that needs to be dried before analysis. (This room gives Warrick the creeps, but Sara finds it calming.) Also called a scraping room, where clothing is preserved against the loss of hair and fibers. It's hung over a paper and scraped by a technician.

- Photography: equipment for digital, ultraviolet, and X-ray photography; a studio for showing mug shots to victims; and a darkroom for developing photos on the premises. This may also be where videos are cleaned up and enhanced, such as from a robbery at a convenience store.

- Identification (aka, Ident): latent fingerprint analysis and examination of impressions such as tire treads and footprints. This area will be set up with computers to link to AFIS or tire-tread databases.

- Chemistry/biology: for screening tissue from an autopsy for poisons, alcohol, and drugs (toxicology); blood pattern analysis and the testing of other bodily fluids (serology); technicians here may even restore serial numbers that have been removed from weapons. They also do DNA analysis.

- Firearms/ballistics/tool marks: this division has a shooting range and a program that accesses databases for firearms, bullets, and cartridges. Technicians can match spent bullets (if not too damaged) to the gun that fired them, as well as determine the distance from which a gun was fired. In addition, they use comparison microscopes to match bullets, which can also be used for tool mark analysis. If Chem doesn't do the serial number restoration, it gets done here.

- Arson/explosives: for analyzing suspicious fires, bomb devices, and debris from explosions. They're equipped for hazardous situations.

- Trace: for examining how evidential material such as metals, glass, soil, fibers, plants, hair, and paint chips function in a crime.

- General instruments: maintenance people for the machines and devices needed for making the different types of analyses.

- Computer analysis: for computer crimes, voiceprint analysis, and other computerized records; also to access databases for information and to process digital photography.

- Questioned Documents: for examination of forgeries, ransom notes, and the materials on which something was written; technicians can also work on impressions left on a tablet from a note written on the top page, in order to read what the note said.

- Polygraph: to detect from physiological responses the level of deception in someone's verbal account. Some offices won't use this because it's not admissible, but others find it valuable to the interrogation.

- Evidence collection unit: specially trained individuals who process a crime scene, collect evidence, and transport it. Not all labs have the funds for specialized personnel, and often those who collect the evidence also analyze it in the lab. The size of the lab and the area crime rate determine how many specialists can (or must) be hired.

- Evidence storage: where evidence gets placed in order to keep control over the chain of custody; freezers and refrigeration are used for biological evidence that may mold or decay.

- Setup rooms: separate spaces where evidence from the victim can be kept separate from evidence from the suspect. (Catherine and Warrick spread out the files from a gunshot case in a room like this.)

■ Administrative offices: those people who oversee the workings of the lab and stay abreast of the latest research. (Grissom has an office, but the other C.S.I.s meet in a general coffee room.)

Access to large data banks, such as those available from the FBI, is essential to a lab's effectiveness. When two shell casings are found next to an unconscious rape victim, Nick checks a cartridge-case database and discovers that the same gun had been used in another crime they'd processed. Now he has a link and a lead.

Four federal crime laboratories have been created to assist in anything beyond the jurisdiction of state and local agencies:

■ FBI (Department of Justice)

■ Drug Enforcement Administration (DEA)

■ Bureau of Alcohol, Tobacco and Firearms (ATF)

■ U.S. Postal Inspection Service

Each offers expertise to local agencies on criminal matters relevant to its responsibilities.

Among the numerous databases offered by the FBI are the Firearms Reference Collection, Standard Ammunition File, Explosives Reference File, Materials and Fibers, Cigarette ID (for butts), Typewriter Standards File, Office Copier Standards File, Automobile Paint File, Hair Types (animal and human), and a Tire Tread File. The list goes on and on. As Nick points out, if criminals were aware of just how much information C.S.I.s have access to, there might be less crime.

Higher-level evidence technicians like Greg need to have certain qualifications. They must have taken basic courses in biology, physical science, and chemistry, along with instruction in crime scene processing and scientific report writing. They need to have knowledge about safety requirements and how laboratory equipment operates. They also need to know how to preserve and handle evidence without corrupting it, and they must display computer skills. Some of them will need instruction on how to testify about evidence analysis in court, and for this, they run moot courts, where experienced technicians can role-play.

The responsibilities of evidence technicians are varied and may include:

- Preparing reagents and solutions for chemical analysis

- Reporting results

- Maintaining supply inventories

- Keeping written records

- Keeping instruments calibrated

- Training law enforcement personnel in proper evidence handling

- Collecting biological evidence at a crime scene

Depending on staffing, some technicians end up in places they never imagined.

The key evidence technician in the investigation of serial killer John Wayne Gacy was Daniel Genty, the first person to enter the dirt-floor crawl space of Gacy's home to determine if there were buried bodies. He went in on hands and knees, drawn to a place where he spotted a hair tuft rising up from the dirt. Then he slithered on his stomach to get to another area and dug his tools into a pool filled with tiny red worms. When bits of hardened human fat floated to the surface, he dug deeper and connected with an arm bone. When he turned up

a kneecap and blackened leg bones in another area, he said, "I think this crawl space is full of kids," and asked for the medical examiner. The remains of twenty-eight young men were turned over to the morgue, where anthropologists and odontologists took over. Later, Genty was called in to testify in court about how the initial evidence was handled.

CRIME LAB INSTRUMENTS

The evidence technicians on *C.S.I.* often use instruments to analyze some piece of evidence, but rarely do they identify the kind of device they are using, except for an occasional reference to "the GC" or some type of microscope. Let's look at the equipment commonly used to process the different types of trace evidence.

The most basic instruments in any lab are the various items of glassware:

- Beaker: for routine mixing, measuring, and boiling of liquids.

- Flasks: volumetric, boiling, and Erlenmeyer flasks, for mixing, boiling of substances, and storing of liquids and cultures. They have a body larger than their necks. Some come with stoppers, some are flat-bottomed, while others are bulbous.

- Buret and pipet: glass tubing for adding specific amounts of liquid to other liquids.

- Graduated cylinder: for mixing and storing liquids where amounts must be accurately measured; there are graduated marks along the side for volume.

- Test tubes: cigar-size glass tubes for mixing and boiling of substances; some are used for cultures.

- Watch glasses: small concave dishes that allow viewing under microscopes and dissolving of materials such as powders.

Then we have the more sophisticated equipment. We'll begin with the microscopes, which operate with light or electron emissions.

The low-power stereo microscope offers magnification of from 6X to 40X, and is often used for the initial examination of substances. It relies on a light source at the base and a stage that holds the specimen. A hollow tube through which the viewer looks magnifies what the naked eye can't see, and the magnification power can be increased or decreased as needed. This works best with transparent objects, but can also bring out details if an opaque object is sliced sufficiently thin.

The compound microscope uses two lenses together, with different adjustment levels, to obtain much higher magnification powers of up to 1500X. Two compound microscopes are joined to make a comparison microscope, which relies on a series of prisms and lenses to join two objects in a common field, viewed side by side. This is useful for hairs, fibers, and bullets. (Greg's "dead-end twins," used to look at a hairbrush and toothbrush, were just two separate microscopes, but Nick examined fibers under a compound microscope in "Cool Change.")

A phase-contrast microscope throws off some of the light waves that pass through a sample, which puts parts of the internal structure into sharper relief, while a polarizing microscope may identify properties of minerals in a soil sample.

Spectrometry is the study of spectra for atomic and molecular structures, using various instruments like the spectroscope, spectrograph, spectrometer, and spectrophotometer. In 1859, two German scientists discovered that the spectrum of every organic element has a uniqueness to its constituent parts. By passing light through a forensic sample to produce a color spectrum, the analyst can read the resulting lines, called "absorption lines." That is, the specific wavelengths that are selectively absorbed into the substance are characteristic of its component molecules. The longest wavelength visible to the human eye is red and the shortest is blue. Yet there are longer and shorter wavelengths, infrared and ultraviolet, which spectrometers detect. The Fourier transform infrared spectrometer (FT-IR) uses curved mirrors to take absorption readings on minuscule samples, and it's often used for paints, explosives, and fibers.

The atomic absorption spectrophotometer works in the opposite way. Elements vaporized in fire absorb specific wavelengths, which are revealed as dark lines in a spectrum. This device can be used on gunpowder residue and can also detect lead and arsenic.

A combination of some of these instruments for the most effective forensic analysis is the microspectrophotometer, or a microscope linked to a spectrophotometer. The microscope locates minute traces or shows how light interacts with the material under analysis. Then the computerized spectrophotometer increases the accuracy. The scientist can get both a magnified visual and an infrared pattern, which increases the number of identifying characteristics for any given material. This method is often used on paint samples and fibers.

Using a different approach, the electron microscopes either pass beams of electrons through samples to provide a highly magnified image or reflect electrons off the sample's surface. The emissions are studied with a closed circuit TV. Electron microscopes extend the wavelength of visible light to increase resolution. The transmission electron microscope can yield an image of a tiny or thin sample that's highly magnified, while the scanning electron microscope (SEM) converts emitted electrons into a photographic image and can magnify up to 100,000X, as well as provide information about the specimen's elemental composition. This technology is often used with gunshot residue on a suspect's hands, and it may be what Greg employs to discover that the glowing metal traces on a fatal head wound are uranium.

Cameras can be mounted on top of the microscopes to record the magnified results for easier comparison and for presentation in court. This even allows large groups to view a televised presentation.

The new technology for storing and transmitting images is fiberoptic video microscopy, which expands the versatility of analyzing very small particles.

Many types of physical evidence are viewed under ultraviolet lighting in the lab. Semen, saliva, and urine will absorb UV rays and fluoresce. Some fibers also stand out, and UV light can indicate when writing on a document has been erased. The coroner, too, can examine a cadaver for bruising, bite marks, ligature marks, fibers, and hair.

While chromatography, which separates the elements of compounds, takes many forms, the real workhorse of a crime lab is the gas chromatograph (GC). Most things encountered at a crime scene are complex mixtures and can be separated into their purest components. Greg uses a GC in the pilot episode when he tries to analyze a mouth swab taken from a victim. We see him inject his prepared specimen into the machine, but it fails to get a reading.

This is how it works: a small amount of the suspect substance or unknown material is dissolved in a solvent and then injected by needle into a hollow tube. A flow of inert gas (helium or nitrogen) propels the heated mixture through the coiled glass tube, where a highly sensitive, computerized detector distinguishes the separate elements at the other end. Each pure element moves at its own speed, so as each crosses the finish line, it can be identified. The amount of pure substance in the mixture is measured as well, producing a chart that offers a composite profile (travel time measured in minutes). Comparison—or control—substances are also put through the GC. This helps to identify suspicious substances, such as an accelerant on a piece of charred wood when compared with a sample of wood without accelerant. GC can be used to identify many things, from poisons to drugs to explosives. It even works in blood alcohol evaluations.

To produce a more specific identification, the GC is linked to another device: the mass spectrometer. This combination is referred to as the GC-mass-spec, or GC/MS. The GC separates the sample into its component parts and then they're ionized by the MS and identified by the fragmentation patterns of the spectra produced. No two substances produce the same pattern. Warrick asks Greg to use this complicated device in "Friends and Lovers" to analyze the contents of the stomach of a maggot.

The mass spectrometer bombards the sample with electrons produced by a heated cathode, breaking it into electrically charged fragments. These fragments pass through the spectrometer, accelerated by an electric field. A magnetic field deflects them onto a circular path, the radius of which varies according to the mass of the fragment. As the magnetic field is increased, a detector linked to a computer records the energy spectra. The position of each fragment on the spectrum measures its mass, and its intensity indicates its proportion in the sample. This comes through as a printed readout.

Among other instruments found in the well-equipped lab, we may find:

1. A device for electrophoresis, which operates on a principle similar to GC. An electrical current is applied to a substance and different parts migrate at different speeds through a gel from a negative to a positive pole. It's primarily used for DNA analysis.

2. A nuclear reactor for neutron activation analysis, which uses radiation. Bombarding substances with neutrons allows the gamma rays of those substances to be detected and measured. Each element has its own characteristic gamma energy level, so this method can help to identify minute traces of elements in substances such as paint, fiber, hair, and metal.

3. Refractometers measure the refractive index in substances like glass or liquid. The refractive index is the ratio between the speed of light through a given substance and the speed of light through air or a vacuum. A beam of light is aimed through the

refractometer, and the measurement of the angle at which it emerges after passing through the test material offers a way to calculate the material's index.

4. A device for liquid chromatography, which separates chemicals in a liquid compound by absorbing them into other solutions with which they have an affinity.

Moving from the equipment to the substances, let's look first at the two most frequently analyzed pieces of trace evidence, hair and fibers.

TRACE SUBSTANCES

Hair

Hairs have been used for more than a century and a half to link people to crimes, like when Warrick analyzes a strand of hair that shows evidence of being pulled out, indicating a struggle that undermines a witness's story. They help to establish the scope of the crime scene, connect a suspect with a weapon, support witness testimony, place someone at a scene, and link separate crime scenes. Since hair that has no nuclear DNA is "class characteristic," an unknown hair shaft must have enough similar properties compared with a known sample to be "microscopically consistent with" the sample; it can't be said definitively to be a perfect match. Hair samples can be used to definitely exclude a suspect but not to convict. Hairs are considered to be contributing evidence.

Yet aside from the shaft, the hair can also carry evidence like dirt or blood that yields important clues. A hair shaft is often mounted with Permount on a slide, which hardens to hold it in place for close microscopic examination.

In an investigation, hair is collected from different parts of the body of the victim and any suspects, including several areas of the scalp. Because different hairs on the same person can show variations, the larger the sample, the better. An average sample ranges from twenty-four to fifty pieces.

Hair analysis can indicate whether the source is human or animal and also whether the source is a member of a particular race. It can determine if the hair has been dyed, cut in a certain way, or pulled out, and where on the body it was located. The hair shaft with a follicle can also indicate length.

Forensic analysis centers on color and structure, determined through microscopic magnification. The shaft has three forensically relevant layers: the cuticle, cortex, and medulla. The cuticle has overlapping external scales, which helps in species identification: animals are different from humans. Within the cuticle is the cortex, made up of spindle-shaped cells that contain the color pigment, and the way the pigment is distributed helps to identify hairs from particular individuals. The center of the shaft is the medulla, which is also valuable for species differentiation: an animal's medullary index (diameter relative to the shaft's diameter) is larger than a human's. However, the medulla is often fragmented or interrupted, and may differ from one hair to another on the same person.

Negroid hairs are kinky, with dense pigments, while Caucasoid hairs are generally straight or wavy, with finer pigmentation. Pigment distribution is also different between the two races. The hair of an infant or young child tends to be finer than adult hair, but it is difficult to establish gender from hair samples. Hair that has follicle tissue was probably pulled out, and that tissue offers the possibility of DNA replication through the PCR method, which can then be tested.

In the 1950s, neutron activation analysis became a valuable forensic tool. A sample is bombarded with neutrons while inside the core of a nuclear reactor. The neutrons collide with the components of the trace elements and make them emit gamma radiation of a characteristic energy level. That way, the scientist can measure every constituent part of the sample, no matter how small. In a single hair, for example, fourteen different elements can be identified.

The first case to utilize neutron activation analysis was the 1958 murder of sixteen-year-old Gaetane Bouchard in Canada. Her former boyfriend, John Vollman, lived across the border in Maine and he was seen with her just before she was discovered dead. Flakes of paint from the place where they had been together were matched to his car. Also, the victim's color of lipstick was found on candy in his glove compartment. However, it was the strands of hair found clasped in the victim's hand that ultimately convinced the jury. These were matched to Vollman via a ratio of sulfur radiation to phosphorus that was closer to his ratio than hers.

Fibers

Like hair shafts, fibers are class evidence. They cannot pinpoint an offender's presence, but certain characteristics can be examined for consistency between a known and unknown sample, like when rug fibers found in a watch are compared to a rug sample from the hotel suite in "Cool Change." A fiber is the smallest unit of a textile material, and they're twisted together to make thread and yarn. Analysts look at diameter, coarseness, machine marks, dye color mix, evidence of wear, and cross-sectional shape. Of the man-made fibers, there are over one thousand, with over seven thousand dye formulas. However, since these formulas are specific to certain manufacturers, some degree of uniqueness in dye lot can be established.

Natural fibers come from plants (cotton), minerals (asbestos), or animals (wool). Manufactured fibers are synthetics like rayon, acetate, and polyester, which are made from long chains of molecules called polymers. To determine the shape and color of fibers from any of these fabrics, a microscopic examination is made.

Generally, the analyst gets only a limited number of fibers to work with—sometimes only one. Whatever has been gathered from the crime scene is then compared against fibers from a suspect source, such as a car or home, and the fibers are laid side by side for visual inspection through a comparison microscope.

Cross-transfers of fiber often occur in cases in which there is person-to-person contact, and investigators hope that fiber traceable back to the offender can be found at the crime scene, as well as vice versa. Success in solving the crime often hinges on the ability to narrow the sources for the type of fiber found, and to find an abundance of them. Like hair, fibers are gathered at a crime scene with tweezers, tape, or a vacuum. They generally come from clothing, drapery, wigs, carpeting, furniture, and blankets.

Agreement of color and shape of a sample based on consistency moves the analysis to the next phase: analyzing the dye and texture. Under a microscope, the analyst looks for lengthwise striations or pits on a fiber's surface, or unusual shapes. Even if fibers from two separate places show a strong similarity, this does not prove they came from the same source, and there is no fiber database that provides a probability of origin.

Yet that's not how such evidence was viewed in one famous case.

From 1979 to 1981, someone was murdering Atlanta's youth. More than twenty-five black males, some as young as nine, had been strangled, bludgeoned, or asphyxiated. The only piece of evidence was the presence of fiber threads on several of the bodies. Technicians isolated two distinct types: a violet-colored acetate fiber and a coarse yellow-green nylon fiber with the type of tri-lobed (three branch) qualities associated with carpets. Searching a suspect's home and car, detectives found yellow-green carpeting, and the microscopic comparisons showed good consistency. The FBI identified the manufacturer and distributor. The problem was to determine that the fibers from the bodies came from the suspect's home. With mathematical formulas, prosecutors calculated the odds to be one in thirty million that they came from any house in the southeast but the one where the suspect resided. In total, twenty-eight fibers were linked to him, and the evidence seemed overwhelming that Wayne Williams was the Atlanta Child Killer.

However, Chet Dettlinger independently investigated the case. He found glaring errors with the fiber analysis. The fiber from the Williams home that was matched to the victims was found in abundance in commercial stores like Wal-Mart. The prosecutor's probability ratio failed to account for visitors to the home bringing fibers in, and narrowing the test area to the southeast failed to account for people from out of the area visiting it on a regular basis. The prosecution also ignored the fact that millions of pounds of the same fiber had been sold undyed to other manufacturers for use in applications such as car mats.

Thus, the probability ratio was too abstract to be meaningful in this case.

Glass

In "The I-15 Murders" Sara and Warrick disprove a breaking-and-entering claim by studying the broken glass of a window at the scene. The hackle and rib marks of the fracture prove the window was smashed from the inside, and a piece of glass found in the butt of a hidden pistol matches the window, pointing to a coverup.

Glass is actually a liquid cooled to the point of solidifying and held between two stressed "skins." Thus it will shatter into pieces. Reacting to impact in a predictable manner, every piece of a shattered pane of glass will have the same properties as every other piece. If a perpetrator smashes glass, some tiny slivers will adhere to clothing, even laundered clothing. It may also get embedded in whatever was used to break it. It is therefore quite useful in an investigation.

There are several methods to determine whether a piece of glass came from a specific broken window. Sometimes large fragments can be fitted back into the window, but if not, a density test can be done. Density is the measure of mass per unit volume. Different types of glass have different densities. To measure the density of a glass fragment, it's dropped into a mix of bromoform and bromobenzine. The density of one is higher than the density of the other.

The density ratio is gradually adjusted by adding one of the liquids while the glass floats. When it remains suspended without going up or down, the density of the glass equals the density of the chemical mix. Then, if the sample to be matched remains similarly suspended in the same mixture, they have the same density.

A refractive index can also be used. That's determined by the change in direction of a light ray passing from one medium to another of a different density, such as the angle it travels passing through air to hit a surface and then passing through the surface. The ratio of the two angles gives the index value, and glass generally has an index of from 1.5 to 1.7. Glass manufacturers develop different kinds of glass for a wide variety of uses, and each has its own refractive index.

Finding the refractive index of a specific piece of glass, even one as small as a sliver, involves placing the sample onto a slide and covering it with a fluid such as silicone oil that has a much higher refractive index. The liquid's index decreases as the temperature rises, so the technician applies heat in a controlled manner until the contrast between the liquid and glass disappears, which means their refractive indices are the same. The microscope itself may be fitted with a heating unit and video camera so that the process can be filmed and examined. Until the refractive indices match, a halo (the Becke line) can be seen around the fragment. When the halo disappears, the match is made.

Broken glass, whether from a window, lamp, mirror, or picture frame, can often furnish clues about how an event took place. If broken by a shooting, it can be determined from which side because the fragments "blow back" to the side from which it was broken. If several bullets penetrated the glass, their sequence can be determined. The fractures made by a second bullet will travel through the glass but end at the fractures made by the first shot, and those fractures will be uninterrupted. Entry edges of the holes are smaller than exit edges, and pieces of glass will fall out (not blow back) on the side from which the bullet exited.

If the glass is shattered by something of lesser velocity than a bullet, the fracture marks are analyzed. When a force pushes against glass, it bends until the point is reached where it can bend no further. Then it cracks, forming radial lines on the surface opposite the exerted force. Concentric stress marks show on the side where the force is exerted, sometimes in the shape of the implement used. So the surface opposite the force breaks first, and the edges of the radial cracks form a right angle to it.

Dust/Dirt

When dust is found on the trousers of a man suspected of murdering a victim who landed on the sidewalk in front of the Monaco Hotel, it's determined to be roof dust, which is used by Vegas hotels to keep buildings cooler in that hot climate. However, when the victim's shoes fail to turn up similar dust, a new hypothesis is required.

It is true that dust or dirt particles picked up on a suspect's clothing can sometimes reveal where he or she has been, and the same goes for where a corpse has been, helping to determine whether a murder victim has been moved. Dust or dirt will be present at most crime scenes. A microscopic inspection can reveal plant spoors, insects, and other microorganisms that provide clues. Dust particles generally yield something about their origins, whether from a concrete floor, bricks, cement, or a particular room. They might offer leads about where someone lives or works.

When collecting dust, a control sample must also be collected that is characteristic of that found at the crime scene. If soil or dust is present on clothing, the clothing is carefully removed and bagged.

Comparison consists of examining the size of the particles and the density gradient. Any number of devices can be used for analysis, but often it's the scanning electron microscope (SEM).

Palynology

Palynomorphs, or pollen data, can be trapped in or found on materials associated with a crime. That brings forensic botanists into the investigation. Because of its production and dispersal in specific regions, pollen can help to link a suspect to the crime scene. In 1969, a murder investigation in Sweden used the presence of pollen in the dirt found on the victim to indicate that she had been killed in another place. There were no plants like that in the area in which she was found. In another case, pollen showed up in the grease of a killer's gun, and in yet another, pollen present in the ink of a document proved it was fraudulent.

Additionally, the study of seeds can offer clues. When jimson-seeds are found inside a dead young man, Grissom wants to tie them to the dealer for a murder charge, but needs the pods to make a DNA identification . . . if that's even possible. DNA analysis of plant pods in one actual murder case did in fact distinguish the specific tree and put the murderer away.

Paint

Some techniques for glass analysis apply to the analysis of paint chips, although the latter also relies on color analysis. Chips from cars can be compared with samples in the National Automotive Paint File, which holds more than forty thousand samples. Undercoats help to narrow down the possible manufacturers. Also the shape of a chip can be matched to an area where a chip is missing, and its chemical constituents can be analyzed by releasing the gases and using gas chromatography. That creates identifying characteristics for each layer and establishes points of comparison.

As forensic science advances with computer analysis and increasingly more accurate means of detecting the component parts of small samples, trace evidence may soon play even more significant roles. As it is, the more trace evidence an investigator can collect at a crime scene, the better the chances of making a case.

Nevertheless, nothing beats a clue with highly unique properties that clearly link a suspect with a crime. Let's turn now to the art and science of making a match.

FIVE

We Have a Match

The usefulness of certain types of evidence depends on making a direct match based on individual characteristics, such as body fluids, bite marks, fingerprints, and certain other impressions. In other words, the suspect impression or stain must be proven statistically beyond doubt to have originated with the designated person or implement. That means careful processing. Then, to be effective in court, the analysis must fit into a case in the right way.

REVEALING FLUIDS

The analysis of the properties and effects of serums—blood, semen, saliva, sweat, and even fecal matter—is called serology. Nick utilizes the tools of serology on behalf of a hooker who needs his help to clear up an altercation with a security guard. She claims the man spit on her, so Nick takes her shirt to the lab and has it tested with a specific type of enzyme test.

Let's break down just what happens during these tests. First, a piece of absorbent paper treated with starch is wetted down. Pressing this over the area where the saliva is located absorbs the enzymes present from the saliva. Then iodine is applied with a spray and the paper turns blue as the iodine reacts with the starch, leaving a clearly defined area wherever there's saliva. It's easy to tell if it's the normal spray or a big globule of spit.

To prove that it came from a suspected source, a C.S.I. must get a sample from that person, just as Nick does when he gets the cop to lick an envelope. A polymarker typing analysis, HLA-DQA1, which is a DNA test for samples of limited quantity, is then used. It's an efficient test but not as highly discriminating as others.

From saliva to semen to blood, biological evidence is often found after crimes of violence. It may be fresh liquid, coagulated, dried, or in the form of spatters, a small drop, or a stain. Each form dictates a different method of preservation and collection, and when it's fresh, time is of the essence.

Let's talk first about blood.

We have about ten pints of blood in our bodies. When someone is wounded, the heart's pumping action makes his or her body leak or spray blood, and the behavior of blood in flight tends to be unaffected by such things as temperature, humidity, or atmospheric pressure. It remains uniform.

Despite how well the crime scene may get cleaned up, even the finest trace of blood can often be detected. Perpetrators may scrub down the obvious places, but they can still neglect areas between floorboards, under pipes, and inside drains. In one actual case in Michigan, the murderer of a teenage girl cleaned everything except a tiny drop that blended with the pattern of the wallpaper. He missed it, but investigators didn't. Merely by pouring water on some tiles at another real murder scene and pulling them up wherever the water flowed beneath them, a detective found blood, which turned out to be the only existing trace of the crime.

One of the earliest ways to link a suspect to the victim was through the analysis of blood types. Although not very discriminating, it was better than nothing. While Type A at the scene does not prove that a suspect with Type A blood committed the crime, it is the case that if the suspect is Type O, then he or she can be eliminated. Once blood types were isolated, other discriminating factors emerged.

In 1901, Karl Landsteiner named and standardized the different blood types. Separating the red blood cells from the plasma in a centrifuge, he added red blood cells from other subjects and found two distinct antigen reactions—clumping and repelling. He labeled them Types A (antigen A present, anti-B antibody present, antigen B absent) and B (antigen B present, antigen A absent). Then a third reaction (both antigens A and B absent) became Type O, and another serum discovered later was labeled AB (both antigens present). In the human population, Types A and O are most common, and AB the most rare.

In 1940, Landsteiner also discovered the rhesus factor, labeling it Rh-positive if the antigen was present in the red blood cells, and Rh-negative if not.

In Britain, scientists came up with a further test for discrimination when they found that the nuclei of female blood cells contain a chromosome-related structure that set them apart from males, which they named the Barr body.

It was an Italian physician, Dr. Leon Lattes, who developed a procedure to apply blood testing to stains on fabric and other materials. He restored dried blood with saline solutions so it could be tested for antigens. Today, blood typing involves many different enzymes and proteins that perform specific activities in the body, and these tests help to individualize the samples. More than 150 serum proteins and 250 cellular enzymes have been isolated, as well as many more antigens.

Yet before applying typing tests, it must first be determined that a stain is blood, or that blood was once present. Nick swabs the trunk of a car that's been recently cleaned and finds evidence of blood. Catherine sticks a swab down a drain where she suspects a body was cut up, and finds blood. Both of them are using what is known as a presumptive test, and there are several that will differentiate between blood and other substances. A positive result from any of them is an indication to go ahead and use other tests to confirm, although care is taken to be sure the tests aren't reacting to some other substance.

The first test involves moving a powerful light, such as a laser, across every surface. That can yield possible traces for visual inspection. If nothing is seen, a chemical reagent called luminol can be sprayed across the scene because it reacts to the hemoglobin in the blood, causing luminescence. It takes only about five seconds to produce a bluish glow. Warrick and Nicky perform this test in "Justice Is Served" on implements belonging to a nutritionist whose dog killed a jogger.

The luminol procedure requires that the room be considerably darkened, and the intensity of the glow increases proportionately to the amount of blood present. It works even with old blood or diluted stains, and can illuminate any smear marks where blood has been wiped away. However, there is a problem with this test: luminol can destroy some properties of the blood, so its use is limited to proving that blood is present. Another problem is that it reacts to common substances such as bleach and some metals, so if these materials are present, there's no point in using it (even if bleach was used to wipe down blood-spattered areas). Yet even with these problems, luminol does not interfere with DNA testing later at the lab.

A newer technique is the fluorescein reagent. It works like luminol, although it uses two successive coatings of different solutions. It's illuminated with a UV light, and since it persists much longer than luminol, it's better for getting photographs.

The Kastle-Meyer Color Test, which is what Nick and Catherine use, relies on a solution of phenolphthalein and hydrogen peroxide.

First, a cotton swab is rubbed through the area suspected to be blood. Then a drop of phenolphthalein is applied, followed by a drop of hydrogen peroxide. If blood of any quantity is present, it turns pink or red within about fifteen seconds. This is the most common field test in use, but it also turns pink in the presence of potatoes or horseradish.

Presumptive tests are quick and can detect even minute traces of blood. Other chemical screening tests include leucomalachite green, which turns greenish blue in the presence of suspected blood, and Ortho-tolidine, which turns an intense blue color. There's also an item called a Hemastix strip, which acts like a urine dipstick. It's moistened with distilled water and turns green when placed in the presence of blood.

From there, investigators can use the precipitin test to determine whether the blood is of animal or human origin. German biologist Paul Uhlenhuth discovered that if he injected protein from a chicken egg into a rabbit, and then mixed serum from the rabbit with egg white, the egg proteins separated from the liquid to form a cloudy substance known as precipitin. In other words, it forms an antibody. In the forensic test for human blood, either a sample of the questioned blood is put into a test tube over the rabbit serum or it's used in the "gel diffusion" test, where it's placed in gel on a glass slide next to a sample of the reagent (antihuman serum). When the slide is stimulated with an electric current, the protein molecules filter toward each other. If a line forms where they meet—called a precipitin line—this means the sample is human blood.

After that, an ABO test can determine blood type, and then work is done on the gender of the person from whom the blood came. Electrophoresis offers a more thorough enzyme/protein profile.

Serology also made another important discovery. Around 80 percent of the members of the human race were found to be "secretors," which means that the specific types of antigens, proteins, antibodies, and enzymes characteristic of their blood can be found in other bodily fluids and tissues. By examining saliva, semen, and even teardrops, analysts can tell the blood type.

These days, thanks to a discovery in 1985, DNA technology has replaced the tests for specific enzymes and proteins.

BLUEPRINTS

DNA profiling becomes integral to an investigation in "Table Stakes" when a semen sample links their case to a ten-year-old murder. But the observer never gets to see exactly how this complicated technology works. Let's look at it more closely.

We've seen how DNA gets analyzed to identify a missing person, and the same techniques are used to link a suspect with a victim or crime scene. DNA can be picked up from many places, including saliva from the mouthpiece of a phone, chewing gum left at a scene, blood flowing from an open wound, and, of course, from semen. The best place to get DNA is from a buccal swab of the inner cheek, because it's rich in shed epithelial cells.

While DNA analysis is relatively new in the crime-fighting arsenal, there have been astonishing developments in its short history. It was a case in England that first linked a detective and scientist together to dramatically affect the future of criminal investigation.

On November 24, 1983, fifteen-year-old Lynda Mann was found raped and strangled in the village of Narborough, England. The only clue was a semen sample that identified the killer's blood as Type A, and the absence of leads left the case unsolved.

Almost three years later and a mile away, Dawn Ashworth, also fifteen, was raped and murdered in the same manner. The blood type was the same.

Soon after, Richard Buckland was arrested and he confessed to the second murder, but denied committing the first. Investigators felt sure they could nail him for both. At the time, they'd heard about a new and untested technique: "genetic fingerprinting" through DNA analysis. They contacted its originator, Dr. Alec Jeffreys, a geneticist who had used it successfully in a paternity suit. This would be his first test in a criminal case.

To everyone's surprise, two different tests failed to make a match between Buckland and either of the samples taken from the two murders. Buckland became the first person to be exonerated based on a DNA test. His confession had been false.

Then the search began again, so the men of Narborough and villages nearby who had type A blood were asked to voluntarily submit to a DNA analysis. Over five thousand men agreed to do it, but the object was to find any man who would not willingly submit.

Colin Pitchfork persuaded a friend to go in his place, providing him with a false passport, but the friend bragged about it, placing the spotlight dead on Pitchfork. His genetic profile proved to be indistinguishable from that of the semen samples, and in 1987 he became the first person to be convicted for murder based on genetic fingerprinting.

DNA profiling has had the greatest impact in the area of sexual assault evidence examinations. Prior to DNA testing, laboratories were limited in the amount of genetic information that could be developed from semen evidence. With the advent of DNA analysis, the genetic content of the sperm itself can be examined.

In a sexual assault, there are essentially three crime scenes: the victim, the suspect, and the place where the assault occurred. There are protocols for the collection of evidence from each, but the victim is often the focal point. That's why Grissom quickly dispatches Sara to process a rape kit on the unconscious rape victim from "Too Tough to Die." The longer it takes to identify a suspect, the greater the chance that important evidence will be lost: clothing gets washed or discarded, people take showers, injuries heal.

Both victim and rapist (if caught) are subject to sexual assault evidence collection kits, also known as rape kits, and a specially trained nurse in a hospital generally administers them. The point of the kit is to prove that sexual contact took place and that the physical evidence is consistent with the described assault. Pubic hairs, semen samples, and vaginal samples constitute the principal evidence.

A rape kit is a large envelope or box that contains a number of items to help collect and separate pieces of evidence. It's perishable evidence, which is carefully preserved against contamination. It must be gathered quickly, before the body's cleansing systems flush it away.

Semen contains a detectable enzyme called acid phosphatase (AP) that doesn't last more than a day outside the body. Sperm cells are gone within three days.

The kit contains:

- swabs for anal, oral, vaginal, penile, and control samples

- smear slides for making specimens on the scene

- filter paper for saliva

- special tubes for collection of liquid samples

- a pair of tweezers for pulling pubic and head hairs from the roots (about twenty-five hairs are needed from each area)

- scissors for cutting close to the root in case the victim resists pulling

- wooden picks and evidence envelopes for fingernail scrapings from each hand

- separate combs and envelopes for pubic-area and head-hair combings

- swabs for saliva, in the event the suspect licked or bit anything

- forms to take patient history and description of the assault (in particular her sexual history)

- envelopes for miscellaneous debris collection

A few drops are taken from the blood that's collected and placed on a cloth, dried, and stored. During the procedure, the vagina and rectum are swabbed for semen and the vagina is washed with saline. (On a male rape suspect, the penis is swabbed for evidence of vaginal cells.)

To process a rape kit, the swabs are cut (extracted) and pieces are dropped into test tubes and moistened with a drop of water. One part is placed on a slide, another analyzed for blood, and a third is mixed with a chemical that indicates the presence of AP. The specimen on the slide is stained for cells, which will make sperm and vaginal cells stand out. Sperm with tails look like tadpoles, while—as Warrick notes—vaginal cells look like fried eggs.

Besides helping with identity, analysis of the kit contents gives an approximate time since intercourse took place. Semen deteriorates at a predictable rate when mixed with other fluids.

When the DNA profile is developed, it's compared with a suspect or entered into the convicted offender index of CODIS. If there's no match, the profile is searched in the forensic or crime science index. If two crimes are linked, the law enforcement agencies in both jurisdictions are notified. All states have databases of DNA for convicted sex offenders.

There is a continuum of sexual victimization, from forced sexual penetration without consent of any orifice to forced sexual contact or harassment, and all rapes get coded. Yet sexual trauma does not always imply rape, as Catherine points out when she tries to clear her ex-husband of a rape charge. Rough sexual activity can leave similar bruises, so it becomes a matter of finding other types of evidence to make a distinction. "He said, she said" doesn't get a conviction, and lab analysis alone won't prove it either way.

GIVING A GOOD IMPRESSION

Making a match with biological evidence is powerful, but certain types of physical impressions can also link suspects with crimes and get convictions. Let's examine some of them.

Bite Marks

In "Friends and Lovers," a young man found dead in the desert is reported missing by his best friend, Bobby. When he scratches a "bite" on his arm, Grissom identifies it as human and an impression from Eric's corpse matches the mark.

In a criminal case, it would be the forensic odontologists (or dentists) who provide information about the formation of teeth and make these types of matches. They may help identify a deceased John Doe or testify in court on the association between a bite mark and a suspect's teeth impressions. Since teeth are the hardest substance in the body and tend to last longest, and since their characteristics are individually unique, teeth are often the first means used for matches.

Why are teeth so unique? As people age, their teeth get worn and broken in ways that make them easier to link to a particular person. Fillings, crowns, braces, or tooth loss further individualize a bite. In one rape case, a young girl bit her attacker, and what confirmed her identification of him was the imprint left by her braces.

Practically all of us get our teeth charted as we develop, and to make it easier to indicate which of them need work, dentists assign a number to each of the thirty-two adult teeth. Each tooth has five surfaces and all dental information about these areas goes into an odontogram (which Catherine and Nick check when matching the teeth of a skeleton from the desert to a local resident). Expert identification relies on a sufficient number of points of similarity between the odontogram and the John Doe or suspect to make an affirmative identification, and they have from thirty to seventy-six comparison factors from which to choose, including:

- width

- curve of biting edge

- shape of mouth arch

- spacing of teeth

In some cases, once a bite-mark match is confirmed, other tests can be done to strengthen the identification. An impression left on chewing gum, for example, may also yield DNA from saliva. Marks left in substances like cheese provide a three-dimensional impression, which offers more points of comparison. According to Dr. Lowell Levine, consultant in forensic dentistry to the New York State Police, analyses of a bite mark is about more than the size and arrangement of the teeth; it also gives details about the musculature of the mouth and the mental state of the biter. Experienced odontologists can provide this information.

That's exactly what happened in the criminal case that finally stopped serial killer Ted Bundy in the mid-1970s. Who would have thought that Bundy would be brought down by his own teeth?

On January 15, 1978, Lisa Levy and Martha Bowman were attacked in their sorority house at Florida State University. A man fatally clubbed them and then fled. He was later identified as Ted Bundy, the notorious serial killer who had cut a brutal swath across the country. Both of the girls were strangled and beaten, and one was raped. While Bundy left no fingerprints, he did leave one identifying mark: he bit Lisa Levy on the left buttock. The impression was clean enough to make a match to a dental impression of Bundy's teeth. His bite mark bore an uneven alignment and several chips, which gave the match from the victim a higher probability of being only from Bundy. In addition, Bundy had bitten the girl twice with his lower teeth, giving the odontologist two good impressions to work with. It was the

first case in Florida's legal history to rely on bite marks for an identification. It was also the first piece of physical evidence that linked Bundy to a victim.

The first step in bite-mark analysis from a crime scene is to determine whether it's human or animal. For example, in "Justice Is Served," something with teeth kills a jogger and bite mark casts from the wounds indicate a dog—a Great Dane or mastiff—missing one tooth. When the probable culprit is located, a mouth impression is cast and compared with the bite mark. There's a match.

Next, the expert must be sure that the impressions did not originate with the victim (self-inflicted or left in food). That means taking the victim's mouth impressions. If it seems that they may have the bite mark of a suspect, then it's measured and recorded, and a swab taken for any possible saliva traces around it (with a control swab from a similar surface, such as another part of the victim's body).

The method for bite-mark analysis on skin is to first take photographs of the impression (with scales) and use computer enhancement to clear it up. If possible, a silicone-based impression material can be used on the indentations. At the morgue, the bite mark is excised and put into formalin for preservation.

Then a dental mold is made of the suspect's teeth and the odontologist uses this to create a transparency. Photos are taken of the suspect's mouth at its maximum opening and of the way he (or she) bites. Casts are made of sample bites, while saliva is collected for DNA testing. If any of the teeth appear to be recently worn down or broken, the abrasion is evaluated for age, because the suspect may have done something to avoid a dental match. The teeth that leave the clearest impressions are located in the front.

Bite-mark evidence can also exclude suspects if the fit fails to match.

One of the key problems with identifying bite marks on skin is that the marks leave bruising, which blurs the definition. If the victim was in motion during a struggle, that can also distort it. The skin's physiology and the victim's position when the bite mark was made affect its detail and shape. With the case of Bobby and Eric, it's likely that if the presumed struggle ensued, the bite mark would have been too distorted for such a perfect match.

Fingerprints

A single fingerprint links two seemingly separate cases in "Face Lift." When a dead burglar is found in a pottery shop, a print from the scene matches one to Melissa Marlowe, kidnapped when she was four, whose prints are in the AFIS database because of a pre-school printing initiative where she lived.

The team gets fingerprints off substances as diverse as plastic, glass, cloth, skin, a steering wheel, and a coin. For most of this century, fingerprints have been central to crime scene investigation, and some real-life C.S.I.s say that processing prints is how they spend most of their time. Yet fingerprinting was not the first means of standardized identification.

In 1883, Alphonse Bertillon was a file clerk for the French police, who wanted their information to be better organized, especially with regard to repeat offenders. As criminals came in, he took eleven separate measurements of each one to classify them as small, medium, or large. He recorded the measurements on cards against which new arrests could be compared. His idea was that no two people would have precisely the same measurements, and he thereby introduced scientific method into criminal investigations. While he called this anthropometry, his system was often referred to as *bertillonage*. While this method quickly became popular in Europe, it wasn't long before fingerprinting, which was more practical, eclipsed it.

To get a sense of the history of fingerprinting as a tool in solving crimes, let's lay out a time line:

- 1000: A Roman attorney showed that a palmprint was used to frame someone for murder.

- 1823: Prussian professor Johannes Purkinje defined nine basic fingerprint types and thus became the first person to devise a fingerprint classification.

- 1858: William Herschel recognized the individuality of fingerprints and used them for authenticating contracts.

- 1880: Scottish physician Henry Faulds discovered that prints could be made visible with powders, and he used a fingerprint at a crime scene to eliminate a suspect and indict the true perpetrator.

- 1892: Sir Francis Galton published the first book about fingerprints and their forensic utility. He proposed that there were three primary features and from them he could devise sixty thousand classes.

- 1901: Sir Edward Henry, head of Scotland Yard, refined Galton's research with a classification system based on five types that influences the one in use today.

- 1903: At Leavenworth prison in Kansas, anthropometry failed to distinguish between two cons who were twins, but fingerprinting did the trick. This case brought fingerprinting into its own as the leading tool for identification.

- 1910: Thomas Jennings was the first person in the United States to be convicted with fingerprint evidence. When he broke into a home and shot its owner, he left four clear prints in wet paint. The conviction was appealed, but the appeals court was satisfied that fingerprinting had a solid scientific basis.

- 1924: Congress established a national depository of fingerprint records at the FBI, and today there are several hundred million sets of prints there.

The reason fingerprinting works is that the undersides of our fingers (and palms and feet) are covered with ridges and valleys, some of which make continuous lines, some of which stop, some of which divide, and some of which make other kinds of formations like pockets and dots. These patterns are classified into four basic groups that have subgroups, making eight overall pattern types:

- Arch: formed by ridges running from one side to the other and curving up in the middle. Tented arches have a spike effect.

- Whorl: a complete oval, often in a spiral pattern around a central point. There's a plain whorl and a central pocket loop whorl.

- Loops: These have a stronger curve than arches, and the ends exit and enter the print on the same side. Radial loops slant toward the thumb and ulnar loops toward the other side.

- "Composites" mix two of the other patterns, while "accidentals" form an irregular pattern that's not classifiable.

As previously stated for matching the prints of unidentified bodies to a missing person, the following facts hold true for criminal investigations as well. While no absolute minimum number of points of comparison between two prints has been established nationwide, the more the better. Some investigators set their own minimum. Only one dissimilar point is sufficient to nix a match between the known and questioned samples.

The way these patterns leave impressions is from sweat mixed with amino acids, or by touching something like oil that clings to the skin. Touching any surface transfers the perspiration present on the ridge and valley patterns, leaving an impression of the minutiae. Sometimes it's only a partial impression, but that can be sufficient to provide a lead. If it's visible, it's a patent print; if not, it's latent.

Making a latent print visible depends on what kind of material it was left on. The more irregular or absorbent the surface, the more difficult it is to lift a good print, although advances have made what was once impossible possible. Fingerprints can actually be taken off skin in some cases.

At first, prints were developed on nonporous surfaces with fine, gray-black dusting powder, and this is still practiced today. It works best with fresh prints, before the oils dry, and the powder is applied with a soft brush. Then the excess is carefully blown off, leaving a clear impression from the powder that adheres to the oils. That makes the print ready to be photographed and lifted with a special tape. It's then placed onto a print card for preservation.

Besides powder, there were other methods for surfaces like paper and cardboard. Prints were located and developed with chemicals like iodine, ninhydrin, and silver nitrate. These chemicals could all be used, but it had to be in the right order, or they would destroy the prints. When the print was raised, it could be photographed through a filtered lens and then lifted.

Then more methods were discovered, including digital imaging, dye stains, and fumes, and now more than forty are in use. Colored powders were developed to contrast with surface colors, and some powders or dyes even glow under certain types of lighting, such as UV. (Grissom's Red Creeper is a fluorescent powder.) Most surfaces are examined initially in darkness under a high-power laser. This may bring up the prints, but if not, then other methods can be used. Even just holding a bright light to the side to provide oblique lighting over flat surfaces can reveal the presence of natural residues from prints. The least destructive method is always tried first.

The Super Glue fuming method was discovered by accident. A British police officer used it to repair a broken heater, and he discovered prints illuminated on its side. He then tried the glue in other areas, with success, because Super Glue adheres to a print's amino acids, and the method now enjoys widespread use. Most labs are equipped for fuming in an enclosed area. Taking it out of the lab and to the crime scene, the Super Glue wand allows for fuming inside cars and for surfaces that cannot be moved. It's also good for bringing up prints on skin. After fuming, the print can be raised further, if need be, with powders.

Vacuum metal deposition (VMD) uses an expensive machine to coat evidence with gold and zinc, which develops latent prints into picture quality. The oils from the prints absorb the gold. Then the zinc bonds with the gold and reveals every place the gold sticks except where it was absorbed. The prints then come forth like a developing photograph, with the ridges highlighted. The process results in a reverse image of the print. VMD reveals 15 percent more of a fresh print than do other sensitive techniques and 70 percent more on older prints. VMD can even detect prints on things that have been submerged in water. It's employed for working with difficult surfaces when other techniques fail, such as on the bags used on victims in the following case:

Along rural East Coast highways in the early 1990s, police found the remains of five middle-aged men. They'd been murdered, dismembered, and wrapped tightly in several layers of plastic bags. Whoever cut them up did so with surgical precision. This seemed to be the work of a single perpetrator, so he was dubbed the "Last Call Killer." A dozen investigators did over five hundred interviews but came up empty-handed, and the cases eventually went cold.

Then VMD was developed. New Jersey investigators sent gloves believed to belong to the killer (but found on a body) and two dozen of the bags from the bodies to Toronto for analysis. The scientists there found prints. The New Jersey police ran the prints through a database and got a match with the prints of a man, Richard Rogers, who'd bludgeoned an acquaintance to death, wrapped the body in a tent, and dumped it along a road. He'd said he killed the other boy in self-defense, and he was found not guilty in that crime. Because his prints matched, Rogers was arrested in May 2001 and indicted for two of the murders.

Not everyone was happy with how prints became such an effective method for solving crimes, and throughout the past century, criminals have tried to distort or eliminate their prints.

Chicago gangster John Dillinger went on a crime spree in 1933–34 that prompted the FBI's J. Edgar Hoover to name him "public enemy number one." Arrested once and heavily guarded, he used a fake gun to escape. Then he went into hiding. He located a team of plastic surgeons, paying them $5,000 to alter his facial appearance and burn off his fingerprints with acid.

Still, people knew him, and the owner of a bordello, the notorious "lady in red," set him up in exchange for reward money. As he exited the Biograph Theater one evening, FBI agents closed in on him and ordered him to surrender. He reached for something, so they gunned him down. Taken to the morgue, he was thoroughly examined. The FBI took his fingerprints and discovered the ploy. However, the doctors hadn't done their job. Around the acid-burned area a sufficient number of ridge patterns remained to make an identification.

Although fingerprint analysis has come under scrutiny in the courts, in all the years that it's been practiced, no one has yet found two people with identical prints.

To compare them, the print technician must first make sure that prints are taken of everyone who was or who might have been at the scene. That includes taking them off any dead bodies. To take a print, an ink roller is run over the fingertips and the tips are then pressed against a card. At the police station, the person dips his fingers into printer's ink and then presses them onto a card, known as a ten-card. Then each handprint is inked and preserved in the same way. The fingers are numbered one through ten, starting with the right thumb. The left thumb is number six. Then they get coded, including any missing or scarred fingers. The database gets a set of ten distinct prints, along with the size of the hand and the shape of the palm.

Since 1972, fingerprints have been compared and retrieved via computer. By 1989, they could be sent back and forth on-line. State and local agencies built up automated fingerprint identification systems (AFIS), and the FBI opened the National Crime Information Center (NCIC), which expedited the exchange of information among law enforcement agencies. They introduced a standard system of fingerprint classification (FPC) so that information could be uniformly transmitted from one AFIS computer to another, although there is still some system incompatibility.

A computer scans and digitally encodes prints into a geometric pattern according to their ridge endings and branchings. In less than a second, the computer can compare a set of ten prints against a half million (although getting matches can take longer). At the end of the process, it comes up with a list of prints that closely match the questioned prints. Then the technicians make the final determination, which involves a point-by-point visual comparison.

Once prints are classified and subtyped, they get stored in the database for future comparisons.

In addition to fingerprints, other types of impressions are considered for database storage, including palm- and footprints. Even ear- and faceprints are getting attention.

Headprints

Catherine and Warrick investigate an earprint left on a wall from which a work of art was taken down and stolen. To get an impression, they apply lotion to the ear of each suspect and then press a handheld piece of glass against it. To set each print they dust it and apply clear tape. This they compare against the print they lifted at the scene. Warrick refers to a case that used this technique for a conviction.

In Washington state in 1999, David Wayne Kunze was convicted of murder based on an earprint. Five years earlier, someone had entered the home of James McCann, bludgeoning him to death and fracturing the skull of his son. A fingerprint technician processed the home for evidence and discovered a partial latent earprint in McCann's bedroom. He lifted and preserved it. Police grew interested in Kunze when they learned that his former wife had upset him by announcing that she was to marry McCann. Then a lab technician compared the earprint with photos of the left side of Kunze's face. He thought they should get an exemplar impression—an actual earprint from Kunze. Using hand lotion, two criminalists obtained seven prints of different degrees of pressure against a glass surface. These were transferred onto a transparent overlay. It seemed a pretty good match and Kunze was deemed a "likely source" for the earprint at the scene.

After a *Frye* hearing, the evidence was admitted. Kunze was convicted, but on appeal, the earprint evidence was excluded because the identification method was not scientific. Numerous earprint analysts have since posted statements to the effect that earprint evidence is indeed scientific and will eventually have its day in court. However, after a mistrial was declared in Kunze's second trial, prosecutors have said that they do not have enough evidence to go to trial a third time.

Besides earprints, Grissom had a case involving a faceprint (the woman who'd been buried in cement in the foundation of a house), sufficiently sharp enough for forensic artist Teri Miller to create a bust for a newspaper photograph.

In that case, the impression helped to identify a victim. In an actual case, such impressions have helped to catch a suspect. In 1984, on an air-force base in California, a woman named Juana Gillette suddenly died. Her husband, Staff Sergeant Ronald Gillette, had claimed she'd died from a combination of medications used when she was feeling ill. However, when he ran off and married another woman within days, another autopsy was performed and it was determined that the drugs in her system were not fatal. A search of the home turned up a plastic laundry bag that appeared to have a nose indentation, so they turned the bag inside out. Using oblique lighting, they were able to see a clear outline of the dead woman's face still impressed on the bag, an indication that she'd been suffocated. Her husband got a new life, but not where he expected to spend it.

Footprints

While footprints made with shoes are class characteristic, and the moulages, or cast impressions, can be compared on databases, they may also yield individualizing traits from wear that can be matched to a suspect's shoe.

The impression is generally left in soft material such as mud, or formed from dust on a flat surface. If they can be seen, they're called visible or residue prints; if they're in something malleable, they're impression prints, and if unseen, they're latent. A visible print is generally made when the shoe is contaminated by something and it steps onto another surface, leaving the outline of an impression, such as the one made by the man in the pilot episode who kicked his own door with a dead man's shoe to stage a justifiable homicide. If the print is made by dust, as in "Blood Drops," an electrostatic dust lifter is used. It operates by using a high-voltage charge on a lifting film that causes dust particles to stick to the film's underside. While mostly employed for flat surfaces, it can even be used on fabric, newspaper, and bodies.

A three-dimensional footprint impression can be taken from soft surfaces like clay, sand, and snow. It's photographed first and then cast with dental stone or silicone casting material. The impression may first have to be stabilized with a spray. Then it's powdered to allow the cast to be lifted easily. To keep the casting material contained, a dam is set up, such as a steel frame. Then the casting material is mixed until it's the consistency of pancake batter. It's poured around the edges rather than directly onto the impression until it's filled, and a reinforcing screen is placed into it about halfway through. It sets for half an hour before it's removed, and is allowed to fully harden before it gets cleaned up for examination.

Tire-track casting is done in the same manner. Warrick uses this technique with the tire impression found outside the Collins residence in "Blood Drops." The tread pattern can be compared with known patterns contained in a database, and if it has an individualizing mark, such as a wear pattern or an embedded nail, so much the better.

Although we probably won't see snow in Vegas, there is a way to cast and lift impressions from snow, using a product called Snow Print Wax. Such prints are extremely fragile and are handled with great care.

Latent shoeprints are treated like fingerprints, and can often be located with oblique lighting or a laser. Sometimes shoes pick up metals or minerals, and the print can be chemically treated to make them visible. A print made with blood but cleaned up can be detected with luminol.

Back in the lab, a shoeprint can be measured for size and inspected for tread patterns that might tie it to a particular type of shoe, and even a brand. Wear marks or other kinds of individualizing impressions should be noted.

While a shoeprint is better than nothing, actual footprints are far superior for individual characteristics.

In "Evaluation Day," footprints made with blood-soaked socks are matched to the dead man's former lover, and Grissom explains that footprints are as unique as fingerprints. From well impressions, at the arch of the foot, to the spacing between footprints when walking or running, to toe step measurements, people leave their own characteristic tread. How did investigators discover this?

In 1999, the Royal Canadian Mounted Police invited thousands of people to participate in the making of a data bank . . . of footprints. Asking subjects to remove their socks and shoes, foot impression expert Sergeant Robert Kennedy had them step onto an inkless pad and then press their feet on specially treated paper. The concept of "barefoot morphology" is based on the idea that individuals have unique patterns to the weight-bearing portion of the foot. Research thus far has shown that no two people have the same barefoot morphology, but the database needs to be expanded to continue to make this claim on a scientific basis.

In criminal investigation, the suspect's foot could be connected to the worn areas inside a shoe, which may be connected to a crime scene via a shoe impression or print.

While some barefoot identification methods match the ridge marks, as in fingerprint technology, when a suspect leaves an impression while walking in socks, no ridges will appear. That makes the weight-based morphology more valuable. To increase individualization, they might also look at crease marks on impressions that are clear enough.

INSTRUMENTAL IMPRESSIONS

It's not just body parts that leave individual marks for a potential match; wounds, too, can sometimes be matched to weapons. A lamp, a knife, and a hammer are all identified as weapons in separate episodes from the shape of a fatal wound.

In "$35K OBO," Warrick pours a silicone casting mixture into knife wounds to come out with a perfect replication of a knife blade. (While bite marks can be thus cast, it's not as credible that a deep knife wound would retain the exact shape of the knife, although with forced injection it's possible to measure the depth.) His replica allows them to see the knife blade's length. Then in another episode, Grissom uses computer simulation to match the claw of a hammer to a man's fatal head wound.

In each of these cases, a match was made between impressions left on a body and some specific implement. Not all weapons leave a mark that can be traced back to them, but the procedure with any mortal wound is to at least attempt a match.

Most wound analysis of this type occurs with blunt trauma wounds, where there are contusions, lacerations, and abrasions. Stab wounds are hard to trace and gunshot wound analysis takes a different route. Blunt-force weapons like hammers and baseball bats leave distinct marks, as do tire irons and fireplace pokers.

Making an actual match to a weapon, however, means finding one with blood, tissue, or hair attached, or some part of the weapon broken off at the scene. The only other way is to see if the implement penetrated bone and left a distinctive mark.

That brings us to tool mark analysis, which is taken up in the next chapter.

SIX

Science v. Intuition

When a scene is ambiguous, reliance on the science of solving crimes can be at odds with a more gut-centered approach. A case in point: In "Pledging Mr. Johnson," Grissom wants to carefully reconstruct a crime involving a one-legged floater (body found in water) in the lab, while Catherine prefers solid gumshoe work, supported by keen observation and sense of intuition. Sometimes one works better than the other, but both are important for solving a crime. Intuition without science is blind; science without intuition is stagnant.

Science is the knowledge gained from careful observation and measurement, based on deduction from physical laws and proven with experimentation. The aim is to approach the facts with a method that can be replicated by peers, which often means to take something into a laboratory to control conditions. In other words, science attempts to objectively prove that something is the case, with a valid method that's appropriate to the thing being studied. Science is not necessarily about certainty. The goal is to devise a hypothesis that best fits the full array of facts, without crunching the facts to fit a theory.

Intuition, also known as the third eye, second sight, or sixth sense, is commonly thought to have paranormal origins. It's a gut feeling on which one acts on faith, and it seems to derive from the fuzzy border between cognitive and emotive skills: something tells you that you ought to act or affirms that your action is correct. It becomes a sort of "knowing," although scientists view it as highly subjective and thus unreliable.

INTUITION

Intuition is about possibility. It often occurs serendipitously, in the midst of some circumstance where it isn't necessarily expected. You might take a train trip and decide to change the seat you had originally picked out. You don't know why, but you do it. Then you meet someone in the seat next to you who tells you something or connects you to someone that opens an important door, and it seems quite magical. Instinct moved you in the right direction.

Intuition can take many forms, such as:

- an inner voice

- a feeling that something is going to happen

- the sense that we must pay attention

- fleeting clairvoyance or sudden energy

- a seemingly significant encounter

- a flow of inspiration

- the easy visualization of a plan

- finishing someone else's thought

- sensing a distant event that later proves to have taken place

- getting the flash of a name

- a suddenly clear sense of direction

The type of intuition employed for criminal investigations seems like this kind of inspirational flash, but a closer look indicates how intuition is not far afield from the observational foundation of science.

It was the summer of 1979. North of San Francisco, California, six women and one man had been shot or stabbed to death along hiking paths in a remote wooded area. The press dubbed the perpetrator "the Trailside Killer." The FBI's investigative support unit was consulted and profiler John Douglas went to the crime scenes. He offered a list of traits to look for: local residence, asocial personality, a criminal record, age thirty to thirty-five, white, employment involving mechanics, above-normal IQ, and . . . oh, yes, he also has a speech impediment.

While local cops were skeptical, they eventually arrested David Carpenter. He was an industrial arts teacher who lived in the area but kept to himself. He'd been arrested before, was white and fairly intelligent. Carpenter also had a severe stutter. Detectives were floored.

As Douglas describes it, his insight did not come as a psychic flash, but was the result of processing at hyperspeed the multiple images and impressions accumulated from years of experience with different types of crimes. From this, he deduces the most likely scenario, and also goes out on a limb—which admittedly can be wrong. Yet it can also provide a solid direction to an investigation. This type of gut instinct relies on reasoning, but the visceral flash is so quick that it seems as if the reasoning process is bypassed. It relies on the ability to recall and quickly process what you already know in a way

that applies to the specifics of the case at hand. "The intuition about the speech impediment," says Douglas, "came from the pattern that I recognized in the facts."

Ideally, intuition and science come together as complementary processes. Grissom offers a case in point, which most forensic scientists know, about an incident that supposedly occurred in ancient China. A group of men were laboring in a ditch when one worker killed another with some implement. No one would confess to the crime, and the questioning of witnesses turned up nothing, so the magistrate ordered the men of the village to gather with their sickles. In time, the flies came, attracted to blood and specks of flesh, and the killer was revealed. The killer confessed.

This tale is attributed to Sung-tsu, who in 1235 wrote *The Washing Away of Wrongs*. He is reputed to have used logic and science to solve crimes, so he's credited with being the father of forensic science. He thought through a problem, used creative intuition to come up with a solution, and relied on the science of observation to play it out.

The fact that criminal investigation techniques like profiling can be taught undermines the idea that they involve psychic flashes. The so-called sixth sense is based in experience, memory, and the ability to reason, which then allows for mental agility and creative thinking. People can come up with new ways of doing things, which can lead to real breakthroughs in a case. Some are better at it than others, but the only "gift" involved is an ability to look at evidence and read the clues.

Observation, which includes mentally seeing things from several different angles, is important to this process. When Catherine visits a home in the pilot episode in which an altercation has produced what is passed off as a justifiable homicide, she notices an inconsistency in the way the victim's shoes are tied. It's a small thing, but it stands out and must be considered when determining what kind of incident actually took place.

Crime scene reasoning involves different types of thinking and the more experience an investigator gets, the more quickly he or she can utilize the right kind.

Dr. Jon J. Nordby, certified by the American Board of Medico-legal Death Investigators and author of *Dead Reckoning: The Art of Forensic Detection,* works as a forensic science consultant. With a background in medicine, art, and philosophy, and extensive training in pathology and death investigations, he has given a lot of thought to how a crime investigator reasons, and he views the concept of "dead reckoning" as central: it's a skill that must be developed with experience, but in the end, it feels like a sixth sense.

The term "dead reckoning" comes from the sea. Sailors rely on it when adverse conditions hinder the use of navigational instruments. From years of knowledge, skill, and experience, they acquire an instinct for guiding the ship under any conditions. That's exactly what the experienced crime scene investigator does.

"Dead reckoning is how you figure out how to navigate when the stars aren't out," Nordby explains. "That's the same kind of problem that I face at a death scene, because we have a lot of things going on all at once. The neat theoretical controls from the science lab are not available, so you have to know how to use your experience and reasoning to distinguish evidence from coincidence. That's a kind of dead reckoning. You smell the air and get a feel for whether there's perfume or gunpowder, and if so, what kind. When you've lost all resources except your brain, you still need to be able to determine your course and position."

Despite the ease of television investigators in locating evidence, many crime scenes are, in fact, filled with a confusing assortment of things that may or may not have some connection to the crime. Investigators learn to make some items stand out for collection and analysis, and to keep their observations highly attuned.

Part of this skill is the ability to think rationally and make distinctions among many variables in order to interpret what specific things mean at a crime scene. They figure it out with forms of reasoning that follow certain patterns:

1. Induction is statistical reasoning toward a probable conclusion based on the frequency of certain occurrences. If five women were abducted and four bodies are found, then it's likely that the person abducting them will kill the fifth victim. Police can safely operate on this likelihood, although they don't know with certainty that it will prove true. It's all based on frequencies.

2. Deduction is a specific conclusion restricted by the actual evidence or claims made in a chain of reasoning that leads up to it. It draws out something that's already contained in the claims. Only a handsaw or a chain saw could have made the marks on these bones. None of the handsaw models fit the marks. Therefore, we're looking for a chain saw. Similarly, it is known that signature killers don't stop killing till they're caught. This guy is a signature killer, so he won't stop till he's caught.

3. Abduction, or retroduction, is the process of proposing a likely explanation for an event that must then be tested. It's an educated gamble that offers explanations and helps to determine what is and what isn't evidence. For example: an etcher made the marks on this bomb fragment, and these etchers are only sold in bulk. A Las Vegas school system bought a shipment of etchers, and that's where the son of one suspect goes to school. It could be that the kid had something to do with the bombs, so let's question him.

Coming up with an explanation that can be tested moves the investigation and guides the accumulation of facts. It links events and develops the overall theory. When a crime scene has investigators stymied, a working hypothesis helps to give it direction. The hypothesis can always change if new evidence demands it, but it's better to have some kind of guidance. Abduction is a structure that forms from making the right links between clues and leads. Making solid inferences streamlines the amount of guessing that goes on, and the more evidence collected, the more precise the reasoning. While a hypothesis provides a starting point, it shouldn't be written in stone.

Sherlock Holmes called his method deductive reasoning, but in fact he actually relied on abduction first. He would observe details, develop links, and interpret them in the context of his hypothesis. Then he deduced what else must have happened.

However, just having the proper chain of reasoning doesn't always produce a conclusion consistent with the facts. The information fed into the structure of the reasoning must also be solid. Catherine and Warrick work on a case in "Too Tough to Die," in which a man accused of murder claims self-defense. The wife of the victim says that she witnessed the second shot. Catherine times how long it takes to run from the spot where the wife says she was and to where she would need to be to have seen the second shot. So far, that's good thinking. However, Warrick points out that a semiautomatic pistol gets off shots quite rapidly, in two-tenths of a second, and Catherine deduces that if two shots were fired in the time frame that Warrick offers, the wife couldn't have seen anything. Her logic runs like this:

1. It takes 3.8 seconds to run from the laundry room to the backyard.

2. The gun can shoot a second bullet in less than a second.

3. If it takes longer to get from A to B than it does to shoot two bullets, then the wife could not have gotten to B before the second bullet was fired.

4. If she couldn't have gotten to B before the second bullet was fired, then she could not have witnessed it.

Therefore, the wife did not witness the shooting.

Warrick and Catherine both dismiss her account based on their knowledge of how eyewitnesses tend to fill in their memories with events that did not occur. Yet their approach to this problem, while logical, rests on a weak premise, which is based on a faulty assumption. While each of the above premises is truthful, the third implies that there's only one possibility: that the suspect did indeed shoot the gun at a rapid-fire rate. Isn't it possible that even though the gun is capable of shooting quickly, the suspect did not use the gun in that way? The witness heard two shots. She claims to have witnessed one. If the two shots were fired seconds apart, which is a real possibility, then why couldn't she have seen the second one?

In fact, as Catherine and Warrick go through their reconstruction of the crime, there's no indication that the killer did fire the gun as quickly as they had first assumed. They can't prove it either way. That means there's a hole in their reasoning. While the deductive structure of their logic is correct, only the limited extent of their reasoning makes the argument work.

Had they brainstormed the case with Grissom, he might have pointed out that science tests all the possibilities. They were too quick to dismiss an eyewitness account, and their dismissal was based on the fact that a percentage of eyewitness statements are erroneous. So the lesson is that logic is a tool; it can get you from point A to point B, but to support an accurate conclusion, the premises must also be accurate.

What Catherine and Warrick could have done was develop two ways of looking at the event. They could have replaced their firm idea about the shooting with possibilities: the suspect might have shot the bullets in rapid succession, in which case the reasoning works. If he did not shoot in rapid succession, then the wife might have witnessed the second shot. Then they need to develop a scenario for this.

Crime investigators must have a guiding frame to interpret the right items as evidence and clues. Using logic to solve the complicated puzzles of crime means the difference between random guessing and the kind of dead reckoning that can steer an investigator in the right direction. "Correctly reading the signs," says Nordby, "is the heart of the process."

Police officers and homicide detectives have to rely on this kind of instinct all the time, sometimes to save their lives, sometimes to crack a case. Let's look at a real-life example.

Ethan Jensen, a field training officer in Nebraska and an expert in defense tactics, was training a rookie one night. Things were quiet as usual, but when they drove through one intersection, Jensen looked to his left and saw half a dozen cars parked on the street. One of them was out a little more from the curb than the others. Something told him to check it out. "Even now, I don't know what made me decide to drive past and then kill my lights before turning around," he says. They rolled slowly back around the corner. Two figures dressed in dark clothes ran from behind one of the cars and dove into the one that had caught Jensen's attention. The car took off, but then stopped, and the men took off running. Jensen called out the K-9 unit to track them and then checked out the car.

"It turned out that these people were burglarizing cars on the street, and the resulting investigation turned up two stolen vehicles, several thousand dollars' worth of stereo components, and ten illegal aliens involved in forgery and smuggling. It closed twenty open cases in four different countries, and it all happened not because something was clearly wrong but because something just wasn't quite right."

THE EVOLVING OF INTUITION

Another time when Catherine jumps to conclusions, it's she herself who sees where she went wrong. Grissom counters throughout the case with the scientific approach. In "To Halve and to Hold," she feels certain they have a murder, while Grissom wants her to be more careful before jumping to conclusions. What they have is an equivocal case—a case in which the findings can have more than one interpretation.

For many investigators, experience sometimes clouds the ability to keep an open mind. They've seen a certain type of case before— perhaps many times—and they assume that they've got a similar type of crime. However, in some way every crime scene is unique.

When a skeleton is discovered somewhere, there can be any number of reasons why. Murder is only one. If bones are scattered, it can be from animals; if bones are cut, it could have happened postmortem from some machine. It's the work of forensic anthropology to determine the approximate age, height, weight, and medical condition of the deceased individual. They can tell from the presence of tissue in the cuts whether the person was dead or alive when the bones were cut, and what type of implement was used. If the teeth are intact, these can be matched on the dental databases for identification.

Once identification is made, the person can be traced back to family, but even if someone close to the deceased failed to report him missing, it still does not imply that a murder took place—not even if human blood is present in the house from which the deceased disappeared. After all is said and done, Catherine ends up admitting that her gut instinct inspired unsupported conclusions.

Reasoning backward from an event like a crime involves risk. It can take false paths and waste time and resources. The experienced investigator adopts the attitude of Socrates, who claimed that what he knew for sure was that he knew nothing. In other words, no assumptions are made and everything gets examined before being accepted as a basis for theory or behavior. Even when everything appears to support the initial gut instinct, scientific reasoning remains cautious.

In fact, in "To Halve and to Hold," while intuition moves the case forward with educated guesses, without the help of anthropol-

ogy, toxicology, and tool mark analysis, the evidence would have
been harder to interpret correctly and could have looked suspicious
enough to a jury to wrongly convict the suspect.

SCIENCE

Let's examine how science answered some of this case's outstanding
questions.

Toxicology

Between drugs, alcohol, industrial chemicals, and poison, the
toxicology section of a lab keeps busy. The results of many poisons
mimic symptoms of fatal illnesses, so if there's anything suspicious
about a death, the medical examiner slices tissues during the autopsy
to send to toxicology. Sometimes there's a distinct odor, such as
bitter almonds in the case of cyanide poisoning, but other times
there's no clear indication.

Toxicology analysis came into its own with arsenic detection,
since that was the poison of choice in seventeenth-century Europe.
First, investigations could detect it in food, and by 1806, a physician
in Berlin named Valentine Rose cut up the stomach of a corpse to
develop a way to detect arsenic in the human body.

Toxicologists await tissue and fluid samples (usually blood and
urine) from an autopsy and then subject them to various tests,
depending on suggestions from the coroner. For example, the tissues
of a kid who'd ingested jimsonweed were sent to see if the recrea-
tional substance had been sufficiently strong to cause death. Even
bones can be analyzed, as was the case with the skeleton in the
desert. A deposit of Digoxin in those bones indicated an overdose.

In the case of sexual assault where a victim believes a strong
tranquilizer drug such as GHB or Rohypnol was used, this section
of the lab does the analysis. These drugs have killed unsuspecting
young women and some labs see increasing numbers of such cases.

The scientists dissolve the tissues in acidic or alkaline solutions and use high-pressure liquid chromatography for analysis. Gas chromatography is also employed for chemical analysis, identified by the mass spectrometer. Thin-layer chromatography works in a similar manner, although samples are placed on a vertical gel film, and then subjected to a liquid solvent that breaks the sample into constituent parts. The plate is then analyzed under ultraviolet lighting, and chemical agents are applied to see what kind of reaction they get from each part.

Yet with the bones from the desert, the toxicology analysts could only indicate the presence of a lethal overdose, not who administered it.

Tool Mark Analysis

This is another section of the lab, often coupled with firearms, since there's some crossover with things like serial number enhancement and the use of the comparison microscope. In this episode, the cutting marks on the bone were matched to the saw found in the victim's garage.

Tool marks are generally viewed on the multiple-prism system of the comparison microscope, called "comparison micrography," which places images close together for a precise visual inspection. Tool mark analysis became key in the 1932 case of the kidnapping of Charles Lindbergh's baby, when a homemade ladder was matched to the tool that made it. Then a study in the 1950s raised this type of investigation to the level of science when it was demonstrated that among five thousand chisels, no two made exactly the same mark.

The idea is that when a tool is both made and used, it acquires tiny nicks and chips that characterize its blade or edges. The nicks produce a pattern of striations that can be traced back to that tool. A questioned tool mark, such as that found on the dead man's bones, is compared to a mark made in the lab with the same tool. (The same goes for matching tool mark indentations.) If the tool cannot be found, then at least it can be compared for class characteristics from an identical model, but identification is most precise when the suspect tool is available.

Another approach is to examine the tool blade for traces of the substance that it was used to cut or pry (in the event that it wasn't wiped clean), or to use a chemical spot test on the cut substance to test for the right type of suspect metal.

All tool marks at a crime scene get carefully photographed, and if possible, the area where they're found is brought into the lab. Otherwise, a mold can be made of the mark. In some cases, a tool mark will link several crimes, such as in serial burglaries.

Of course, as Catherine learns, matching a saw to the cutting marks does not necessarily imply murder—it only means that someone cut the body with a particular tool. Sometimes, even science and intuition together can't resolve everything.

TUNNEL VISION

One thing the scientific method seeks to avoid is a personal involvement that can put blinders on investigators. This happens to Catherine in "Justice Is Served" when her rage against child molesters prevents her from spotting clues that point to a surprising murder suspect.

Everyone has biases and if those biases corrupt the investigation process, then pains are taken to keep that person off the case, if possible. Yet that doesn't always happen. Even the most experienced investigator is prone to making this mistake.

Sometimes certain suspects look so obvious that no effort is made to follow up on other suspects. That means that assumptions have been made in forming the hypothesis that may be weak or wholly inaccurate.

In fact, Catherine had only to think of a rather famous and shocking case to realize that another very good suspect might be right in front of her.

When Susan Smith strapped her two young sons into the backseat of her car in South Carolina in 1994 and then pushed it into a lake to drown them, few people spotted her deception as she tearfully told the story that someone had kidnapped her children. The media was completely behind her. Even when she finally revealed that she herself had murdered them, few people wanted to believe it. Why would a mother do such a thing? Some citizens of the area were so traumatized by her act they couldn't sleep and needed psychiatric care. Because such a murder seemed so incomprehensible, it wasn't even considered a possibility during the initial stages of the investigation. Yet mothers do kill their children. So do fathers. Since all theories are to be considered, investigators must keep open minds. What one *wants* to believe may be the greatest hindrance to finding the truth.

INTUITION FEEDS PERSPECTIVE

It bears repeating that intuition without science is blind, and science without intuition is stagnant. Even Grissom gets a "flash" that enhances what science is able to do, when he agrees to reopen a capitol double murder case in "Fahrenheit 932."

The basis for his persistence is that what passes for "facts" may be only half of the story. A second look may overturn an initial interpretation. Science is never about facts alone, and facts are always understood in a context. That means that it's not just about observation and replicable results, but about forming the right guiding idea. This is not a subjective feeling but an awareness based on his experience of how investigations can get sloppy and shallow, and evidence can get mishandled or ignored.

When Grissom smashes a coffeepot, it allows him to envision the crime scene in a new way. This is often exactly what investigators do to help prisoners on death row. They envision the evidence in a way other than how it is was presented in court, and if they succeed, the person might get a new trial or be freed altogether.

It's likely that someone in Grissom's position would be aware of the recent controversy over death-row inmates. A journalistic investigation of 285 death penalty cases in Illinois turned up the fact that half of them involved incompetent defense attorneys, questionable jailhouse snitches, questionable hair analysis results, or obvious racial biases. DNA analysis exonerated thirteen of these men, prompting Governor George Ryan to place a moratorium on executions in the state. And Illinois was not the only place to have serious problems with the way such cases are handled.

This momentous event started with the situation of four black men, two of whom were slated to die because of their alleged involvement in the 1978 murder of a white couple near Chicago. A couple of journalists (not lawyers or criminalists) turned up evidence that they were innocent. Then DNA tests exonerated them altogether. Shortly thereafter, three other men confessed. Had the journalist not been curious, it's likely that at least two innocent men would have died.

It's chilling to think that four men were unfairly imprisoned, but soon there were other cases—thanks to the legwork of journalism students at Northwestern University (again, not lawyers). Another man, with an IQ of fifty-one, was only two days from execution when his conviction was overturned based on a reexamination of evidence. He should never have been that close to the death chamber, and it wasn't the evidence that put him there; someone's erroneous interpretation did. According to a report in the Associated Press, two-thirds of death penalty appeals from 1973 to 1995 were successful, which is a shameful testament to the enormous number of mistakes made in some very serious cases.

It's important to understand that not everyone involved in investigating or prosecuting a criminal case is a scientist. And, not all scientists are concerned about doing careful work. For some, the priority is efficiency and closure, not truth. In many real-life criminal cases there are problems with witness perception, with the jury system, with confessions, and even with the effects of expert witnesses who might be influential but are nevertheless wrong. One experiment run in the mid-1990s by a nighttime magazine show, for example, pitted two tire-tread experts against each other in a murder case. The older and more experienced man had a greater air of authority. He testified that the tire-tread pattern from a hypothetical crime scene matched the tire of the car driven by the suspect. The other expert refused to make such a strong statement. He was right, the older man was wrong, and yet the jury sided with the one in error. Why? According to a poll of the jury members, he just seemed more convincing. Unfortunately, this problem is not rare.

After Governor Ryan learned about the thirteen exonerated prisoners, he expressed shock at the idea that innocent men may have been executed. Thirty-seven other states use the death penalty and it's no secret that the court proceedings are not always about justice. Too many convictions rely on questionable eyewitness testimony. Lack of funding and the large number of bad lawyers—and even bad judges— also top the list of reasons why someone is falsely convicted.

In Texas, Roy Criner received a prison sentence of ninety-nine years for the rape and murder of sixteen-year-old Deanna Ogg. Apparently he'd hinted at his involvement in the crime, and so he was arrested and convicted. In the mid-1990s, DNA testing excluded him as being the contributor of the genetic material found on the girl. Yet the appeals court decided that the DNA evidence would not have made a difference in his trial, so they did not release him. Then a local reporter found a cigarette butt, previously discounted. It was tested for a DNA reading and found to contain DNA from the same person who had raped Ogg—and that person was not Criner. After serving ten years for a crime that he did not commit, he was finally set free.

When properly used and understood by the court, DNA appears to be an important safeguard, and yet many states resist postconviction testing. Those few that grant inmates the right to it are in the minority. From 1982 to 1999, over seventy men were freed from death row based on exculpatory DNA evidence.

Barry Scheck, coauthor of *Actual Innocence* and director of the Innocence Project in New York, has stated that many of the cases he takes on for DNA testing are "literally wars," because the courts tend to resist getting the testing done. To assert that a person already convicted is innocent is tantamount to an attack on the entire justice system, and getting anyone to see the truth can be a torturous process. Yet a person can be convicted based simply on the fact that someone "saw" him near a crime scene. The witness can be wrong, but evidence that gets collected may be interpreted to support the eyewitness, because this will likely be the most compelling testimony for the jury. (No one takes the time to educate juries on the error rate of eyewitnesses, which we'll take up in chapter 7. They can get so caught up in the idea of righting a wrong that they ignore real evidence.)

"In thirty-three states in this country," Scheck said in 2000, "there are statutes of limitations of six months or less on newly discovered evidence of innocence motions. We have to fight that." He compares DNA testing in criminal trials to what the telescope did for the stars: it was a way to see things as they really are.

One thing that the DNA revolution in the legal system has proven, he goes on to say, is that there are far more innocent people in prison—sometimes awaiting execution—than we might want to believe.

Janet Reno, then attorney general, heard the message, and in 1996 she called together a Commission on the Future of DNA Evidence. Everyone who attended agreed that such tests ought to be available, yet in reality, court personnel in many places continue to close their ears to the possibility that mistakes have been made. Few laypeople understand the ramifications of this controversy, but in essence, those who are fighting for better statutes for postconviction hearings and testing are working on behalf of people whose innocence can be proven by science—a far more reliable standard than eyewitness testimony or the rhetoric of lawyers. Nevertheless, it appears to be an uphill battle.

Grissom's intuition about what happened at the scene of the fire is inspired by too many unanswered questions in the scenario that another C.S.I. devised. This doesn't sit well with a scientist. So with that uneasiness as a starting point, he uses scientific methods to substantiate it.

He's correct that all possibilities must be kept in mind until science narrows the scope, but it's also true that intuition, based on knowledge and experience, develops frameworks that offer ways to solve cases. As long as the investigator remains flexible on both counts, and uses the strengths of each to complement the other, the case can move forward efficiently and with accuracy.

Now let's see how intuition, logic, and science team up in what's central to crime scene investigation: reconstruction.

SEVEN

The Elements of Reconstruction

There are many different types of crime scenes. Some can be processed with general expertise, while others require a specialist. As painstaking as it is, only by putting themselves at the scene and thinking through all the possibilities do investigators get to the heart of a mystery. They listen to witnesses, process evidence, develop a feel for the crime scene, and reason backward from the event to come up with likely ways to replay what happened. While at least a partial reconstruction occurs with every serious crime, analyses involving blood spatter patterns, multiple suspects, and equivocal crime scenes reveal how complicated the process can be. In whatever manner the questioned events are simulated, nothing can be taken for granted, because C.S.I.s must be able to prove in court each piece of the chain of evidence.

CRIME SCENE RECONSTRUCTION

In "Friends and Lovers," Nick and Catherine use multicolored strings to interpret blood-spattered patterns, and with the help of a special computer program, effectively reconstruct how a victim received his fatal wounds. This type of crime scene reconstruction uses scientific methods, physical and testimonial evidence, and different types of logical and inventive reasoning to determine the sequence of events at a given time and place. Blood spatters, bullet holes, or a smashed bottle may speak of violence, but it generally takes a lot of work to reveal not only how the crime went down, but who was involved.

Rick Workman has been processing crime scenes for over twelve years, first as a police officer and now as the criminalistics bureau supervisor for the investigations division in the police department in Henderson, Nevada. In other words, he basically does what Grissom does (except for the bugs). Since he actively works crime scenes, oversees the lab, and attends autopsies, he's developed an expertise in crime scene reconstruction.

Workman defines reconstruction as "locating and examining potential evidence to help determine what happened and to determine who was, or was not, involved."

The initial step is to get briefed by the first responding officers at the scene and then make a summary of statements given by anyone involved. After that, some members do a walk-through, observing everything and making preliminary conjectures. Experienced investigators are aware that appearances can be deceiving. "When we keep an open mind," says Workman, "we often find that what we first believe occurred did not actually happen, and vice versa. If you form an opinion and only look for evidence that supports that opinion, the scope of the investigation may narrow in focus too early, overlooking potential evidence."

While they want to avoid collecting a lot of garbage that can burden the investigation, they have to collect anything that might be useful. "Just when a victim seems to have died of a heart attack, the autopsy X ray reveals a bullet in the head. So . . . that expended cartridge case on the ground fifty feet from the body might be related, in spite of the fact that the deputy coroner failed to find any indication of a bullet hole." Even an empty beer bottle across the street might reveal important fingerprints. "I like to use the 'so what?' or 'what is the significance?' test," Workman explains. "If we're not sure, it's best to document, collect, and process it. The most trivial item may become a key factor in reconstructing a crime scene, and if we don't collect it at the initial investigation, it may be lost forever."

Even eyewitnesses can be a productive source. "We never want to ignore any eyewitness account that may lead us to potential evidence. However, we keep in mind the fact that witnesses see or hear things from a particular point of view and may relate what they believe happened rather than only what they actually witnessed. Independent statements from witnesses who have not talked to others—especially those who corroborate evidence or statements of other witnesses—may carry more weight."

Workman feels that the importance of reconstruction cannot be overestimated. "Crime scene reconstruction has helped us solve many crimes that would have otherwise gone unsolved." He gives the example of a man in Las Vegas, named "John," who told police that someone had shot a bullet into his car as he was driving. The crime scene analysts went to the parking lot where this event occurred and found the body of a nineteen-year-old male. He'd been shot and his car was in the lot, two parking spaces away. John admitted that he'd struggled with the victim, who'd pointed a gun at him, and it went off, "slightly injuring" the victim in the neck. John drove away and it was then that a bullet struck his car (he said).

Workman recovered a bullet, brain matter, samples from bloodstains, and small paint chips that matched John's car. He noted what looked like bloody shoeprints leading away from the body and toward the parking lot exit. Since they had a homicide victim, they were now looking for a suspect, which could be John. Both John and the victim's vehicles were transported to the crime lab, where additional evidence was recovered. Workman and his team then did an extensive reconstruction, which demonstrated that:

1. The "bloody footwear impressions" were actually repetitive transfer impressions, in blood, from the suspect's left front tire.

2. The victim was upright (possibly standing) and adjacent to the suspect vehicle when he received one of his gunshot wounds.

3. The victim was lying on the ground adjacent to the suspect's vehicle when one of the rounds was fired. The same round struck the suspect's vehicle.

4. The victim was on his back, adjacent to the suspect's vehicle, when he was shot by someone positioned above him.

5. The victim was adjacent to the suspect's vehicle when he received the fatal gunshot wound.

6. The victim was moved after he was killed, and prior to the suspect's vehicle being moved.

7. The suspect's vehicle was backed from the parking stall, through the victim's blood, and then traveled forward toward the exit.

Thus the evidence undermined John's story.

"Crime scene reconstruction can be surprising," says Workman. He's aware that poor training, incomplete evidence processing, and preconceived ideas can contribute to an incorrect interpretation, but the procedure has proven many times over that an "accident" was a homicide, and vice versa.

The basic steps in a reconstruction are:

1. Observe everything.

2. Recognize evidence (note anything out of place, suspicious, or obvious).

3. Document it with notes, diagrams, and photos.

4. Collect it and place markers where it was found.

5. Evaluate it for as much information as possible.

6. Come up with a working hypothesis of how the incident occurred.

7. Test the hypothesis against the evidence, often by simulating what is assumed to have happened to see how it plays out.

8. Use everything available to reconstruct the action at the scene and write up a report.

The type of reconstruction undertaken is based on the nature of the crime, the incriminating factors, and the questions that need to be answered. Some analysts say that there are five common ways to approach reconstruction:

- Specific incident (traffic accidents, homicide, arson, rape)

- Specific event (how some part of the incident happened in a sequence, or determining positions of participants)

- Analysis of a specific type of physical evidence (firearms, glass, handwriting, blood spatter)

- Partial case reconstruction (perhaps concentrating on only one room and approaching it with more than one method)

- Specialized determinations within a crime scene (criminal profiling, *modus operandi*, signature analysis)

With any of the above approaches, a large amount of data must be processed and integrated into a theory. In particular, scenes in which several people moved around are difficult to sequence, and several different hypotheses may be needed. To help with accurate reconstruction, evidence has to be "recognized," i.e., separated out from debris at the crime scene that plays no role. For example, fibers in the aisle of a plane where a body is found may help; a magazine open on a table may not.

Analyzing the evidence may involve technology from any part of the lab, from Firearms to Trace. It may be that a comparison must be done between a questioned sample and a known standard—an anonymous ransom note with a suspect's actual handwriting, or fluorescing chips of paint with various known metals.

Pattern evidence is also key in reconstruction. It's the kind of evidence that's produced from forcible contact with an object or person. That means some type of violence, and among the kinds of pattern evidence, we have:

- Blood spatter patterns

- Glass fractures

- Print impressions

- Psychological patterns (signature)

- *Modus operandi* (MO)

- Fire burn or powder residue patterns

- Projectile trajectories

- Skid marks

These must all be documented and then examined against a hypothesis. Obviously, if there's an MO that matches other similar crimes, it can provide valuable clues as to who did it and what the sequence of events was, based on past details. The point of crime scene reconstruction is to identify a suspect, link the suspect to the victim or crime, and be able to prove with evidence what occurred. Toward that end, reconstruction can provide important leads.

To make an accurate and detailed reconstruction, all evidence, measurements, diagrams, autopsy findings, lab reports, and photographs or videos are submitted to the team. Those undertaking the reconstruction generally visit the scene at least once to get perspective on where each evidential item was found. Once all of the reports are available for review, the reconstruction gets under way, although a tentative hypothesis will have already been proposed: "This was a crime of passion," or "Maybe the victim was on drugs."

As the evidence accumulates, it's tested against the working hypothesis, keeping in mind that while evidence beats theory, evidence may also be ambiguous and thus open to more than one interpretation. The hope is that as more evidence emerges, the interrelationship among all the items will be clarified.

To get a sense of how crime scenes present themselves and how C.S.I.s jump right in, we'll examine crimes involving blood spatter patterns, reticent eyewitnesses, and evidence that speaks, as it were, two languages.

BLOOD, BLOOD EVERYWHERE

Interpreting blood spatter patterns (BSP) is a both a science and an art. As a liquid, blood obeys the laws of physics, and when force is applied, the amount of blood, shape of the drops, angle of impact, and location of a spatter at the crime scene will indicate everything from velocity to weapon used to how many people were involved. In "Friends and Lovers," the BSP analysis is crucial to the reconstruction. The same is true for "Blood Drops," which involves four victims killed with a knife. Since these reconstructions approach blood evidence with different questions and different methods, we'll compare them to demonstrate the varied uses of BSP.

In the first one Catherine and Nick map multiple spray patterns to establish:

1. The position of the victim when hit

2. The position of the assailant relative to the victim

3. The victim's and offender's respective movements in the crime scene

4. The types of blood drops or spray that are present

5. The number of blows struck

6. How hard they were struck

7. The weapon used

8. What the absence of blood in an otherwise continuous pattern means

9. Who else was present

While it's not difficult to prove to the suspect that she's lying, or even to establish that another person was in the room, it's trickier to determine if that person just happened by or served as an accomplice.

In "Blood Drops," Grissom arrives at a house where Scott Collins, his wife, and two sons have been brutally slaughtered. With four separate victims and two survivors, BSP analysis becomes a crucial tool.

What Grissom needs to know for reconstruction is:

1. The different type of injuries the victims suffered

2. The order in which the wounds were inflicted

3. Whose blood is present where

4. The exact type of weapon that caused the injuries, and whether it's present

5. Whether the victims were in motion or lying still when the injuries were inflicted

6. Whether the victims were moved after the injuries were inflicted

7. How far the blood drops fell or flew before hitting the surface where they were found

8. What the shapes of the various blood drops indicate about the assailant

While BSP analysis is not an exact science, some facts about blood and injuries always hold true. For example, the greater the force striking someone, the smaller the size of the spatter. Punching someone in a way that draws blood will result in a larger surface than a bullet produces. Blood with more weight travels farther, and it only travels so far in a straight line before it curves downward.

In the 1930s, Scottish pathologist John Glaister classified blood splashes into six distinct types:

1. Drops on a horizontal surface

2. Splashes from blood flying through the air and hitting a surface at an angle

3. Pools of blood around the body

4. Spurts from a major artery or vein

5. Smears left by movement of a bleeding person

6. Trails from a body dragged or carried, or a bleeding person in motion

Any of these can be traced back to the point of attack by considering such factors as the surface on which the blood fell, the angle at which it hit, and the distance it traveled. That's what the stringing is all about, and this involves mathematical calculations. Different colored strings are used to trace the paths of different blood drops from their point of origin, devised from the angle at which they hit. A computer program does the math, using length and width of the spatter patterns and factoring in a body to indicate the victim's position when hit. Where the strings converge indicates the point of impact, and several converging points mean several hits drew blood.

Brian Kennedy, a sergeant with the Sacramento County Sheriff's Department in California, has specialized since 1984 in blood spatter pattern analysis. For more than a decade, he's been teaching this technique to other forensic investigators.

Bloodstain patterns, Kennedy points out, help investigators understand the positions and the means by which the victim and suspect moved, interacted, and struggled through the crime scene. When they see the sequence of how events occurred, investigators can then look for fingerprints, footprints, hairs, fibers, and other forms of trace evidence. The BSP assessment also minimizes the need to collect a lot of blood samples for DNA, and a crime scene reconstuction helps determine which of the witnesses and suspects is telling the truth.

The shape of the blood drop itself can produce important information, because its proportions can reveal the kind of energy needed to disperse it. The shape of the stain indicates the direction in which it was traveling and angle at which it struck the surface. Choosing several stains and using basic trigonometric functions allows analysts to do a three-dimensional re-creation of the bloodletting event.

For example, a path of drops several feet apart that show an elongated shape indicates that someone who was bleeding was also running. If they're closer together and more rounded, but still in a path, the person was moving more slowly. Drawing a line through several successive stains will indicate the direction in which the person was moving. If elongated, the narrow end points in the direction of the travel. One can also see where an assailant was standing in relation to the injured person.

The disruption of a blood drop on impact with a surface is directly related to the texture of the surface. A smooth surface, such as glass, records a stain with clean edges. A rough surface, like concrete, will break the surface tension irregularly and generate a star burst pattern. Some blood spurts, when compared to where the wound is located on the body, indicate the victim's position when the injury was inflicted and any subsequent movement by that person. Blood drops that are thrown off of a swinging instrument in the arc of the swing, show the assailant's position when swinging the weapon.

According to other bloodstain experts, the shape of a blood drop can reveal a lot about the conditions in which it fell. It's all quite complicated, but a flexible rule of thumb when dealing with a generally smooth and nonporous surface might be the following:

1. If blood falls a short distance—around twelve inches—at a ninety-degree angle, the marks tend to be circular.

2. If blood drops fall several feet straight down, the edges may become crenellated, and the farther the distance from the source to the surface, the more pronounced the crenellation.

3. A height of six feet or more can produce small spurts that radiate out from the main drop.

4. If there are many drops less than an eighth of an inch across, with no larger drop, then it may be concluded that an impact produced the blood spatter.

5. If the source was in motion when the blood leaked or spurted, or if the drops flew through the air and hit an angled surface,

the drops generally look like stretched-out exclamation marks. The end of the stain that has the smallest size blob indicates the direction in which the source was moving.

All of the above help in the reconstruction of events. To briefly review, spatter patterns reveal the nature of the force and position of the victim. Cast-off patterns reveal the position and the possible size of the assailant, as well as how many times he drew a weapon back to strike. One also gets an indication of the size of the implement and whether the assailant is left- or right-handed. The absence of blood where one would expect to find it is called a "shadow," and this suggests that an object that blocked the path of the spatter was moved. That means the blood that completes the pattern will be found on some person or object.

Nick and Catherine remember this in "Friend and Lovers," and that's how they locate the accomplice to the crime. The missing blood helps reveal the person's size. They also note cast-off patterns that prove the weapon was raised several times, throwing blood against the window.

The clue in "Blood Drops" is subtler. It is only when Catherine examines the blood's directionality indicators in the hallway that she realizes that the killer moved opposite of their original supposition, helping the team develop a new hypothesis about the case.

These kinds of expert analysis of blood spatter patterns involves many variables. It was easy to use it to undermine the killer's story in "Friends and Lovers," but more difficult to determine how the Collins family killer proceeded through the crime scene in "Blood Drops." Yet leads were developed that filled in the gaps.

No matter what kind of analysis is used on blood at a crime scene, it must be handled properly to prevent putrefaction. Photos and notes are taken before any blood is lifted. Samples are protected from heat, moisture, or bacterial contamination, because these things shorten the survival time of proteins, enzymes, and antigens.

Delays can diminish its evidential value, so blood evidence is sent to the lab post-haste.

While physical evidence like blood is instrumental in crime scene reconstruction, so are the accounts given by witnesses. The trick is to get an accurate one. Sometimes eyewitnesses remember things erroneously and sometimes they have reason to mislead. Yet even the way they report an event, true or false, can help with reconstruction.

EYEWITNESS ACCOUNTS

In "Unfriendly Skies," nine passengers and a flight attendant are sequestered (and surprisingly allowed to sit together), offering a collective story that a dead passenger had a panic attack and died before landing. It is the physical evidence, however, that does not fit, and a reconstruction based on this contradicts the passengers' later claim of self-defense. In fact, it is likely that the cause was something much more complicated.

Incidents of "air rage," clinically known as disruptive passenger syndrome, have increased dramatically in recent years, in part due to the deteriorating conditions aboard many flights. Over one four-year period in the mid-1990s, they increased by nearly 500 percent. A disruptive passenger is anyone who interferes with the flight crew or creates unsafe conditions. The syndrome generally is the result of a combination of alcohol or other substances, antisocial behavior, and the perceived loss of control. Between dehydration and exposure to hypoxia, the physiological effects of alcohol are more pronounced in flight. People can act out of character.

In fact, the incidents can be astonishing. A banker defecated on a food cart, while another man simulated a sexual act with the back of his seat. One passenger tried strangling a flight attendant and others have tried to open emergency doors. On a flight between Bangkok and Budapest, the crew and passengers had to tie a man to his seat with headset cords while a doctor injected him with a tranquilizer. The man died right there on the plane. Another man disrupted an Alaska Airlines flight out of San Francisco when he removed his shirt, barged into the cockpit shouting threats, and nearly caused the pilots to lose control of the plane. Once on the ground, he had no memory of the incident and was soon diagnosed with encephalitis.

One of the worst cases of air rage remains a mystery, and this is what appears to have inspired "Unfriendly Skies."

Jonathan Burton, nineteen, boarded Southwest Airlines Flight 1763 on August 11, 2000, bound from Las Vegas to Salt Lake City. When the plane landed, it was a crime scene because Burton was dying, the victim of a disturbing and bizarre attack.

The other first-class passengers were interviewed to try to make sense of how this apparently healthy young man had suffocated to death. Their accounts of the events differ. It is reported that during the flight, his behavior was rude and aggressive and even showed signs of mental instability. He paced the aisles with a glassy-eyed look on his face. At six feet and nearly two hundred pounds, he frightened them. Suddenly he kicked a hole into the cockpit door, yelling, "I can fly this plane." The pilots managed to push him out.

Then a group of men surrounded Burton in an exit row and someone shouted that the young man was going to open the emergency door. Instead, he sat down. The others watched him carefully. He sat without a word until the plane began its descent. At that point, he exploded again. He began to hit and spit on people, so the men who'd surrounded him earlier wrestled him to the floor and pinned him there. Four guys sat on him. According to only one account, passengers were urging them to hurt him and beat him up. According to a different account, some people began to hit him, and a large man in black boots repeatedly kicked him and stomped on his chest.

As the plane landed, Burton was left unconscious in the aisle.

Police officers boarded and found him beneath other passengers, who had their feet on his head, throat, and arms. He was bleeding from the mouth. Transported to a local hospital, Burton died within an hour. Some of the passengers gave written statements, but others just left the scene, including some crew members.

An autopsy report found traces of cocaine and THC, but the cause of death was "compressional or positional asphyxiation." The report also showed multiple contusions and abrasions on his neck, face, and torso. The U.S. attorney, after reviewing the case, decided that this homicide was justifiable, committed in self-defense, and he declined to file charges.

In almost any unexpected situation, but especially where there's fear and trauma, eyewitness accounts are notoriously inaccurate. People on juries tend to believe them, in part because they think their own memories are always accurate, but that's often not the case.

Most of the psychological research on witnesses indicates that they're poor sources of information. Many people seeing the same incident will report it differently. False memories feel just as authentic as real ones and are difficult to shake.

In fact, there are many cases in which an eyewitness has placed a person at the scene of a crime and that person was later exonerated by physical evidence. The only people who actually know what went down are those who participated. If they're victims, the trauma may have caused them to miss important details, and if they're perpetrators, they'll probably withhold some or all of the information. They may even deflect the investigator with false leads.

Psychologists have found that there's no correlation between confidence in one's memory and its accuracy. Over the past thirty years, research has developed around two main issues:

- "Event memory," in which a witness recalls something that happened

- "Identification memory," or the ability to recognize the perpetrator in a lineup or photo spread

Both types of accounts can be corrupted with suggestions or misleading questions, because memory is malleable and can be shaped by events occurring after the fact. In other words, if a witness saw a man assault someone and run, and was then shown a photo of someone who resembled him, the witness's memory may actually shift toward the photo. Then if the witness saw *that* man from the photo in a lineup, the witness would identify him, even if he's not the same man that the witness saw running from the scene. In other words, it's easy to make a mistake. Witnesses can inadvertently incorporate new information and even testify about it in full confidence, as if they'd actually seen details of an event that they never saw.

One study with three hundred subjects explored conditions that produce faulty eyewitness testimony. Researchers misled eyewitnesses and then elicited information in a way that committed that person to what the researcher had suggested. This is how the experiment was set up: the subjects viewed a slide depicting a crime and then listened to a narrative about the crime that contained misinformation. After that, they were asked to write a statement. The results showed that memory becomes impaired, not so much by the misinformation but by the act of retrieving it. Retrieved misinformation can actually block accurate information about what was witnessed, and it then tends to become the dominant memory. What the subjects saw and what they recalled were two different things.

Several prime-time magazine shows, such as *48 Hours* and *Dateline,* have run experiments on eyewitness accuracy among law students. Each time a "crime" was committed in front of the students, there were people who not only identified the wrong guy but clung to their identifications even after they were told they were wrong. The percentage of eyewitnesses who got the details right was shockingly low.

Eyewitnesses identify more than two hundred people per day as participants in a crime. Trial lawyers like to have this type of testimony on their side because juries weigh it heavily when considering a suspect's guilt or innocence. However, psychologists have identified those conditions that increase the chances of mistaken identification, and they're fairly common to many investigations:

1. Surrounding an innocent suspect in a lineup with people who fail to resemble details from the witness statement

2. Failing to instruct witnesses that the actual perpetrator might not be in a lineup

3. Using lineups that encourage relative judgments ("He looks more like the one than that other guy.")

4. Showing witnesses photographs of suspects before lineups

5. Suggesting that the police have someone they feel sure of and all they need is a good identification (which places pressure on the witness to deliver)

As previously noted, recent work with DNA evidence to exonerate people has highlighted the problems with eyewitness testimony. By the year 2000, DNA testing had freed more than seventy people, a surprising number of them from death row. Of the first forty cases, mistaken identification was involved in thirty-six. In 205 wrongful convictions without the use of DNA testing, nearly half were attributed to mistaken eyewitness accounts. There have been cases in which an eyewitness saw a stranger for less than three seconds from a distance and the jury *still* believed that person's identification!

While eyewitnesses can certainly offer crucial information to help solve a case, such as giving a description for a composite sketch, whatever they say should always be measured against the physical evidence—especially if they have reason to lie.

RECONSTRUCTING EQUIVOCAL CRIME SCENES

Officer Joe Tyner claims in "Who Are You?" that after pursuing a Jeep into a parking lot, pulling out his gun, and ordering the driver to put his hands on the wheel, the driver reached for a gun and shot himself in the forehead.

In order to substantiate or disprove the cop's story, the following factors must be determined:

1. The bullet trajectory in relationship to both parties involved

2. The number of bullets fired

3. The location of the spent bullet(s)

4. Whether the cop's gun was fired

5. What the shooting distance was for both weapons

6. The position and location of the victim

7. Whether the bullet matches the victim's gun or the cop's gun

Unless bullets lodge in something obvious, like a victim, they can be difficult to retrieve at a crime scene. They take paths that defy anyone's predictions and end up in the oddest places. If something deflects them, they can arc away from where they were fired, and then get deflected again. Detectives use metal detectors (as Sara does), brooms, and vacuums to try to locate them. It takes as much luck as skill.

One way to determine a trajectory path is to find two surfaces through which the bullet passed and use a laser or dowel to line them up. This is also done according to an angle of penetration. Once a bullet hits something and ricochets, the angle can't be precisely determined because the bullet's shape has been altered, but lasers and mirrors can approximate the trajectory path if the ricochet spot is located.

The bullet in this case must be found because it's the only thing that can resolve the ambiguity of witness testimony. Only by finding the bullet can they determine its point of origin and trajectory.

It's in the face of such ambiguities that brainstorming makes its greatest contribution. Reconstructing complex scenes requires a guiding hypothesis, but when evidence fails to clearly support it, and the person who devised it comes up empty, someone else involved may have an inventive new direction. Reconstruction is a team effort, involving detectives, criminalistics, lab technicians, and medical examiners. Each participant can check the feasibility of others' theories, and anyone can offer a new perspective on some part of the analysis.

One thing Warrick and Sara could have done in the absence of clear physical evidence was a psychological autopsy, also known as an equivocal death analysis. That is, when the circumstances surrounding a death are unclear, information can be collected about the victim's state of mind prior to death to distinguish between accident or homicide and suicide. This is another form of reconstruction, but it's specifically about events during a time frame prior to the death. The situations in which equivocal death analysis is often used include:

- driving fatalities

- explosions with numerous fatalities

- suspicious suicides

- deaths of new inmates

- autoerotic accidents

First used in the 1950s in Los Angeles, psychological autopsies are now a more standard option, although some courts still question their rigorousness as a scientific technique.

To proceed, the investigator examines numerous factors, and the database generally consists of information from:

- an examination of the death scene

- a study of all documentation pertaining to the death, such as witness statements and police reports

- the presence or absence of a suicide note (which may have to be authenticated by document experts)

- interviews with family members and associates

- medical autopsy reports

- history of medications and of institutionalization

- reports about conflicted relationships or other stressors

- unusual recent behavior, especially suicide threats

- the appearance of getting affairs in order or giving things away

- all relevant documents about the individual's life history, like school or employment records, financial statements, letters, and diaries
- changes in wills or life insurance policies

A close examination of the death scene may indicate the degree of intent and lethality—a secluded place and the use of a gun exhibiting a higher degree than using slow-acting pills in a house shared by others. The case that Warrick and Sara have before them is not a likely suicide scenario, but a further investigation could turn up a reason why the victim wanted to die. In that case, the incident could have been a stress trigger.

Sometimes acquaintances of the deceased have reasons to conceal what may have happened, so the investigator needs to be proficient in deception detection as well. In some cases, the analysis will be clear, while in others, the deceased's state of mind remains uncertain. Some forensic psychologists estimate that this type of investigation demands about twenty to thirty hours of work.

What ultimately matters is to be able to prove a theory in court. If it's too ambiguous and can support reasonable doubt, there's no point using it. There are times when Grissom is certain that, given more time, the evidence for some crime will become crystal clear, but he doesn't always get more time to work on it. Those in a police department who watch the budget have to make decisions about resource allocation and they base such decisions on two things: how well what they currently have will play out in court and whether more evidence or better analysis will make much difference. Sometimes, as in "Unfriendly Skies," a case must be terminated before it's finished.

That's one reason why criminalists spend time experimenting. While not working directly on a case, they may work on setting up different types of crime scenes and acting out various scenarios. That's what simulation dummies are for. They're used in place of people to better role-play an event, such as when Grissom slammed a weapon against a dummy's head to replicate blood spatter from blunt-force head trauma. Dummies might also be pushed off buildings, strapped into cars, shot, stabbed, and used as place-holders for people who were at a scene but are no longer present.

The results of such experiments can be photographed and analyzed for comparison with future crime scenes—especially those that fail to present themselves clearly. The more a criminalist learns about BSP analysis, for example, the more prepared he or she will be when confronted with tricky evidence.

Some crime scenes, however, have a strong psychological component, and a different type of specialist may be needed for this.

EIGHT

Criminal Logic

What seems obvious during an initial inspection may not be how a crime went down. Only a thorough reconstruction of the scene gets close to the real story. This brings up the subject of how offenders think, especially when they attempt a cover-up. That means examining the criminal mind, which introduces psychology as another forensic discipline. Studying clues at the scene, victim traits, and criminal behavior during and after a crime can indicate complex motivations. Combining these things with knowledge of past crimes and what those convicted perpetrators have revealed helps to figure out the kind of person who did the present unsolved crime and what that person might have done to bring it about. We'll look at mass, serial, and individual murders to understand how criminology contributes to crime scene investigation. Often, it's through the methods of profiling.

PROFILING AND RECONSTRUCTION

Reconstruction forms the foundation for surmising who the perpetrator was. Reconstruction is the "what" and "how," while profiling is the "who" and sometimes the "why," as well as the crucial question "Will this happen again?"

Let's return to "Blood Drops," the scene of a mass murder and a perfect example of how profiling can play a role in an investigation.

Because of the presence of strange spirals drawn on a mirror and wall, the first hypothesis to be examined is a possible cult killing. Catherine mentions the Manson murders:

In 1969, Charles Manson urged cult members to go on a killing spree. He'd formed this group from wayward kids in the Haight-Ashbury district of San Francisco, giving them a home on a ranch outside Los Angeles and a sense of belonging to something. His disciples were known as "the Family," and his vision of "Helter-Skelter" meant that blacks would rise up to massacre whites. However, they would need the help of a white tribal leader to govern things, and Manson was the man for the job. On August 9, he sent his disciples to kill some prominent Hollywood people, telling them to make it look like the job of black militants. At the home of Roman Polanski, they used guns and knives to slaughter five people, including pregnant actress Sharon Tate. Then one of the killers used blood to write the word "pig" on a door.

The following night, they did the same to a married couple, Leno and Rosemary LaBianca. They carved "war" into the man's chest and used blood to write "Death to Pigs" and "Healter Skelter" on the walls. Then they had a snack before leaving.

One of them, Susan Atkins, spilled the beans while in jail for another crime, and the killers were arrested, tried, and convicted.

From appearances, Catherine smells a copycat, and the ability to reconstruct the psychological angles of a crime scene derives in part from familiarity with such cases. The most notable copycat of the Manson murders was the MacDonald family massacre.

On February 17, 1970, the Fort Bragg military officers answered an emergency call and went to the home of army doctor Captain Jeffrey MacDonald. He was conscious but lying on the floor of his bedroom. His twenty-six-year-old wife, Colette, lay next to him, dead from multiple stab wounds. Above them both, written in blood on the headboard of the bed, was the word "pig." Investigators then found MacDonald's daughters. Kristen, two, had been stabbed thirty-three times, and her five-year-old sister, Kimberly, had been repeatedly stabbed and hit. Both were dead.

MacDonald's wounds were minor. He told the officers that he'd been sleeping on the living-room couch when he woke up to the sound of Colette crying out for him. He saw three men and a woman standing over him in the living room, dressed like hippies and chanting, "Acid is groovy . . . kill the pigs." He struggled with them, but they stabbed him with an ice pick and knocked him unconscious with a baseball bat. When he came to, he found his wife and daughters unresponsive to his attempts to revive them.

The detectives who made the subsequent investigation sensed from the lack of significant disturbance to the living room that MacDonald's story just didn't add up. Even more suspicious was the fact that one of the magazines on the table contained extensive coverage of the Manson murders. The whole thing looked staged. The detectives wondered why this gang of hippies on acid who'd stabbed MacDonald's family in such a frenzy had allowed him to survive relatively unscathed. Although he was acquitted in a military court, he was tried again in a civilian court and found guilty.

Because it looks like an attempt to deflect suspicion onto a cult, rather than actual cult activity, Grissom seeks a better hypothesis. He needs to think through how the killer committed the crime by devising a possible motive. Thus, from the different degrees of brutality against the victims, he might surmise who the key target was and why the others were killed the way they were. Along with other evidence found, he can get a sense of the killer's age range, gender, method of transport to the home, and *modus operandi* (the action taken to commit the crime). Perceiving the crime in this way offers leads that will either confirm or contradict developing assumptions. If this crime can then be linked to other previous crime scenes, investigators might also see the "signature," or the personal gesture inserted into the crime that was unnecessary to do it but satisfied the killer in some way.

In a crime scene of this type, the questions that might be asked to help understand the offender include:

Why would a killer come without a weapon?

Did he know where to locate a weapon in the house?

What does it mean that there's no sign of a break-in?

Why were some family members spared but others killed?

Why did he come at the time he did?

Is there evidence that this is a first crime or has he killed before?

What was his intent in drawing the designs in blood?

Where might he have gone from this scene?

What kind of post-crime behavior will he exhibit?

Did he have an accomplice?

Reading the killer's specific psychology from a crime scene, as Grissom does, can help to 1. identify the person; 2. question identified suspects; 3. determine if the crime was a single contained incident; and 4. coordinate the evidence. From the available clues, Grissom can easily hypothesize that the assailant is familiar with the family routine, knows one of the survivors, is not very bright or experienced in crime, lives nearby, and may have orchestrated it with an accomplice.

Let's look more in depth at the way criminal profiling works, as developed by some of the FBI's original profilers.

IN THE BEGINNING

When media personalities bandy about the unsavory term "racial profiling," they're talking about police officers who calculate the odds of a person of a certain age, gender, and race being involved in a criminal act. Criminal profiling is altogether different. The former targets a certain person and makes probability assumptions, while the latter tries to compile information about an unknown person from a thorough crime scene analysis.

The FBI began its profiling program in the early 1970s when Special Agent Howard Teten used what he knew about crime analysis to teach a course called Applied Criminology at the FBI National Academy. He talked about the criminal character and the factors that contribute to certain types of crimes. It was Teten who rendered the first official FBI profile, offering an analysis about a case in Texas. Then he teamed up with Pat Mullany to look more specifically at the abnormal aspects of the criminal mind. Their profiling techniques were first taught to FBI hostage negotiators. Then in 1972, they started the Behavioral Science Unit (BSU) and used their methods to solve criminal cases. Numerous requests came in for assistance from law enforcement agencies around the country, so they trained more agents to go out and teach the program.

Special agents like John Douglas, Richard Ault, and Robert Ressler were often on the road, so some of them decided to use their downtime to interview hard-core criminals at the various maximum-security prisons around the country. "We were talking about these cases as part of our instruction," says Douglas, coauthor of *Mindhunter* and *The Cases That Haunt Us,* "so I figured, why not see if they'll talk to us?"

Their goal was to collect information about the criminal mind from the criminals themselves, and then incorporate this into a data bank. Between crime scene analysis, psychiatric and prison records, and interviews with killers like Richard Speck, Ed Kemper, and Charles Manson, they began to get impressive results. "They talked so much," Douglas recalls, "sometimes you couldn't get them to shut up." Nevertheless, the interviews taught the agents to refine their interviewing techniques, and the information they gained contributed to the pattern they would use to make predictions from a crime scene.

They learned a great deal about motive, MO, fantasy-driven acts, and behavior that occurred before and after a crime. They began to better understand how to link crime scenes to ascertain whether a rape or murder was the work of a serial offender, and to narrow down the possibilities of what such men were like and where they might reside. "Most serial killers," Douglas points out, "are motivated by a desire to create and sustain their own mythology." Knowing this helped the profilers develop their ideas.

While profiles often accurately state an age range, mental condition, type of car used, and level of employment, profiling is not a special kind of perception. As stated previously, it's based in experience and knowledge about previous crime scenes and offenders. According to former Special Agent Roy Hazelwood, one of the early FBI profilers and coauthor of *Dark Dreams,* to be good at it requires a few basic qualities. "Number one is common sense," he says, "or practical intelligence. Then you need an open mind—you have to be able to accept other people's suggestions. Number three is life experience. Number four is an ability to isolate your personal feelings about the crime, the criminal, and the victim. And number five would be an ability to reason like the offender."

In other words, what profiling is *not* about, contrary to what Thomas Harris writes in *The Silence of the Lambs* and *Red Dragon,* is becoming so absorbed in the mind of a killer that one is only a thin veil away from being a killer oneself. Profilers can understand that another person finds a certain behavior both tolerable and desirable without wanting to do it themselves. People who engage in this type of criminal psychology may get stressed out from the long hours and endless analysis, but they're not in danger of turning into psychopaths.

Eventually the BSU became the Investigative Support Unit, and then part of the National Center for the Analysis of Violent Crime (NCAVC) at Quantico, Virginia. Now the Instructional Services Unit of the FBI also has a criminal profiling division, along with ViCAP (Violent Crime Apprehension Program) and Engineering Services.

ViCAP was inspired by Los Angeles police officer Pierce Brooks. He was assigned to some homicide cases that struck him as being the work of someone with a history of violence, so he spent hours in a library looking up information about other cases. He realized that if the police were going to stop repeat offenders who crossed jurisdictions, a national computerized database was necessary. In 1983, he testified before Congress, and the result was the establishment of NCAVC in 1984. ViCAP became available the following year, with Brooks as program manager. It's a computer-automated data center that collects and analyzes information from police departments about solved, unsolved, and attempted homicides from around the country so that linkages can be made among crimes in which the perpetrator is transient. They also have data about unidentified bodies where the manner of death is suspected homicide, and missing-person cases in which foul play is suspected. In Canada, a similar database is known as ViCLAS (Violent Crime Linkage Analysis Systems).

The methods of profiling have become a regular part of law enforcement. Not everyone does it like the FBI, and many forensic mental health practitioners have developed their own styles, but it was this small group of agents—who later put together *The Crime Classification Manual*—who formed the basic program.

One of the first official profiles for law enforcement was done in 1957 by psychiatrist James A. Brussel in the case of New York's "Mad Bomber," George Metesky. For sixteen years, he'd exploded some thirty bombs in various places around the city and sent angry notes to the newspapers (which were not published). The police had few leads and no idea how to stop this man, who signed many of his notes "FP." Brussel studied photos of the bomb scenes, analyzed the content of the letters, examined the handwriting, and managed to draw several quite specific conclusions:

The bomber was male, middle-aged, foreign (probably Slavic), paranoid, hated his father, was obsessed with his mother, had worked at Consolidated Edison and had a vengeful grudge against the company, had a heart condition, was self-educated, lived in Connecticut with a brother or sister, and was heavyset, single, Catholic, overly sensitive, and meticulous. When they found him, he'd be wearing a double-breasted suit, buttoned.

The police officers were skeptical, but as it turned out, Metesky matched this profile pretty closely. He was a middle-aged, unemployed Eastern European who lived with two sisters in Connecticut and felt that his onetime employer, Con Edison, had caused the tuberculosis from which he suffered. When fired without being given disability, he'd threatened "dire consequences," but no one had taken him seriously. "FP" meant "fair play." Although investigators actually found Metesky in a bathrobe, when they requested that he get dressed to come with them, he came out wearing a double-breasted suit . . . buttoned.

Douglas is now retired from his stint as the head of the FBI's BSU, but he has written and lectured widely about the profiling methods he helped develop there. He states his basic formula as "How plus Why equals Who," believing if the motives and MO of a crime are clarified, the solution is just a matter of good logic. Even so, he doesn't dispute that profiling is a complicated process. "The profiler's best weapon is his or her mind," he states. It's a form of mental gymnastics.

Developing an assessment of a criminal prior to actually questioning a suspect involves looking at such data as the following:

- The weapon used

- The killing site (and dump site, if different)

- The position of the body and whether it was moved

- The type of wounds inflicted

- Details about the victim

- Any risks the offender took

- The offender's method of controlling the victim

- Any evidence of staging the crime or overkill

Based on the idea that people tend to be slaves to their psychology and will inevitably leave clues, a profile is an educated attempt to provide parameters about the type of person who committed a certain crime. The information that a good profile will offer includes the offender's:

- Gender and approximate age

- Specific MO and signature

- Living situation and vehicle condition

- Evidence of significant relationships

- Educational level and military history

- Evidence of an organized or disorganized personality

- Type of travel pattern

- Psychological traits like being impulsive or compulsive

- Type of fantasy involved (S&M, homosexual, pedophiliac)

- Tendency to take a trophy

According to Douglas, the signature or "personation" (behavior done for emotional satisfaction) is key: "I've found that signature is a more reliable guide to the behavior of serial offenders than the MO. That's because the MO evolves, while the emotional reasoning that triggers a signature stays relatively rigid." In other words, an offender may change the manner in which he breaks into a place or pursues a victim, but he will continue to perform his ritual. There are investigators who specialize in signature analysis, and we'll revisit this subject in chapter 10. For now, let's stick with profiling.

Although a profile can be developed from a single incident, it's more commonly used as a way to link serial crimes, especially serial murders. The FBI coined the term "serial killer" in the 1970s during the "Son of Sam" spree in New York, and their official definition is someone who has killed at least three times with a cooling off period between attacks. They're unlike mass or spree killers in that mass killers seek to exterminate a large number of people all at once (as in "Blood Drops"). A spree killer slaughters people 1. in a ceaseless frenzy in more than one locale; 2. episodically in one locale; or 3. over a period of time in more than one locale with nonviolent activity between events that is not equivalent to the cooling off period of the serial killer. Each type of killing pattern is given a different type of analysis.

The mass killer generally has a clear agenda and often uses the crime to send a message. A spree killer may just be on a rampage, which in itself could be suicidal. Serial killers are different.

They kill compulsively and they don't stop; instead, they die, get hospitalized, or get caught. They account for about 10 percent of all the murders in the United States, and it's estimated that our country is home to 75 percent of the world's serial killers. It's generally the case that serial offenders act out of a compulsion fed by an active fantasy life. The older a killer gets, the more sophisticated the fantasy. The victims are more or less just props who happen to have the right characteristics for the scenario. Nevertheless, many serial killers devote a lot of planning to their crimes.

Responsible profilers gather as much information as they can, looking at crime scene photos, autopsy reports, witness statements, police reports, and sometimes even going to the crime scene itself or learning how it was reconstructed before providing an analysis. And they will always caution investigators about profiling's limitations.

A profile is most easily developed if the offender displays some evidence of psychopathology, such as sadistic torture, postmortem mutilation, or pedophilia. Those who leave a signature help to link crime scenes and predict such things as future possible attacks, the most probable pickup or dump sites, and victim types.

Between June 14, 1962, and January 4, 1964, thirteen single women in the Boston area were victims of a serial killer dubbed "the Boston Strangler." Within ten weeks, six were killed, the first four within twenty-seven days, then two were killed in the same month, August, nine days apart. All were elderly. A second wave began in December, with two dead, and not again until the following September, then November, then January. These women were younger than the first six, but there were two more elderly women in the spring of 1963.

**All were murdered in their apartments, had been sexually mo-
lested, and were strangled with articles of clothing. Sometimes the
killer tied the ligature with a bow. There were no signs of forced entry,
and the women apparently knew their assailant, voluntarily let him
in, or failed to lock their doors. Most of these women led quiet, mod-
est lives. The killer's MO was to gain undetected entry through the
front door, and his signature involved the way he molested the victims, searched through their personal items, and made it clear from
notes or bows that the same killer had visited each woman.**

Generally, profilers employ psychological theories that provide
ways to analyze mental deficiencies, personality characteristics, criminal thought patterns, and character defects. They also utilize actu-
arial (statistical) data such as the age range into which certain types
of offenders typically fall, the rate of repeat for certain offenses, and
the influence of an unstable family history.

While serial killers are classified in many different ways, from
geographic mobility to state of mind, one of the most common divisions is the organized vs. disorganized killer, suggested by Special
Agents Hazelwood and Douglas when they wrote a now classic article called "The Lust Murderer."

Basically, disorganized killers are loners whose personal appearance, vehicle, and place of residence are somewhat messy. If employed at all, they generally hold menial jobs and often live with a
relative. They tend to be insecure underachievers and may be voy-
eurs. They go into a crime unprepared—without a weapon, for example—and use whatever they can find for what's known as a
"blitz" attack. They may also indulge in overkill and do things af-
terward to the corpse. Their crimes tend to be inspired by opportunity yet still driven by fantasy, and they often fail to cover their
tracks. Some suffer from mental illness and have a psychiatric history.

On the other hand, organized killers carefully plan what they will do, wait for the right time, come prepared, and have a great need to keep their victims firmly within their control. They're brighter than average, mix with people, tend to dress well and be educated, and they often have normal relationships and occupations. They'll travel away from where they live to commit a crime and may carry a torture kit. The organized killer is more of a stalker and likes to practice verbal manipulation for maximum power. Quite often, organized killers are versed in police procedure and will read endlessly about their crimes. They will also learn from the investigation and try to perfect their techniques. Unlike the disorganized killer, they may use bondage and will have sex with their victims, either before or after death, depending on their fantasy. They're often looking for the maximum level of excitement and their killings tend to become ritualized. If they get away with a crime, they feel more empowered to do it again. For some, the goal is to feel invincible, and they generally cover their tracks quite well.

Both types may take "trophies," which is an item that belonged to the victim or a part of the victim, and they use these objects to relive the crime. While few killers are purely one type or the other, but rather are "mixed," they will tend to show more traits of one or the other pole on the continuum.

NARROWING IT DOWN

Grissom and Catherine demonstrate profiling in "The I-15 Murders" when they pinpoint a specific truck driver associated with stores where five women have been abducted. At each place, a message was written on the door of a restroom stall, challenging authorities to catch the killer. To do this, the team turns to a graphologist to analyze the handwriting.

A graphologist speculates about people's character from such things as the shape and slant of their writing, which is not to be confused with the scientists who analyze handwriting style in a Questioned Documents section of the lab. Aside from the shape of the writing on the stall doors, the content is important as well. To anyone experienced with criminal cases, the communications in "The I-15 Murders" are reminiscent of a conflicted serial killer from the 1940s, who was caught through a study of his patterns.

> Burglarizing apartments excited sixteen-year-old William Heirens. His first victim was a forty-three-year-old woman who caught him robbing her, and the deed proved utterly intoxicating. He obsessed about it, and six months later killed another woman, using her lipstick to write a message on a bedroom wall: "For heaven's sake catch me before I kill more. I cannot control myself." Less than a month after this, he dismembered a six-year-old girl and distributed her parts in sewer drains. When he walked into another apartment, the police were ready. They chased and subdued him. He confessed, blaming the influence of an alter ego, and received three consecutive life terms.

The graphologist's determination in the "The I-15 Murders" that the notes found at the crime scenes were written by a woman is not as shocking as it may seem. In fact, there are many couples on record in which the female complied with whatever the male demanded, including luring the victims.

> In 1978, Gerald Gallego of Sacramento, California, persuaded his wife, Charlene, to help him fulfill his most violent sexual fantasies. He told her he wanted a pair of teenage girls that he was watching from his van, so Charlene lured them inside with the promise of some marijuana. When they went with her to the van, Gallego tied them up, raped them, and beat them. After driving for a while, he let the girls out and told them to walk in front of the van. Then he shot them and left them on the road. This scenario was repeated several more times, sometimes with one, sometimes two. After ten murders, they

were on the run. Charlene wired her mother for money and instead got the FBI. Charlene struck a deal in both California and Nevada: she admitted to participation in two murders in each state, getting a sentence of only sixteen years in exchange for her testimony against Gerald, who was convicted and sentenced to death.

According to Hazelwood, who participated in a definitive study of such women, men who seek a companion in their crimes generally target certain types. "These men have the ability to recognize vulnerable women," he says, "and they manipulate them into doing the crimes. The behavior gets reinforced with attention and affection, gifts, and excitement. Eventually these women are doing things that isolate them and further lower their self-esteem. All they have is this guy, so they cooperate."

Expert profiling depends on knowledge of such cases. It is the awareness of the range of criminal behavior that helps investigators remain open to possibilities. In the end, the most effective weapon in "The I-15 Murders" came from a subspecialty of profiling known as geographic analysis. These profilers use specific types of information to try to identify where a serial offender lives.

Vancouver criminologist Kim Rossmo developed an effective computer program called Criminal Geographic Targeting (CGT). He uses it to link information about a serial offender's hunting behaviors and geographical information about where the crimes take place. "Spatial patterns are produced by serial killers as they search and attack," he explains.

In order to best utilize geographic profiling, investigators want to know:

- Where a victim was selected

- Where the crime was actually committed

- The travel route used for body disposal

- Where and how the bodies were dumped

- The relative isolation of the dump site

Gathering this information reveals something about the suspect's mobility, method of transportation, and ability to cross barriers (such as state lines). In other words, if many houses within walking distance of one another are getting burglarized, then it's likely the suspect lives in the neighborhood.

Familiarity is part of one's comfort zone and many murderers begin a crime spree in areas where they feel relatively safe. When analyzing data for geographic patterns, the principal elements are:

- Distance

- Mental maps

- Mobility

- Locality demographics

A disparity between perceived distance and actual distance can affect the commission of a crime, and how distance is perceived can be influenced by the availability of transportation, the condition of roads, and familiarity with a specific region.

Another significant factor is the "mental map." This is a cognitive image developed through travel routes, reference points, and centers of activity. Catherine and Grissom use a satellite tracking computer in order to map the trucker's route in "The I-15 Murders," indicating his routines. The places where people feel safe are part of their mental maps. As offenders grow bolder, their maps expand.

Some criminals are geographically stable (stay in a certain region) and some are transient. Whether they tend toward stability or mobility depends a lot on their experience with travel, their vehicle, sense of security, and predatory compulsion.

Rossmo lists offender styles as:

1. Hunter (stays in home territory)

2. Poacher (hunts away from home)

3. Troller (has opportunistic encounters)

4. Trapper (creates a situation to draw a victim to him)

Any of these types might attack the victim upon encounter, follow a victim before attacking, or entice the victim toward a more controlled area.

In general, geographical profiling looks at data about the neighborhood in which serial crimes have occurred, where victim dump sites are located, other things along the travel route that might interest the offender, potential escape routes, and whether a suspect vehicle might have been abandoned in the vicinity. Profilers believe that plotting the routes of serial offenders makes their mobility predictable, which also makes it easier to pinpoint the places where the offender most likely hangs out. A series of rapes in Louisiana that were analyzed with Rossmo's system turned up a suspect who lived in the general vicinity—and he was eventually convicted.

No matter what angle the profiler takes, an important part of any analysis is to gather details about the victim. In fact, many types of crime analysis must take the victim into account. How a victim crossed paths with an offender provides clues to the offender's character and intent.

VICTIMOLOGY

Two approaches to how victims figure into a crime are shown in "Sounds of Silence." One relates to a murdered deaf boy and the other to a mass murder.

Some crimes are opportunistic but others may have been planned and rehearsed for a long period of time. If a connection can be made, then it's possible not only to establish the offender's identity but also to predict if he'll strike again and who the next potential victim might be.

Living victims who are conscious may be able to provide a description of the offender's appearance, voice, odor, or means of attack, and can say precisely where and when it occurred. Yet much can be read from the bodies of those who did not survive.

In the case of Brian Clemonds, Grissom learns that the boy was a student at a nearby school for the deaf, who was out buying beer from a convenience store, before being found dead on the road. Doing a victimology means discovering how many students go to the school, how they coexist, who Brian's friends were, and whether he was having academic difficulties. Grissom also knows that solving the crime hinges on understanding the victim as a deaf person.

A comprehensive victimology involves gathering enough information to have a sense of what the victim was like as a person. Profilers may end up knowing the victim's habits, preferences, ideas, and fears better than they know those same things about their own friends or family. They may even feel the victim's feelings as their own. This is emotionally dangerous territory, but it's territory that often must be traveled.

The victim's history and personality can offer context to a crime as well as leads. Somehow, someplace, that victim encountered the killer or rapist, which can mean at a job, a video store, or even a Bible-study class. Except in totally random or opportunistic hits, he or she was chosen for a reason. Even with a random hit, the way the victim is treated is revelatory.

Basically, the profiler needs to know:

- The victim's physical characteristics

- Significant aspects of the victim's lifestyle that might attract the attention of a killer (daily schedule, hobby, social life, marital status, financial affairs)

- The victim's occupation and employment history

- Items that were meaningful to the person (books, music)

- The victim's last known movements (creating a time line and even traveling the route to make note of all background details)

- Personal papers/communications (letters, phone calls, E-mails, diary)

- Mental and physical health assessment and history

- If the person ever was arrested or incarcerated

- State of mind (depression, anger, fear)

- What the wound patterns reveal

- Possible compliance (knew the killer or was forced into the crime)

- Risk assessment of victim's lifestyle (drugs, alcohol, prostitution, consorting with criminals)

- Opinions of family and friends about the person (get a range)

- If any belongings are missing

It's also important to note how the victim's body was found at the crime scene (in this case, he was run over postmortem by another car that came later). Where the victim was assaulted, abducted, and/ or killed determines the degree of risk taken by either the victim or offender, as does the victim's age and occupation. Risk is calculated in terms of the chances of someone getting harmed. Among low-risk victims are those who live fairly normal lives and are assaulted in daylight or in their homes. High-risk victims include prostitutes, women who travel alone, substance abusers, highly volatile people, and people who work at night. Medium risk is somewhere in between, such as a normally low-risk person who decides to visit an isolated ATM machine in the middle of the night.

If the scene of abduction is relatively busy, it may be that the offender is sufficiently familiar with the area to know when he or she can get away with the crime. It may also be the case that he's familiar with the victim's schedule. Thus investigators check out potential spots for surveillance. First crimes by offenders are generally committed in familiar territory or against someone with whom they are acquainted.

Profilers lay out a sequential and detailed chronology of events of the victim's known movements up to the point of the crime, relying on diaries, witness statements, phone messages, purchases made, and acquaintances.

Unfortunately, careful attention to victimology can be fruitless if it turns out that the victim was killed randomly, as in Brian's case. But another investigation in the same episode demonstrates how important it can be to painstakingly research victimology. When a prominent man and his bodyguard are shot along with two employees and a customer in a coffeehouse, Catherine and Nick focus attention on who might have wanted to have the man killed.

There are five victims here, however, each of whom needs attention and any one of whom could have been the actual target. To make assumptions before the crime scene reconstruction is completed is to potentially miss the killer's trail, as the team learns when evidence reveals that the "connected" man was just an innocent bystander. Only careful attention to the lives and relationships of *all* the victims can reveal the true target and her killer.

Thus, in a single episode, victimology is shown from the angles of 1. a random crime that can't easily be solved from victimology; 2. assumptions about a victim that result in tunnel vision; and 3. an obvious association between a victim and a perpetrator.

PROFILE PROBLEMS

Sometimes a profile can be misleading. In "Boom," the most obvious suspect in a bomb investigation, based on information about past bombers, is Dominic, a security guard at the target building who happens to be an amateur bomb enthusiast. Often people who use bombs as their way to "communicate" have learned to make a particular type of bomb, which means they've practiced and have a good grasp of the mechanics. Unlike just grabbing a gun or knife, these people have some fascination with explosives, and probably with crime and law enforcement. They tend to be organized, since making bombs requires planning and care. They're often angry and socially withdrawn, so bombs are their calling cards.

From the security guard's appearance and eagerness to help, and from the way the police handle him, the case of Richard Jewell comes immediately to mind.

In the early morning hours of July 27, 1996, a crude pipe bomb that was placed inside a backpack exploded in Centennial Park at the Summer Olympic games in Atlanta, Georgia. One hundred and eleven people were injured, and one was killed. Richard Jewell, a thirty-four-year-old security guard, alerted police about the backpack before it exploded and had already begun to evacuate people. Jewell had a passion for police work, and it wasn't long before the FBI pinned him as a suspect. They used a psychological profile of the bomber as a former law enforcement officer, single, who longed to be a hero. Raiding his apartment, they found evidence that he'd attended lectures about explosives and bomb-making instruction. They also came across his collection of newspaper clippings describing him as a hero. The pieces all seemed to fit. To get more information, the FBI deceived Jewell into believing that he could be integral to one of their training videos, which they believed would appeal to his desire to be

one of them. When no physical evidence supported these suspicions, Jewell was cleared.

As all profilers know, the method of character analysis from a crime scene is just one of many investigative tools, and should always be used in the context of the evidence. Otherwise, innocent people can become victims.

Profiling is a subspecialty of the broader discipline of forensic psychology. To see how the analysis of a criminal mind gets its context, we should see what's involved in the general study of deviant psychology and crime.

FORENSIC PSYCHOLOGY AND PSYCHIATRY

In "Face Lift," Grissom consults Dr. Philip Kane, a mental health expert, about a young homicide suspect, Melissa Marlowe. Using what he knows from the psychological research of such children, Kane warns Grissom to beware of the possibility that she's a sociopath. Since there are several types of mental health professionals who can draw such conclusions, let's see what differentiates them as forensic experts.

First we must consider what forensic psychology is and then narrow it down to studies of antisocial personality.

Forensic psychology involves psychology *in* the law, *by* the law, and *of* the law. Practitioners might be psychiatrists, psychologists, neuropsychologists, or social workers. Such professionals use their expertise in human behavior, motivation, and pathology to provide psychological services in the courts, play roles in criminal investigations, develop specialized knowledge of crimes and motives, assist with counseling, and conduct forensic research. Psychologists are generally called on to present findings in court from test data and clinical interviews, specifically in terms of whether a defendant understands the charges and the legal process, or what his mental state was at the time he allegedly committed a crime.

Psychiatrists have medical degrees in addition to their clinical training in psychology and tend to make diagnoses based on the categories offered in the *Diagnostic and Statistical Manual of Mental Disorders—IV,* which lists and describes various mental and behavioral dysfunctions. From references he makes to Freud, it can be fairly assumed that Dr. Kane is a psychiatrist.

Likewise, forensic psychologists can do personality assessments for use in diagnosing a case, but their range of theoretical approaches is often broader. They tend to deal with patients on a more individualized basis and to figure out treatments or therapeutic tools relevant to the unique aspects of the case rather than relying on a strict catalog of traits prematched to treatments. Psychologists cannot prescribe drugs.

While any forensic behavioral expert can deal with criminals and will thereby encounter antisocial personalities, there's been some confusion about what to call these people. Dr. Kane uses the word "sociopath," but that's just one label in a rather haphazard history of research.

First, it should be noted that a sociopath and a psychopath, while sharing the same traits, are not to be labeled "psychotic." Psychosis is a gross impairment in one's sense of reality, which involves the creation of an alternate reality. This can result in paranoid delusions, hallucinations, and schizophrenic manifestations that show up as disorganized or catatonic behavior.

Back to the psychopath. In the early part of the century, "constitutional psychopathic inferiority" was a catchall term for most mental and physical deviance and defect. Then brain damage and physiological conditions were separated out, but there was still a diverse body of problems grouped under one heading, leaving the unworkably broad "psychopathic personality," or just plain psychopath.

Then in 1941, Dr. Hervey Cleckley published *The Mask of Sanity,* an attempt to analyze the specific traits of a psychopath. Coming up with sixteen distinct clinical criteria, Cleckley described these people (who are not always criminals) as hotheaded, manipulative, irresponsible, self-centered, shallow, lacking in empathy or anxiety, and likely to commit more types of crimes than other offenders. They are also more violent, more likely to repeat their violence, and less likely to respond to treatment.

In 1952, the word "psychopath" was officially replaced with "sociopathic personality," and the two names eventually were used interchangeably under the heading of "personality disorder." Then "sociopathic personality" yielded to "personality disorder, antisocial type." Those persons exhibiting an antisocial personality were described as unsocialized, impulsive, guiltless, selfish, callous, and failing to learn from experience.

Yet as the terminology evolved, some researchers believed that the field of behavior research was losing focus on the true nature of the psychopath. The work of Canadian psychologist Robert Hare, documented in *Without Conscience,* clarified a set of diagnostic criteria that offered a practical approach to both assessment and treatment. Based on Cleckley's ideas, Hare devised a list of traits and behaviors for his Psychopathy Checklist (PCL, and then later the PCL-R). He listed twenty-two items to be evaluated by clinicians working with potential psychopaths. With this scale, psychopathy was defined as a disorder characterized by such traits as lack of remorse or empathy, shallow emotions, manipulativeness, lying, egocentricity, glibness, low frustration tolerance, episodic relationships, parasitic lifestyle, and the persistent violation of social norms. In other words, these people are narcissists who feel no regard for others and no remorse. They do what they must to survive, as Melissa Marlowe demonstrates in "Face Lift." Her strategy introduces the next subject: how to tell when someone is lying.

NINE

Varieties of Deception

From forgery to fraud to fabrication, criminal deception can take many forms. An offender might stage the crime scene, lie outright, or feign an illness. Sometimes the C.S.I.s just know when they're getting rolled, but other times they're unaware until the evidence tells them. That means they must be alert to both gut instinct and physical clues. Between unyielding evidence and sophisticated techniques, deception can often be exposed.

Vernon J. Geberth, author of *Practical Homicide Investigation,* says that staged crime scenes and planted evidence are on the increase because people are "learning more about the process of death investigation through the media, true crime books, television mystery shows, and movies." They know that to get away with a crime, they have to cover their trail, and that will often mean creating elaborate stories or disguising the scene.

Let's look at how one of these crimes was taken apart and revealed for what it was, then examine some of the methods investigators can use to dismantle a lie.

STAGING THE SCENE

In "Crate 'n Burial," Laura Garris and her lover, Chip Runyon, plot to run off together with $2 million of Jack Garris's money, so they stage a kidnapping using a taped ransom message. The C.S.I. team uses a spectrograph to match a sample of Runyon's voice to the voice-altered ransom demand. Then, with audio enhancement, they separate out different elements to hear each one distinctly.

Bell Telephone Laboratories developed voiceprint technology in 1941, for processing communication information during World War II. A voiceprint is a pictorial representation of the human voice. It first came into forensic use in the early 1960s for bomb threats against major airlines. The FBI could not pin down the culprits, so they asked Bell Labs to help. They assigned senior employee Lawrence G. Kersta to the task. He was a physicist who had worked extensively with voiceprints, and after analyzing over fifty thousand voices, he felt the technique was 99.65 percent accurate. Soon the Michigan State Police adopted voiceprint technology for criminal investigations. They formed a Voice Identification Unit and hired Kersta to train the officers. Today the procedure is in wide use in law enforcement, because the human voice has individualized features.

Kersta noted that qualities unique to each person's voice can be processed and charted on a graph. Individuality derives primarily from differences in physical vocal mechanisms. The size and shape of the vocal cavity, tongue, and nasal cavities contribute to this, as well as how that person coordinates lips, jaw, tongue, and soft palate to make speech. No one's voice is like anyone else's. Yet are voices affected by changing conditions? Kersta insisted they remain stable over a lifetime, but other experts disputed this: if the body changes, so does the voice. It deepens, and it's affected by climate, illness, stress, and other factors.

Then Kersta got a test case.

In 1971, Clifford Irving cut a deal with a publisher for what he claimed was Howard Hughes's autobiography, ghosted by him. He had letters from Hughes, he said, and he handed them over for authentication. Handwriting experts confirmed that Hughes had written them. McGraw-Hill paid Irving an advance of $765,000 for the manuscript. Irving gave them 1,200 pages.

What Irving thought he had going for him was the fact that for the past fifteen years Hughes had been a recluse. Who was going to find him and ask if this manuscript was for real? In fact, several people who had known Hughes read it and felt convinced it was genuine.

Hughes, however, surfaced from his Bahamas retreat to have representatives denounce the book: he'd never met Irving and did not know where he'd gotten his information. When asked to say this in person, Hughes agreed to a phone interview. That meant he could be identified only by his voice.

Reporters familiar with him from his early days asked questions designed to trip up an impostor. The man on the phone responded in convincing detail. Irving insisted the man was a fraud, so NBC hired Kersta to make a voiceprint analysis of the recorded Q&A. He compared the pitch, tone, and volume to a speech that Hughes had made in 1947. Despite the time difference of twenty-five years, Kersta was able to announce that the matching spectrographic patterns proved that the voice was indeed that of Howard Hughes. Irving was arrested and convicted of forgery.

Many law enforcement laboratories are equipped with at least one sound spectrograph, although there are several types to choose from, including digital models. Tom Owen, who runs Owl Investigations, Inc., is a certified voice identification examiner who teaches at the New York Institute of Forensic Audio. He also consults with law enforcement agencies and for more than twenty years has served as an expert witness. His processing laboratory has five different types of spectrograph machines, and he attests to their forensic utility.

"It's not uncommon," he says, "that at a murder scene or shooting, you have a tape made from a 911 call where the victim might have been calling for help, or else they might have been on the phone talking to a relative. Someone shoots them, they die, and the shooter doesn't realize that the machine was recording. I would get that tape and see if the intruder said anything before they shot the person. Sometimes we get results. Then there are civil incidents, like someone calling to threaten you. We can analyze those calls."

He did a study on twenty-five female voices of varying races and ages, doing a one-to-one analysis to determine the degree of error. The results were striking: "When you're comparing a known and an unknown voice using a verbatim exemplar [the samples contain the same verbal communication], there are no errors. That's 99 percent of what we do today. We don't try to pick a voice out of a pack."

Yet because of error rates among interpreters, this technology is not always accepted in court. Even so, it can contribute to an investigation.

How does it work?

The vocal column begins in the vocal folds and ends at the lips. The vocal folds provide a closed end, so that the vocal column becomes a resonator, with vocal fold tension determining the frequency of the vibrations. When a sound is produced, those harmonics nearest the vocal column's resonant frequency increase in amplitude.

The spectrograph converts the voice into a visual graphic display, the voiceprint. With an analog spectrograph, a magnetic high-quality tape is fastened to a scanning drum, which holds a measured segment of tape time. The process takes about eighty to ninety seconds to complete. As the drum revolves, an electronic filter starts up and acts as a gatekeeper: it allows only a certain band of frequencies to get through. They're translated into electrical energy that gets written by a stylus onto special paper. As the process continues, the filter moves into increasingly higher frequencies and the stylus records the intensity levels of each defined range. The final print shows a pattern of closely spaced lines that represent 2.5 seconds' worth of all of the distinguishable frequencies of the target person's taped voice.

The horizontal axis on a voiceprint registers how high or low a voice is. The vertical axis is the frequency. The degree of darkness within each region on the graph illustrates intensity or volume. These prints can be filed into a computer after being coded, or can be produced as a bar print, which is useful for identification.

For most forensic purposes, comparisons are made between known and questioned samples. When sufficient similarity exists between the patterns that both voices make on the graph, they have a "high probability" of originating from the same person. To work with a known sample, interpreters need a clear recording. The best cases have the suspect repeat what was said on the questioned sample, or at least include some of the same words.

For accurate identification, voiceprint analysts use two methods:

1. Aural: listening to the known and questioned samples to compare single sounds and series of sounds, and to listen for breath patterns, inflections, unusual speech habits, and accents

2. Visual: reading the voiceprints on the graph

The highest standard for court requires the identification of twenty distinct speech sounds that possess similarities.

Another audio process is tape enhancement. The idea is to use "cleansing" algorithms to remove noises from noise-laden tapes in order to zero in on specific sounds that need to be identified. This was used to determine how many shots were fired in the assassination of President John F. Kennedy, and to try to see what was on the missing eighteen minutes of the tapes involved in Richard Nixon's Watergate scandal.

Enhancement improves the listenability and intelligibility of an audiotape. This may involve noise reduction, or the attempt to restore or heighten nearly inaudible sounds. The technique is also used to identify sounds. For better listenability, technicians apply compression, equalization, and an increase in amplitude. Intelligibility requires more complex engineering. It may involve zeroing in on a specific region of the tape or selective elimination—removing one sound to enhance another. The desired signal can be separated as long as it doesn't share the same frequency as the one to be eliminated.

The engineers in "Crate 'n Burial" managed to find a voice beneath the sound of a car motor and enhance it well enough to identify. Although they didn't need to, at that point they could have used a voiceprint comparison as well.

Yet voices are not always recorded, and voiceprint analysis, while valuable, is just one type of evidence that can contradict a story and uncover deception.

LIE DETECTION

A suspect's fabrication can be undermined by both gut instinct and evidence. In "Crate 'n Burial," Catherine and Warrick have an instinct that a willing confession for a hit-and-run is a coverup, and continue investigating even after the confessor breaks down, because his story still sounds false. The ultimate evidence that cinches the case would never have been discovered without this gut instinct.

Conversely, in "To Halve and to Hold," Warrick and Sara doggedly check out the stories of three women who were with a male stripper when he died, only to realize they are lying when the evidence fails to corroborate their stories. In fact, had a piece of trace evidence not realed the truth, the "confession" would have helped the true perpetrator get away with homicide.

Some people think they can always spot a lie—as Warrick implies about his radar regarding white people. Yet one study indicated a problem with professionals who felt confident of their skill: not only were they wrong, but many actually showed a decreased ability. However, since they were confident, they failed to realize their mistakes. In this study, degree of confidence was inversely related to true ability. What happens is that those who believe they know a lie fall into relying on stereotypes, but success with this skill actually depends on experience with specific situations.

Detecting when someone is lying is a source of endless theories. From simple questioning to full-scale interrogation, investigators of any level must have methods to tell when they're being duped. Let's look at some techniques:

Statement Analysis

Rather than using a question-and-answer format that gives away what is known about the crime, the investigator simply asks, "What happened?" and leaves the person to fill in the blanks. This is usually in the form of a written statement, either a description of a specific event or an alibi, but it can also be delivered verbally or on a recorder. The subject is allowed to pick the starting and ending points, which indicates more to detectives than if they asked, "What happened at three o'clock on Sunday, the fifteenth?"

The interrogator feels that determining the truth of an account by analyzing certain aspects of a suspect's narrative presents a reliable way to check for deception. In short, they look for what's revealed and what's left out. Statement analysis focuses on three parts: what was said about events leading up to a crime, the crime itself, and what was said about the aftermath.

What investigators note is whether subjects provided more information than was requested or skipped over something crucial.

Also, if their tone or speed of delivery changed, it could indicate something about their feelings. Another clue is a change in language regarding another person, or sensitivity at some point, indicated by something like a shift from first to third person. The listener pays attention to the nuances.

Statement analysis can also be used on ransom notes, such as the one left in the Ramsey's home when their daughter, JonBenet, was murdered. While the "foreign faction" demanding a ransom sometimes referred to themselves as "we," there were also a few singular self-references. In addition, "Mr. Ramsey" shifted to "John," and the note was excessively long and wordy. There is some indication that the writer already knew that the child was dead according to one statement analyst, and as clues they include the letter's unusual length, which hints at something amiss, and the phrase that they are "watching over" (like God) rather than merely watching (keeping an eye on) the child.

Reading Body Language

When Catherine and Sara investigate the death of a child at an amusement park in "Justice Is Served," they question the mother. Her hesitations and bland response could have been a tip-off, but Catherine instead uses a popular understanding of the association between deception and eye movement. According to some versions of a theory known as Neuro Linguistic Programming (NLP), moving one's eyes to the left means recalling a real event, while moving to the right means creating an event. While this is not actually correct, it does introduce some background in interrogation training.

NLP was developed in the 1970s by John Grinder and Richard Bandler as a way to help people make patterns of thinking into maps for success. They did this by evaluating how people communicated. The basic premise is that we use words that reflect the way we subconsciously perceive our problems. Our phrases frame and also limit the way we see the solutions, which makes the problem persist. Thus our thinking creates us, and too often traps us. Because of diverse backgrounds and attitudes, two different people will process the same signal two different ways. We program ourselves to be and think a certain way, but that means we can program ourselves to be and think differently, too.

People in law enforcement who have adopted NLP as an interrogation tool have oversimplified the notion that certain eye movements always mean the same thing:

Myth: Breaking eye contact means a person is getting ready to lie.

Truth: It could mean any number of things, from deception to getting focused to feeling anxiety over being questioned. People respond according to their own patterns.

Myth: Looking up and to the left means recalling a real event from the past.

Truth: It's not an exact science. Looking to the side is often about accessing an auditory clue, but it could also be a personal habit. The eye movement should be interpreted in the context of other indicators.

Myth: Looking to the right means imagining or creating a story . . . seeing an image a person has never actually seen.

Truth: Again, it's not an exact science. Looking to the right does not necessarily mean that a suspect is making something up, although interrogators using NLP believe that responses given while looking to the right are more likely to be fabricated. However, the careful interrogator won't jump to conclusions. Some people do exactly the opposite of the expected patterns. Each of us stores memories based on certain triggers, negative or positive. Sometimes recall is quick, other times difficult and piecemeal.

Nothing about memory is simple, so methods of accessing it can hardly be interpreted rigidly or with a formula.

One idea about lying is that it is a more complicated activity than truth telling and thus produces certain physiological reactions, such as a heightened pulse rate, dilated pupils, and certain behavioral manifestations. This is especially so if the stakes are high, such as going to prison. However, people telling the truth under such conditions may also display emotion. They may be anxious about whether they are believed or may be embarrassed to be there under those conditions. To further complicate the problem, psychopaths and pathological liars are very good at lying, and their skill makes the typical modes of detection irrelevant. They appear to have lower levels of autonomic nervous activity and are not as adversely affected by the idea of punishment.

In general, the conditions under which people tend to be apprehensive about lying include when the interrogator has a reputation for reading lies, when the interrogator is suspicious, when the deceiver has little experience lying, and when the consequences of being found out are serious.

The types of behaviors that may signal deception include:

■ language with more negative than positive statements, over-generalizations, deflections away from the self, increased pitch

■ uninterrupted talking

■ Speech hesitations and pauses, taking longer to respond to questions, appearing to think through what they will say, answers that seem too long or are irrelevant, no apparent spontaneity

■ Increase in number of shrugs, blinking, and nervous habits like stroking

■ Increased leg and foot movements

■ Decreased number of specific verbal references; fewer sensory details

■ Hyperventilation, blanching, flushing, breath holding, sighing

■ Asymmetrical, miserable, or fearful smiles

- Reduced use of hand gestures; lack of head movement

- Increased behavioral clues when feedback appears positive

None of these is definitive, but they occur more often in those with the greatest motivation to deceive—possibly because they are trying hard to plan and control what they say.

Polygraph

When a teenage boy helps his girlfriend murder her family in "Blood Drops," he's asked to take a polygraph. The results are mixed, which means that Grissom must continue to dig. Since polygraph interpretations can be erroneous, it's not clear whether the boy is lying or the interpretation is problematic. That's why investigators need to find corroborating evidence for the result.

Richard Bruno Hauptmann, charged with the 1932 kidnapping and murder of the son of Charles Lindbergh, repeatedly requested a polygraph. J. Edgar Hoover said that under no circumstances would that be allowed. Two polygraph examiners came forward, eager to test this budding technology on such a high-profile case. The trial judge refused them access. Who knows what the results might have been?

It was a prototype of the polygraph that inspired the landmark court decision in *Frye* v. *United States* that became the benchmark for decades on the admissibility of scientific evidence into court, and polygraph exams are still inadmissible in most jurisdictions. Some investigators use them for interrogations, but some won't touch them.

The polygraph in use today is a compact portable device. Rubber tubes are placed on the examinee's chest and abdomen and a blood pressure cuff on the arm. Small metal plates attach to the fingers. A moving paper feeder and stylus record the simultaneous input from three involuntary physiological responses:

- galvanic skin response

- relative blood pressure

- respiration

Some instruments add peripheral blood flow (obtained by placing a plethysmograph on the finger).

The moment when a question is asked is marked on the paper, just before the response gets recorded. The data are then interpreted through a numerical scoring system, according to deviations from a baseline that occur when the subject shows a physiological response to a question. The examiner interprets the data according to the magnitude of the deviation and may also use his observations of the subject. He then concludes one of three things:

1. The subject was truthful.

2. The subject was deceptive.

3. The results were inconclusive.

The first stage of an examination involves gathering data—the subject's medical background, physiological condition, and psychological history. Examiners must decide whether subjects are competent even to take the test, and then they proceed.

One method is to ask two types of questions: "relevant" questions are related to the crime, and "control" questions are based on common misdeeds such as betrayal, which are calculated to inspire an emotional reaction. The assumption is that subjects will deny such misdeeds, but are likely to be lying. That provides the baseline "deception response." When lying, then, innocent subjects are more aroused by the control questions, while guilty subjects react to the crime-relevant questions.

In 1981, psychologist David Lykken developed "the Guilty Knowledge Test," meant to detect the presence of covert knowledge of a crime in the suspect's mind. He believed that participants in a crime are aroused by a meaningful stimulus that has some association with the act, which he called the "orienting response." The procedure is based on the facts gathered by investigators, and known only to them, the victim(s), and the perpetrator. The examiner uses this information to create a series of multiple-choice questions. Supposedly, a guilty person reacts to certain details, especially if he believes that he is the only one who knows something.

Regardless of the approach, the main issue is accuracy. Critics contend that the pressure of taking a polygraph can produce both false confessions and false physiological reactions. The error rate more often involves calling an honest person dishonest than the other way around.

The American Polygraph Association states that a survey of over eighty studies proves that the polygraph's degree of validity is high, but accuracy depends on having a properly trained examiner using a good instrument, and an accepted testing procedure and scoring system.

Brainprints

A recent development in deception detection is the brain-fingerprint, used on a deaf suspect in "The Sounds of Silence." Grissom straps the roommate of a victim to the device to chart his responses to specific images before clearing him.

Psychiatrist Lawrence Farwell developed this technology in his brain research laboratory in Fairfield, Iowa. He claims that it's 99.9 percent accurate. The idea is that the brain is central to all human activities and it records all experiences. If it's possible to trigger memories of an event, it's possible to connect that person to the event. In other words, a crime scene is stored in the brain of the offender and a brainprint offers evidence of this fact.

It works like this: the electrical activity of the brain of a crime suspect is monitored via a headband with sensors while the subject is exposed to words or images that are both relevant and irrelevant to the crime. If his brain activity shows recognition to the relevant stimuli—a distinct spike called a MERMER (memory and encoding related multifaceted electroencephalographic response)—it means he has some record of the crime stored in his brain. Innocent people will display no such response. Their brain activity will remain constant because nothing in the stimulus photos or phrases is meaningful. If the suspect offers an alibi for the time of the crime, scenes from that can be displayed as well to see if it registered in his brain. A computer analyzes the quality of the patterns and determines whether a MERMER is present.

One flaw, which is also true with fingerprints, is that if the person was at the crime scene but did not commit the crime, there's no way to make a distinction. They may also recognize some part of the scene, or the victim. The best images are designed to trigger the memory of someone with very specific knowledge about a crime.

Stress Evaluator

Another type of deception detection device, which was used to evaluate a phone call to 911 about a kidnapped baby in "Gentle, Gentle," is the Psychological Stress Evaluator (PSE). People who advocate the use of this method claim that the voice itself reveals deception, even if the person is unaware that someone is evaluating the communication.

The PSE does measure variations in emotional stress, although there is little evidence that it is accurate for deception. The idea is that when subjects lie, their voices reach a higher pitch. The advantage of this machine is that it avoids physical contact with the subject, but instead uses a microphone or tape recorder into which the subject speaks. The machine then analyzes the sound of the voice and prints the results onto a graph. Technicians say that it can detect differences in the voice not available to the human ear.

The analyzer can be used over the phone and in a variety of conditions as long as a tape of good quality exists. That means that the test can be done without the subject knowing.

The American Polygraph Association, however, did a study on a similar device, called the Computerized Voice Stress Analyser (CVSA) and concluded that for deception detection the voice stress analysis is no better than chance. They also pointed out that while the Department of Defense uses polygraphs, it does not employ voice stress analysis in any investigative context.

Aside from evidence analysis and machines, there are psychological tests for deception, especially when someone is trying to feign a mental illness. That's called "malingering," and it's been tried in some high-profile criminal cases.

MALINGERING

Tammy Felton, actually Melissa Marlowe, is charged with her father's murder in "Face Lift," and to escape punishment she attempts to convince detectives that she has dissociative identity disorder (DID), more commonly known as multiple personality disorder (MPD). Dr. Philip Kane explains that if this is a case of DID, the dominant personality knows about both, but the subjugated personality would be ignorant of whatever the dominant one did—such as the murder.

Unfortunately, viewers never get to see the verdict or how psychologists may try to disprove her claim in court.

Malingering is a deliberate attempt to create the impression that one is mentally ill, specifically to avoid a charge of criminal responsibility. Many people believe that psychosis is the same thing as insanity, which means to them that if they can fake something like schizophrenia or dissociative identity disorder, they will incur no legal penalties. They'll just walk.

Yet insanity simply means that one was suffering from a mental disease or defect *at the time of the offense* that blocked an understanding of the nature of what one was doing or kept one from conforming one's actions to the law. Even people who are considered mentally ill may still show comprehension that what they were doing was illegal or wrong.

With malingering, psychologists are looking for:

- An overplayed presentation

- Inconsistent information

- Deliberateness of manner

- Endorsement of obvious symptoms

- Inconsistency with past psychiatric diagnoses

They may check the defendant's past history of psychiatric confinement (if any) and statements from witnesses (friends, family, prison guards, hospital staff) as to the person's condition, current and past. They may also observe the subject in various settings and encounters over a period of time.

Another way to assess malingering is to compare the symptoms presented by the defendant with those that fit a typical clinical profile. Schizophrenia generally manifests in auditory hallucinations, but someone trying to fake this illness may "see" visual hallucinations, which are more likely to happen with toxic conditions from drugs or alcohol.

Some assessment devices are sensitive to malingering, such as:

- The Minnesota Multiphasic Personality Inventory (MMPI-2), which picks up "faking bad" and "faking good."

- The Rorschach (inkblot) test, which assesses thought disturbances and deviant responses.

- The Structured Interview of Reported Symptoms (SIRS) specifically detects malingering and deception.

Malingerers make a point of ensuring that people pay attention to their illness, while most truly mentally ill people would rather not be the focus of attention. If they say the delusions or hallucinations were sudden, this is inconsistent with the clinical picture of mental illness—except for drug-induced psychosis. Malingerers also tend to overact, especially when presenting many personas.

Multiple personality disorder is not considered a psychotic condition, although it has been confused with schizophrenia as a split identity. Two or more subpersonalities develop in a single human being, each with its own identity, and each takes turns controlling the personality and behavior. The "core" person generally experiences periods of memory loss and may even "wake up" in a foreign place with no idea how they arrived there. This is called an "amnesic barrier between identities." One "person" may have full access to the memory bank, while others get only partial access. In some cases, the subpersonalities know the core personality.

Dissociative identity disorder often develops after an early childhood trauma, such as sexual abuse or violent beatings. People who suffer from the disorder learn to dissociate—to mentally remove themselves from full awareness of the situation—and this form of psychological flight then becomes a survival mechanism that disturbs the integrative functions of identity. Poly-fragmented DID may involve several hundred different identities in a single body.

Experts talk about how a memory that is not recalled may still have the power to emerge in symptoms like depression, numbness, hypersensitivity, and reactions to certain environmental triggers. There may also be vague flashbacks, or the memory might return years after the incident. These people may "trance out," feel out of touch with reality, ignore genuine pain, and experience sudden panic attacks. They may also act out with eating disorders, abuse of others, self-abuse, or addictions. Generally, they have trouble with intimacy and may experience sexual dysfunctions and sleep disturbances.

It's important to collect data from people who have seen the subject in an altered personality state under normal conditions. While other personalities can be elicited through hypnosis, it's also possible to affect a suggestible person with hypnosis in such a way

that they will act as if they have different personalities—especially
if they have something to gain. Malingering DID is a popular ploy
among those facing serious prison time, but such people tend to
believe that this involves a mere split personality—as was the case
with Melissa Marlowe. However, that's a mistaken notion. As popular as the idea is, DID is not about a good person and an evil
person living in the same body—as one serial killer found out.

When Kenneth Bianchi was arrested in the late 1970s as part of the
two-man team dubbed "the Hillside Stranglers," he convinced his lawyer that he was suffering from amnesia. Then a social worker diagnosed him with multiple personality disorder. He'd seen the classic
movies, *The Three Faces of Eve* and *Sybil,* so he devised an insanity
defense. He allowed a psychologist versed in MPD to believe he was
under hypnosis, and then went into his evil persona, "Steve Walker."
It was Steve, not Kenneth, who killed those girls.

Yet sometimes when he was supposed to be "Steve," he referred
to Steve in the third person. The expert didn't notice, but the detectives did. A second expert also bought it, so one detective did some
research. He thought the evil twin's name sounded familiar, so he
went through Bianchi's papers and found it: Steve Walker was a pseu-
donym that Bianchi had used to apply for a diploma. Now they had
fuel for the prosecution's fire. The prosecutor had an expert, too, Dr.
Martin Orne, who set a trap. He told Bianchi that it was rare to have
only two personalities for MPD, figuring that now a third one would
suddenly erupt. He was right: Bianchi introduced him to "Billy."

Armed with this, the DA offered him a deal: roll on his partner in
crime and escape the death sentence. He took it.

Malingerers who fake DID have a hard time retaining the voice
and personality of the one they want to blame for their crime.
They're also not confused by their criminal behavior, as would be

true of an authentic case. In addition, they generally cannot show a history of the kind of fragmenting characteristic of MPD/DID.

Tammy/Melissa doesn't stand a chance in court.

Yet a strategic use of deception is not limited to the perpetrators of a crime. Sometimes law enforcement officers find it works to their benefit.

TURNING IT AROUND

Like many of the criminals they chase, investigators may also rely on deception. For example, Catherine posed as a street-smart hooker to bait a criminal and make an arrest. Yet even with all of their savvy, at times there are crimes that no amount of physical evidence or psychological expertise can easily solve. Sometimes special knowledge is necessary.

TEN

Forensic Puzzles

While physical evidence can confront liars, contradict witnesses, and undermine hypotheses, understanding the evidence is not always straightforward. Some cases are convoluted, others a challenge to even comprehend. Whether it's fire, bullets, or two-legged beasts, some crimes contain surprises.

Let's look at these puzzles and see what science has to say.

NATURAL OR SUPERNATURAL?

In "Face Lift," Nadine Winston is discovered in a chair, burned to ashes. Sara, despite Warrick's disagreement, thinks Nadine's death may be a case of spontaneous combustion.

The fact is, there are several odd cases of people apparently catching on fire. In April 1990, smoke poured forth from four-year-old Tong Tangjiang, and his parents discovered that his underwear had ignited for no apparent reason. They rushed him to the hospital, and over the course of two hours, he erupted again several times, causing burns on different parts of his body. The doctors thought he was generating electrical current in amounts high enough to ignite his clothing, and they pronounced him "fire-prone."

The apparent phenomenon of spontaneous human combustion (SHC) is even more dangerous because it starts inside the body and reduces a person to ashes in less time than the hot fires of a crematorium. One man in England—a nonsmoker—supposedly experienced this in 1985. He survived because he got to a hospital in time to be extinguished, but he said he felt like he'd been plunged into a furnace. People have attributed SHC to some preternatural cause.

One such incident in the States in 1951 started such persistent rumors that the FBI stepped in. This was the case of Mary Hardy Reeser. Like "Nadine," Reeser was found immolated in an easy chair in her home in St. Petersburg, Florida. She had taken a dose of Seconal, a sleeping pill, to calm herself over a stressful situation, and then sat down to have a smoke. That was her last night alive.

It was her landlady who found her. Reeser's ashes lay on the barely burned chair, along with teeth, bone fragments, and a clump of soot that turned out to be her left ankle and foot inside an undamaged shoe. Oddly, the fire had failed to disturb items sitting only a few feet away, including newspapers, though it had to have burned quite hot.

The police surmised that Reeser had dropped a cigarette onto her rayon nightgown, and because of the sedative, had not awakened. Yet it seemed impossible that such an intense fire could consume a body but nothing around it. They tested for an accelerant, thinking murder, but tests were negative. The investigators were stymied, and rumors of SHC turned up in the media, so that's when the FBI took over.

The police chief sent a box of evidence to J. Edgar Hoover,

which contained glass fragments found in the ashes, six teeth, part of the carpet, and several other items. He also sent photographs. To his mind, none of this made sense.

However, the FBI had an explanation. They theorized that Reeser had died from "the wick effect." According to their report, a small spark grew into intense heat, fueled by body fat. With the increasing heat, the fat seeped out onto whatever the victim was wearing and fed the fire. Thus, the woman burned like a candlewick. The heat went straight up, so items next to her failed to catch fire. Reeser had been obese, so clearly there was enough fat to produce this effect. The cause of the fire, they decided, was the cigarette dropping from her mouth as she nodded off.

In 1991 a murder case gave scientists the clues they needed to support this theory. A police officer came across a burning body near Medford, Oregon. He took photos as the body continued to burn, which offered documentation on how tall the flames would be. They proved to be exactly as the theory predicted: sufficient to burn the corpse to ash but not to ignite nearby objects.

Yet not everyone accepted that explanation and rumors persisted, so Dr. John de Haan of the California Criminalistics Institute decided to test it. He did exactly what Warrick ended up doing to prove the theory to Sara: he wrapped a pig in cotton and used a little gasoline to set it on fire. As expected, the pig's body fat leached into the material and caused the fire to burn hot and then simmer long enough to reduce the corpse to ashes. The fat apparently rose to the temperature of a cremation, and thus had a greater effect on the body than would fire from an external source.

Warrick and Sara, who duplicate this test, watch the pig burn into the same kind of ash as Nadine, with only a strip of cloth left over—just as they'd found at the scene. Grissom happens along and explains the wick effect, although his definition is a little different. He says a piece of clothing acts as a wick and is left scorched but unburned. Those who devised the wick theory state that the clothing and body fat act as an inside out candle, with the clothing burning like a wick to temperatures high enough to combust the fat and reduce bone to ash. It's not the unburned piece that's the wick, but the ignited material. In fact, not all suppposed cases of SHC do have this unburned piece left over. Sara questions why Nadine didn't wake up when she burst into flame, and the answer comes from Toxicology: like Reeser, she'd taken Seconal.

TRICKY TRAJECTORIES

In "Too Tough to Die," Catherine and Warrick must turn to reconstruction to find out whether or not a victim was shot in self-defense. When nothing at the crime scene provides a clue, they take it to the lab. That involves:

1. The shooting range

2. A self-healing simulation dummy

With innovative thinking and the tools of science, they come up with a crime scenario that the evidence best supports, solving the mystery.

Yet without a certain type of specialized knowledge—ballistics—they'd still be pondering how this crime went down.

Ballistics is the study of the impact of various conditions on projectiles in motion. It's linked with the Firearms Identification section of the crime lab, which compares, examines, and identifies firearm evidence. This case draws on their contributions.

Ballistics was born in 1835 in England when the ridge on a bullet taken from a victim was matched to a bullet mold in the suspect's home. Confronted with the evidence, the suspect confessed.

The first time an expert proved in court that a specific gun was used for a murder was in America in 1902. A gunsmith fired the gun into a basket of cotton, and using a magnifying lens, he matched the bullet from the victim to the fired bullet.

It was a firearms case, the St. Valentine's Day Massacre on February 14, 1929, that led to the opening of the first scientific crime detection laboratory in America. Two men, disguised as police, had gunned down seven bootleggers, leaving behind seventy cartridge casings. The weapon was identified as a type of submachine gun, and when another case produced two submachine guns, Dr. Calvin Goddard proved they were the weapons used. His work inspired two businessmen to back him, and his lab opened in Illinois in 1929.

From years of experiments, firearms scientists can:

1. Compare bullets and match them to a specific firearm

2. Accurately estimate the distance of a shooting

3. Detect gunpowder residue around wounds and on shooters

4. Restore obliterated serial numbers

Let's look at each in turn:

Guns and Ammo

Briefly, firearms are of two basic types: handheld and shoulder. Of handheld pistols, there are single-shot or multiple-shot, like revolvers and self-loading pistols. Shoulder firearms have long barrels and include rifles, machine repeaters, and smoothbore shotguns. There are many variations on these basic types.

In mass-produced guns, different makes and models have standardizing characteristics. Since the eighteenth century, guns have been made with internal helical grooves cut into the barrels that are similar to the threads of a screw. They form "lands," or metal ridges, between the grooves. The lands grip the bullet and give it accuracy, range, and spin.

The interior part of a gun barrel is the bore, and the caliber of a bullet is determined by the bore's diameter, expressed in hundredths of an inch or in millimeters. When a bullet travels through a gun barrel, its softer metal gets worn in a unique pattern by the harder metal of the barrel. Any bullet fired from a specific gun will show the same marks, unless there's been some intentional alteration.

"Rifled" weapons (rifles and many handguns) fire single bullets, and the weapon may also eject shell casings. If no casings are found at the scene, it may indicate that the shooter used a revolver, which retains spent cartridges until manually reloaded. Smoothbore shotguns fire multiple pellets.

Bullets found at the scene (or in a victim) can present plenty of information, and investigators are looking for two specific parts. People often refer to a cartridge as a bullet, but in fact it's made up of several components:

- The bullet (lead or lead alloy, and may be jacketed in another metal)

- The compartment containing the propellant (black or smokeless powder)

- The cartridge casing that wraps around all of this (straight or bottlenecked), stamped with manufacturer's mark and caliber

- The soft metal cap at the cartridge head containing the primer

When triggered, the gun's firing pin hits the cartridge in a place that has a shock sensitive primer, or explosive. That charge sets the gunpowder in a rapid burn, which builds pressure until the cartridge can't contain it. This forces the bullet outward and the cartridge backward against the weapon's breech. The impact stamps a distinct impression onto the cartridge head. In addition, the mechanisms that extract and eject the shell leave their own characteristic marks. Whatever scratches the cartridge picks up are unique to that gun.

It's often difficult to match a spent bullet, since it's generally mangled, but sometimes it leaves a trace, such as from a Teflon jacket (remember "Sex, Lies, and Larvae"?). It's usually the casings, if located, that are matched.

Matching a casing to a gun may mean shooting the suspect gun (if recovered) in the lab's firing range. Then a comparison can be done between the casing from the scene and the one shot by the scientist. People sometimes mix different brands of ammunition, so it's necessary to use the brand under investigation. Since the bullet must be recovered, the gun is fired either into a tank of water for very soft metals or into thick cotton batting for others. Then it can be compared for microscopic scratches.

On a comparison microscope, the views are linked optically and can even be rotated to line up the scratches. It takes skill and experience to make a definitive match, but it's possible to say that a certain bullet came from a certain gun, and only that gun.

Yet suppose the police don't recover the gun? What then?

It's possible to tell something about the make from the type of cartridge case or bullet found. The direction of twist refers to the way the rifling gives a right- or left-handed spin to the bullet when fired. Smith & Wesson guns have five lands that twist to the right, for example, and a Colt .32-caliber revolver has six that twist to the left. To get this determination, the analysts point the casing away and examine how the lines of striation angle from base to nose, and they add up the number of marks around it. To say that two bullets are from the same gun, the land impressions must match on the angle of twist and in the number.

These days, crime labs can use a computer analysis to make some comparisons. Computers are networked to statewide and national (even international) databases, similar to an AFIS system for fingerprints. One is called Drugfire, sponsored by the FBI. The ATF has something similar, called Bulletproof for bullet images, and Brasscatcher for cartridge cases. IBIS, by Forensic Technology, also offers automated comparisons of evidence images.

For example, when there's a shooting in one locality and the casing is recovered, it's put into the Drugfire database. (If the gun is recovered, it may be test fired and that spent casing used.) To get a comparison on the way a mark is left by the firing pin of that gun, the ejected case is placed in a device with a video camera that links to a computer. A magnified image of the marks are run through the database to get the closest matches. If the case matches the firing pin's mark, an image of the base is positioned on the screen and the computer then lines up the other images for comparison, twenty-four at a time. They can be moved around to get better side-by-side views. Examiners eliminate all but those that seem likely candidates, and these go to a microscope for a more precise comparison of all angles.

Distance

The firing range also has another use, which Catherine and Warrick employ. To measure muzzle to target, the gun is shot from varying distances at a thick cardboard target. The shooter then examines the size of the hole and the diameter of gunpowder residue, because when guns are fired, fragments of unburned powder fly out of the barrel. They don't travel far, only a few feet, but if they're close enough to hit something, they leave a distinct circular pattern. Thus, if a person is shot at close range, the GSR will produce what's called stippling, a gunpowder burn. The pattern's residue diameter depends on the distance the victim was from the gun. Replicating the powder burn from the person on the target yields the distance measurement: how far away the shooter was standing when the gun discharged. (If blood has obscured the pattern on a body, IR lighting in a darkroom can bring it out for better comparison.)

GSR Detection

The GSR can also be swabbed from the skin or clothing of the suspected shooter (as long as it didn't involve a gun where the primer chemicals eliminate metals). For example, if a man kills himself with a handheld gun, he will undoubtedly have GSR on his hand. It can be subjected to analysis for its composite content under the scanning electron microscope. (Some labs use a different method.) One of the problems is that just standing near a gun when it is fired can result in GSR. Yet the experts can still examine relative amounts and make educated guesses.

Restoration

Another aspect of firearm examination is the ability to trace a serial number to a registered owner—even if the number appears to be gone. Although some criminals file it off to prevent a trace, it may still be recoverable.

This works because the stamping process actually goes deeper than the surface numbers indicate, and when criminals can no longer see the number, they believe they've obliterated it. The examiner grinds the metal down past the deepest scrapes to get a strip of polished metal. He then applies a solution of copper salts and hydrochloric acid, and that makes the strained area just beneath the stamped number dissolve at a faster rate than the metal around it. That temporarily brings up the number (or a partial), making it available for a photograph before it disappears.

While knowledge about bullet trajectories in a human body comes from pathology, not Firearms Identification, these scientists do know it's not impossible for a bullet to behave wildly, and that awareness influences trajectory studies. In one Oklahoma case where a bank robber decided to eliminate a witness, for example, he put a .357 Magnum to the back of her head and fired. The bullet entered the skull, made a sharp turn, went around the head, and exited out the forehead. The girl was knocked unconscious but not badly hurt. She was able to testify against him. In another case, a bullet entered a vein at the wrist and traveled all the way up the arm to the heart. Anatomically speaking, as Warrick and Catherine find out, no bullet wound case is cut-and-dried.

Neither are cases that involve a crafty predator.

THE CLEVER KILLER

Because some serial killers have been resourceful, they've raised the stakes for law enforcement and spawned cultural myths of larger-than-life predators like Hannibal Lecter who can elude even the best efforts to catch them. They create puzzles for their pursuers because it's the game and their ability to one-up the best detective minds that excite them. Few killers have actually been that clever, but because they were never caught, Jack the Ripper and San Francisco's Zodiac Killer come quickly to mind. Both killed one victim after another, both taunted police, and both eluded arrest. The Zodiac, in particular, used complicated codes and clues.

Grissom must match wits against an equally perplexing serial killer, Paul Millander, in "Anonymous" and the pilot episode. He's a highly organized killer, murdering for his own unique needs, and for him, the fun of this game is to let Grissom know who he's dealing with while remaining unstoppable.

The type of puzzle that a killer like Millander devises often cannot be solved from evidence because it's conceived to deflect and confuse. The killer creates the maze, and he'll extend it as long as his skill and interest hold out. Only the detective who figures out his next move can get close.

An even more organized killer than Millander is "the Strip Strangler," who murders three attractive brunette women in quick succession. The deaths are linked via the killer's signature. While certain things are different, such as the type of location and the MO, the personation factors remain the same.

Although certain behaviors of a signature crime may evolve, the theme does not, because it's inspired by the killer's core pathology.

If object rape or posing addresses a primal need, these acts will always be evident.

This, however, is the forensic puzzle. Since they don't know the killer's history, as is the case in most investigations, they can't be absolutely sure what his core pathology is. That means they can't be certain which parts of the scenario might change. A truly organized and witty killer can keep them guessing, even as he feeds his need.

Grissom says that the way to predict what a signature killer will do next is to study his past. That means a process called signature analysis, a term coined by Dr. Robert D. Keppel. He led the Ted Bundy and Green River Killer investigations in Washington state, interviewed Bundy about serial killers, and wrote the definitive *Signature Killers*. To Keppel's mind, the issue is control. These men are life's losers, who feel powerless. The need to feel better about themselves generates a compulsion to find and control victims in a specific way. They act out the same compulsion repeatedly.

A killer who is also a stalker, for example, generally passes through predictable phases:

1. Spinning a fantasy that builds pressure and inspires action

2. Anticipation: seeking a victim who will fit into the fantasy

3. Blitz attack, trapping or capturing

4. Torture and killing

5. Removing a trophy

6. Cooling off that generates the need to repeat the fantasy

According to Keppel, the killer will either use the scenario to build sexual tension and ejaculate at the scene, or will delay it and substitute certain rituals, such as posing the victim, to indicate sexual subservience. "Signature killers are sexual offenders at the far end of the violence continuum," he says, "who leave their psychological imprints at crime scenes to gratify their sexual needs." Since what they do sets their murders or rapes apart, they provide patterns that indicate how best to hunt them down. Even when a clever killer tries to throw off the investigation, certain repetitions give him away. As Keppel explains, "It lies within the very nature of the killer that his signature will be recreated in each and every murder he commits."

These murders involve progression and escalation. Either they become more intense, with bolder expression of the ritual, or they are done increasingly more often. The way the killer selects, approaches, kills, and poses a victim reveals his "psychological calling card." Those who can read signatures have a higher success rate in stopping these criminals.

Let's look at an example of an actual signature killer.

Early in 1990, a man stalked the San Diego, California, area in search of victims. Three women who lived in the neighborhood of the Buena Vista Garden apartment complex were murdered, including one who was simply visiting her brother. A fourth victim turned up in her own Clairemont home, which sent the community into a panic and made the press dub the intruder "the Clairemont Killer." By September of that same year, he killed a mother and daughter in their home. The man left a distinct signature that indicated his victims were deliberately chosen rather than being random hits of opportunity, and that he enjoyed a certain form of sexual gratification known as "piquerism." That is, he liked to stab, gouge, or cut in a way that tore the skin, shed blood, and penetrated the victim.

Signature analysis closed in on the psychological fingerprints, which seemed to be provoked by anger. The issue of control dominated the killings and inspired overkill—doing much more than necessary to bring about death. This also implied a ritual that reinforced the thrill.

The Clairemont Killer committed his crimes exclusively indoors, removed most of his victims' clothing, stabbed them multiple times, and left them on their backs, posed provocatively. He also moved in and out of a victim's home with relative ease, left articles from the home strewn about, and he often discarded the knife right there. All of the victims were white females. Evidence of his boldness was the way he moved from apartments to the more risky entry of homes, a hint that he was familiar with burglary. He became stimulated through violence, and the knife was thought to be a substitute for penile penetration. Only one victim had been raped. When stabbing the victims, he always focused on the breast and heart area, and stabbed with deep penetration. It was aggressive but not frenzied.

A failed break-in led to the arrest of a black man, Cleophus Prince Jr., twenty-five, who had lived in the areas of all the murders. He had also joined the same health club as some of his victims, leading to speculation that he'd seen them there and then had followed them to their homes. He often took a piece of jewelry from them as a trophy. Later he was convicted of special circumstances murder under California law and was given the death penalty.

In such cases, Keppel emphasizes the need for signature analysis over the more general activity of profiling. For this, he established the Homicide Investigation Tracking System (HITS), located at the Washington State Attorney General's Office, which contains a database of thousands of homicides and sexual assaults for that state, as well as information about violent crime. Over two hundred query capabilities help to narrow down crime scenes to link crimes by signature. The program has had much success.

Keppel's approach is psychological, yet another way to do signature analysis, which is getting more attention, is by studying blood spatter patterns (where available) from one crime to another. In the case of the Clairemont Killer's six murders, a description of the blood spatter from each crime scene was entered into a computer, and the crimes were shown to be linked through common patterns, time periods, victim positions during and after the attacks, and manner of stabbing. This method involves less psychological "reading" but does depend on fairly rigid ritual behavior.

Even when the MO changes, the signature links the crimes and reveals the killer's essential vulnerability. Such killers are compelled to leave their imprint: some always choose a victim with the same hairstyle; some always abuse the corpse after death; some always ejaculate next to the body. Whatever the compulsion, it will be—must be—repeated. In essence, signature reveals intent, and the intent is always the same, because it never gets fully satisfied. This is how the Strip Strangler case was ultimately solved.

There's no database for dissecting a case like the next one, however.

UNUSUAL BEASTS

A jogger dies from an animal attack in "Justice Is Served," yet no amount of sleuthing would have solved the "why" of this crime, since the motivation is off the radar of typical crime scene analysis . . . except for one case that was remarkably similar. The animal's owner, health consultant Dr. Hillridge, is placed under suspicion because the victim's organs were removed with a scalpel. Dry ice found at the crime scene points to a gruesome, but not altogether unheard of, phenomenon.

Organ harvesting was big business in the 1980s for David Sconce's Lamb Funeral Home in Pasadena, California. While people came in to arrange funerals, tissue technicians in the back were busily removing hearts, lungs, eyes, gold fillings, and uteruses from other corpses, which were then sold to medical schools. Whenever the home received a death call, the pickup crew rushed to get the body while the eyes were still valuable. Sconce figured that no one would be the wiser. He then started stuffing as many as thirty bodies into an oven at a time, which produced an overwhelming stench and surge of black smoke that made neighbors complain. When inspectors responded, they found a sludge pile of human fat and cans full of remains behind

Sconce's building. Sconce was arrested and tried. He pled guilty to twenty-one charges related to the desecration of human remains and got a five-year prison term. The funeral home was never charged and remains in business.

However, it is only when blood matching the jogger's DNA is found in the suspect's *blender* that a classic case of vampire psychosis comes to mind.

In December 1977, in Sacramento, California, Richard Trenton Chase shot and killed a man for the thrill of it. A month later, he walked into a woman's home, killed her, cut out her entrails, stuffed her mouth with feces, and used a yogurt container to drink her blood. He took some parts to chew on later. Next, he killed a family, including a two-year-old that he took with him for further experiments, and was quickly identified through a police search. In his apartment, police discovered evidence that he seemed to be planning to kill over forty more times that year. In fact, he had quite a strange history.

During a stint at a psychiatric facility, he'd purchased rabbits and drunk their blood. At times, he tried to inject rabbit blood into his own veins. He also bit the heads off birds and was known to the hospital staff as Dracula. Once he was free, he stole dogs and cats to torture them and drink their blood, because he believed that his blood was turning to powder and he had to replenish it. A search of his apartment turned up several plates holding bones and body organs, and a bloodstained blender that smelled of biological rot. As he discussed his crimes with investigators, he said he drank blood for therapeutic reasons. He had no awareness that his victims were even human.

Sentenced to death, he overdosed on drugs and died in his cell in 1980.

In custody, Hillridge explains that she has a rare blood disorder, porphyria, and needs to enrich herself with a fresh supply of heme, a substance found in blood.

Porphyria, also known as King George III's disease, is an abnormality of the hemoglobin. In the king's case, it began with abdominal pain, fever, and constipation. Then he grew weak and his urine turned dark red. He couldn't sleep, and had headaches, convulsions, and delirium that might send him running naked through the palace corridors at any moment. Just when he seemed hopelessly mad, he recovered. Thirteen years later, he suffered again, and eventually the disease forced him into a stupor. Some historians blame the American Revolution on his condition.

Porphyria tends to be hereditary. The absence of an enzyme sends part of the blood pigment hemoglobin to the urine rather than to the cells. Porphyrins accumulate to toxic levels and attack the nervous system. While seven separate enzyme deficiency disorders fall under the name porphyria, the acute types are the most severe. As Hillridge points out, some include skin symptoms, such as thickening, darkening, and blistering in direct sunlight. The most severe form manifests in scarring and an increased growth of hair, along with infections that damage facial features and fingers. Some treatments involve removing blood to diminish its iron content, while others inject heme. Porphyria has been related to legends of both vampires and werewolves, although scholars of mythology refute the connection.

From special knowledge to special crews, the C.S.I.s also solve crimes that require a particular type of expertise. That means working with other teams.

ELEVEN

Evidence Response

Some crimes require a special way of handling evidence. That can mean involving a trained team of other professionals—even dogs. Sometimes they get to the crime scene first, sometimes they're called in later, and C.S.I.s need to know how to coordinate efforts to best tap their range of expertise. When things heat up with fire or bombs, or when they must track a suspect through the woods or on paper, there's a wealth of personnel available to help.

FIRE RESPONSE

In "Fahrenheit 932," Frank Damon is arrested for the murder by fire of his wife and son. He insists he's innocent, saying that he returned to find the house in flames and could not save his family for fear of "flashover." This phenomenon occurs in the development of a contained fire when surfaces exposed to thermal radiation reach ignition simultaneously and fire spreads rapidly throughout the space. It's an extreme form of fire behavior, when heat is given off faster than a piece of ignited material can burn. Smoke rises to the ceiling, and as it gets hotter, it reaches flash point. Fire then races across the ceiling and radiates heat downward that rapidly ignites all combustibles. Anyone in such a room will die from the extreme heat and toxic gases. Understandably, dangers such as these make safety a firefighter's first priority.

"Fahrenheit 932" shows the difficulties involved in the investigation of a crime scene fire. First, the fire can destroy a lot of evidence, and second, the firemen and other officials can, too. Their job is to put the fire out, not preserve the crime scene, although there is currently more emphasis on training them to avoid evidence "spoilation."

Arson is the willful or malicious burning of property for some improper or illegal purpose. Property losses from arson are in the billions of dollars every year. Fire investigations can be more complicated than a typical crime scene because they involve three separate groups of authorities:

- Fire officers

- Police and crime scene technicians

- Insurance companies

All of them are looking for the cause of the fire, specifically for signs of arson, which is generally motivated by insurance fraud, thrill seeking, revenge, or to conceal something like a robbery or murder. Some fires are accidental, too, but all leave clues about the heat source that kindled them. Generally, hot fires are started with accelerants, which may also be used to spread the fire, and the most common are ignitable liquids like gasoline and kerosene.

Before the evidence search, the fire team first ensures that the building is secure. Fire burns upward and outward, so the seat is likely to be at the lowest point in the place where there's most damage, and that's where the search begins. Since fires need a source of fuel, investigators look to determine this, and since different types of fire burn at different temperatures, they burn with different colors of flame and smoke. Witness statements can help to ascertain these things.

Cooking oil causes a yellow flame and brown smoke. Gasoline yields a yellow or white flame with black smoke, and phosphorus has both a white flame and white smoke, while wood and fabric fires burn with reddish-yellow flames and gray or brown smoke. However, some substances share the same colors, so it can be difficult to pinpoint one with certainty.

Certain patterns are also indicative of the seat of a fire, and they're influenced by the availability of oxygen and combustible materials. Some patterns are fairly predictable, and because of that, the scene can be reconstructed. An inverted V pattern points to a seat at the apex of the V, and the depth of charring indicates the point of most intensity. Chipping and splintering (spalling) are caused by hot spots on a wall or floor. Wood beams or floors tend to carbonize into a pattern that looks like alligator skin, with the "scales" that are closest to where the fire started being smaller than other scales.

At this point, officials may use accelerant swabs or look for a pile of flammable material, a fuse, or any type of timing device rigged to set the fire at a specific time of day. (Burned carpets give off pyrolysis by-products that can be confused with accelerants, so unburned samples are brought to the lab, if possible, for comparison.) Grissom indicates that with arson, "trailings" show an attempt to spread the accelerant around to make the fire burn faster.

One test that reveals the presence of accelerants is the J-W Aromatic Hydrocarbon Indicator. This can be carried into the scene of the fire, where it registers positive in the presence of any type of accelerant not ignited by the fire. Hydrocarbons are organic compounds containing only carbon and hydrogen, and the three simplest molecules are methane, ethane, and propane.

It's also possible to use an arson detection dog, trained to point wherever it "hits" on an accelerant. Its nose is often more sensitive than any detection device. Wherever the dog points, samples can be gathered for lab analysis.

Fire evidence is collected into cans that look like paint cans, with the same kind of sealed top. After a set period of time, the charred material is removed from the cans and put into a glass flask with a few drops of carbon disulfide, and all of this goes through the GC for analysis. The added solvent has its own characteristic peak on the GC chart, which is known, but anything else indicates a substance to consider as an accelerant. Comparison samples, if available, go through first to separate out carpet shampoo, fire retardant, or glue backing.

Other suggestive evidence includes telltale odors, a gas can or petroleum packaging, material designed to spread a fire, tools left behind, a pile of documents near the seat, and footprints.

It's likely that any C.S.I. on the "Fahrenheit 932" case would first approach the firefighters to ask if they had observed anything indicative of arson. They would ask about:

- The type of fire

- The type of security on the premises

- Whether there were signs of a break-in

- If there were any witnesses

- If anyone was seen leaving the premises

- If there was more than one seat, and the location(s)

- The amount of combustible material in the premises

- The fire's source (wood or paper, hydrocarbons, wiring, metals, radioactive materials)

- Whether the fire was caused by smoldering or by flame

The presence of more than one point of origin is a clear indication of arson, as is evidence of breaking into the building, particularly through the roof. (Arsonists believe that this evidence will be quickly eliminated because fires often burn roofs as they move upward.) Accidental fires generally have an obvious cause, such as flammable materials stored near a heat source.

Accelerants fall into two categories: petroleum distillates and nonpetroleum accelerants, such as turpentine, lubricants, and alcohol. The petroleum-based accelerants are mixtures of hydrocarbons that can be found in oils like lighter fluid, kerosene, and gasoline. Sometimes a certain grade of gas can be traced to a specific point of purchase. Infrared spectroscopy can be run on pure liquid samples and compared with known substances. Then their boiling and flash points can be determined.

Another method for detecting minute traces involves passing vapors through a charcoal tube that absorbs the components. A solvent is used to extract them for GC injection.

If bodies are found burned by the fire, it's important to determine whether they died before the fire was started or from smoke inhalation or loss of oxygen. Usually the intense heat causes the muscles to contract, and they're found in a position with arms raised, fists clenched, and knees bent.

At the morgue, the pathologist samples the blood and checks the lungs to determine if the victim was still breathing when the fire started. The presence of soot and carbon monoxide tells that tale. The autopsy may also reveal any injuries to the body, such as blunt force, stabbing, or a bullet. Bodies are often not burned so badly as to conceal the cause of a violent death. The gathering of white blood cells indicates the presence of a wound in a living person, which blisters in heat. Postmortem burns tend to be hard and yellow. Toxicology on the burned tissues can still detect the use of poisons.

If a suspect is apprehended, then not only should their premises and vehicle be searched for accelerants, tools, or devices, but their clothing and shoes should be confiscated for analysis in the lab.

Fire investigations have several things in common with the post-explosion evaluation of a bomb, including a mess at the crime scene.

TOTAL DESTRUCTION

Bombs are weapons of chance. Not all people who get injured are targets, which makes anyone vulnerable. Bombs are created for one purpose: to blow something up. They're cheap to build and easy to hide, but potentially more lethal than any other weapon.

An explosion is the effect produced by a violent expansion of gases from a chemical change, such as igniting a flammable gas or detonating an explosive substance. Within a microsecond, a power source causes shock, heat, or friction (the initiators) to start the reaction. The substance breaks its chemical bonds to release the gases. The wave of pressure that results destroys everything in its immediate path until it equalizes with the surrounding pressure. Then there's a negative phase in which the gases draw back and may cause further damage.

The explosive limit is the lower and upper concentration of air and gas mixture in which combustion will be supported. The most hazardous fuels are those with the broadest explosive limits, and the deadly impact has more to do with placement than size. In 1988, the bomb that exploded Pan Am Flight 103 over Lockerbie, Scotland, and killed 271 people fit inside a portable radio, yet only six people died in the 1993 World Trade Center bombing, which used a thousand-pound explosive.

Types of common explosives are gunpowder (potassium nitrate, charcoal, and sulfur), fertilizers, and weedkillers (nitrates and chlorates), nitroglycerine (carbon and nitrate), TNT, tetryl, PETN (Semtex), cyclonite, and picric acid. Explosions can be triggered with a shock, a match, or electrical discharge . . . anything that raises the temperature of the components. All are designed to be unstable compounds. Detonation waves can reach temperatures over nine thousand degrees Fahrenheit and pressures as great as 1,200 tons per square inch.

To control the explosive, it's put into a casing of some type, like a metal pipe. To complete the circuit from power source to explosive involves timers, relays, switches, and shunts.

An explosives investigation is similar to that for a fire, although the investigators may be searching for more suspects. Explosives response units look for the bomb maker, as well as the person who set off the charge, and possibly for accomplices who purchased the parts. To find the seat, they look for the way things like nails and window frames bent away from the shock waves. Holes and scars in surfaces can also point the way to the center, as can the clothing on bodies.

Then, to mark off the crime scene, they estimate the distance from the seat to the farthest piece of debris and add 50 percent more to get a safe radius. Photographs are taken everywhere, although bombs obliterate evidence as much as fire does, and by Grissom's standards, the bomb squad can be just as careless at the crime scene, as Catherine notes in "Boom."

A suitcase bomb explodes in the lobby of an office building, killing a security guard. Since bomb parts survive an explosion, they can be found in the scattered debris. That means a painstaking search, but once the parts are recovered, investigators can try to determine their source.

Traced on the bomb are the enigmatic initials F.P. As insignificant as they may seem, initials can provide an important lead, as they did in several high-profile cases. We've already looked at the George Metesky case in New York in the 1950s. He also used the initials F.P., and his case inspired a more contemporary terrorist, the Unabomber.

It took nearly two decades before Theodore John Kaczynski was identified as the man responsible for the "Unabom" explosions sent
through the mail to selected targets. His attacks followed an erratic
pattern, with unpredictable gaps in time, so it was difficult for investigators to pin him down until after he'd already killed three people
and injured twenty-nine.

His bombs were made by hand. The first one in 1978 injured a
security guard. Within a year, there were three more bombs, and the
first actual fatality occurred in 1985 when a computer-store owner
opened a package. That same year, the "Junkyard Bomber" sent a
communication to the *San Francisco Examiner* and identified himself
as "F.C.," a terrorist who belonged to a group called the Freedom
Club, which was taking a stand against technology and science. The
initials F.C. were then used on the bombs.

After the sixteenth bomb killed Gilbert Murray, a thirty-five-
thousand-word manifesto arrived at the offices of several major newspapers, sent by "the Unabom." Only if his manuscript was printed in
full, he insisted, would the bombings cease. The papers printed it and
there were no more bombs, but that may be because the FBI closed
in on him. On April 3, 1996, Ted Kaczynski was arrested in his isolated cabin in Montana. Evidence found there linked him to the bombings.

A bomb investigation involves five distinct activities:

■ Identify the components and try to find out who bought or
made them. (A piece of clock can be matched to a purchaser.)

■ Determine the size of the bomb and how it got there. (For
example, Grissom and Sara detonate bombs in a safe area and
measure the distances the various parts flew to test the pipe size
of the bomb used.)

- Figure out the bomber's signature and see if there are case links. (As done in the Unabomber case.)

- Find evidence associated with the bomb, such as a transport vehicle. (As done with the Ryder truck in the Oklahoma City bombing case.)

- Identify the motive for the bombing to develop a suspect type. (Do a profile based on the building type and location, and time of day the bomb was detonated; see if it links to other sites.)

To identify an unexploded package as a bomb, it must have a power source, an initiator, and an explosive. After an explosion, investigators must first determine that a crime has occurred, rather than an accident. In any event, the area must be secured as a potential crime scene. Then, since 95 percent of the shattered bomb will be preserved rather than disintegrated, debris is collected in the hope of gathering the pieces—especially a piece with a fingerprint, tool mark, or some other identifying factor.

To determine a bomb's components and initial size, investigators analyze the color of the flash, placement of soot, type of damage, residual smell in the air, and extent, speed, and direction of flying debris. They also examine damage done to human bodies, because it's been the case that a bomber got caught in his own mechanism and died, or that bombers have been suicidal. (From the way the security guard's ears were blown off, Catherine realizes he was looking right at the bomb.) Witnesses might be helpful, as they were in the quick apprehension of a suspect after the 1995 Oklahoma City bombing. Someone might have seen the person bring in the package or overheard a suspicious conversation. Video cameras in buildings may also have recorded a suspect.

Before a search, the scene is divided into numbered grids so that each piece of evidence can be tagged according to the grid in which it was found. In most cases, the debris gets sifted through screens by hand, although sometimes an evidence vacuum with a filter is used. Anything can be significant in solving the case, so this is patient work, and sometimes solving it is just a matter of luck. Yet the bomb fragments have a distinct look that makes identifying them easier. They're often coated with soot or residue and have jagged edges. Investigators with experience can pick through the damage fairly quickly.

Explosives technicians know what substances are generally used in bomb construction, and often some undetonated substance will be found close to the seat, possibly embedded in soft or porous material. Swabs are taken from various areas to pick up minute residue, and investigators may use a portable vapor detector. After the physical examination of the scene is complete, the chemical analysis begins.

Back in the lab, the substance is analyzed by means of gas, thin-layer, or liquid chromatography. Each of these uses a different process to achieve the same end: separating the elements of a compound to compare them with the readings of a known substance.

There are many ways to make a bomb, but watches and clocks are commonly converted into timers. Wires are attached to the moving hand and to a pin stuck at the time at which the bomber wants his device to activate. One wire connects to the power source and the other to a detonator. The moving hand ticks along until it makes contact with the pin and detonates the bomb. Any small miscalculation can prevent the circuit from closing, and then the bomb won't go off.

Most bombs bear their maker's signature, not necessarily as obvious as initials, but obvious to the expert analysts in terms of what the perpetrator chose to do in the bomb's construction. To link crime scenes, points of similarity are used to determine whether the same person is behind them. Even the courts accept such signatures as evidence.

To disarm a bomb requires separating the power source from the detonator. Many bombs are movement sensitive, so they must be disarmed in place. Some can be frozen with liquid nitrogen or the explosion can be aimed to cause the least amount of damage.

When suspects are found, traces of the bomb components may be on their hands, clothing, possessions, or in a room in which they stayed or car they drove. Even if they wore gloves, there may still be penetration to the skin.

Yet even as the bomb investigation goes on, another member of the team arrives: the forensic engineer.

Forensic engineering is the discipline of checking buildings for structural safety and understanding the behavior of structures under catastrophic loadings. Forensic engineers are responsible for determining how a building might have brought harm or death to a victim. After extensive examination, they can see specifically how a building failed and whether intentional damage, such as from a bomb, might have caused the collapse. (In "$35K OBO," Catherine shows some of what can be involved when she investigates the collapse of a building.)

Forensic engineers analyze buildings after fires, explosions, collapse, damage from natural disasters, and damage due to neglect. They engage in reconstruction based on what they know of a building's behavior under diverse conditions. With terrorist damage, as in the World Trade Center and the federal building in Oklahoma City, they engage in blast physics—they determine what must have happened based on the extent and pattern of the damage.

A man from Decker, Michigan, quietly drove a yellow Ryder rental truck through the streets of Oklahoma City on the morning of August 19, 1995—two years to the day after the tragedy at the Branch Davidian compound in Waco, Texas. He parked outside of the seven-story Alfred P. Murrah government building and walked away. By the time the estimated four-thousand-pound bomb exploded at 9:02 A.M., he was blocks away, with earplugs to protect him from the noise of a huge building collapsing. Then he got into a beat-up car without a license plate and drove away. He considered himself a hero, without

a thought for the 168 men, women, and children who were dead or dying, and the more than 500 who would turn up injured.

Trooper Charles Hagan was called into the city, but on his way, he passed the car and decided to have a look. Timothy James McVeigh, twenty-seven, got out. He had a concealed weapon, a 9mm Glock, so Hagan took him in and charged him with four criminal counts.

At the same time, the Ryder truck was found and traced to the rental agency, where employees gave a description to the FBI artists. The resulting composite drawing sparked recognition in the owner of a motel, who named Timothy McVeigh as an occupant on his property and said he'd been there with a Ryder rental truck. The FBI closed in, and there was no escape for this American terrorist, who had committed the costliest crime to date on American soil.

Once the dust was clear, forensic engineers went to work to help determine where areas were still unsafe and to study the extent of the bombing. Working with the FBI Explosives Unit, they had to evaluate from the way the building had collapsed what type of bomb had been used and whether there was more than one. In that case, McVeigh might have had accomplices.

The first step is to talk with the building engineer of record, and then conduct a visual inspection. The forensic engineer looks for ground zero, or the point of origin of the collapse. That's where the best evidence will be found of how the damage came about. Engineers use instruments like the dialectrometer to locate imperfections inside walls. It works with an electronic impulse and records the absorption of energy to indicate significant changes in some part of the structure not readily visible. Engineers also have devices for simulating various conditions in the lab that need closer study.

By developing sophisticated calculations in any crimes involving a building, they can estimate the probable weight of the explosives. They can also project estimates of damage that might be done from different distinct forces, which means they can supply a prosecution team with accurate information in cases where the attempt to damage a building was thwarted.

In short, there's a lot that can be learned from the scene about bombs and fires, despite the extent of the damage.

Not all special teams get involved in dangerous investigations, yet some have expertise that can have equally vital results. Moving from fire to paper, let's leave the arson and exlosives unit and visit QD.

PAPER TRAILS

When Grissom tells Sara to take a ransom note to QD, he means the section of the crime lab known as Questioned Documents. This covers any kind of crime involving writing, writing implements, and a writing surface . . . including one where the writing is no longer visible. A questioned document is a graphic communication involved in an investigation about which questions are being asked, such as: Who wrote this? Is it authentic? Where did it come from?

A short list of crimes for QD's involvement includes:

- Forgery

- Counterfeiting

- Money laundering

- Ransom demands

- Espionage

- Extortion

In the context of these (and other) crimes, the types of things these experts examine are:

- The ink used to write something

- The type of paper or surface used

- The handwriting style

- The content, especially codes

While there are sophisticated pieces of equipment for special tests, the basic tools for comparing a questioned document with a known exemplar are a magnifying lens, microscope, camera with filters, and good lighting. QD also examines printers, copiers, and typewriters for anything that will make a document produced on that particular machine stand apart: odd marks or impressions, an imperfection, or the stamp of a machine part.

One of the C.S.I. team's more interesting cases involves getting QD to bring out the message written on the missing sheet of a pad where only some illegible impressions were left. This happened in "$35K OBO."

While indented impressions can often be brought out with oblique lighting (changing the light angle can make the invisible visible), the technique used in this case is an electrostatic detection apparatus (ESDA). This device was invented as a means of detecting fingerprints on paper, but it didn't work well because indented writing interfered with the readings. Here's how it works: the sheet of indented paper is placed over a glass plate and under a sheet of Mylar, then placed on a machine, the bottom of which is a brass plate. The machine lid is charged with high voltage, and a fine electrostatic substance, like toner, is sprinkled onto the paper. The tiny pieces move toward the brass plate, filling in the paper's indentations.

What QD is probably best known for is matching handwriting samples, and that happens in this episode as well. They match the handwriting of one of the victims and realize that he had given the murdered girl money to hire a hit man to take out his wife.

Let's see how handwriting analysis solves crimes.

• • •

The first time that the method of handwriting analysis played a major forensic role in American history was in the trial of Richard Bruno Hauptmann for the kidnapping and murder of the son of world-famous aviator Charles Lindbergh. Several experts made extensive examinations, and Hauptmann was forced to repeatedly write the set of ransom notes to the point of exhaustion. Ultimately, the experts announced that he was the only person who could have written them. How could they narrow it down to just one person?

Most people learn to write by imitating a certain style, usually the Palmer or Zaner-Blosser method, but as they develop their own style, idiosyncrasies appear in the way letters are formed and connected. This is influenced by education, artistic ability, physiological development, and sometimes just by a specific preference (such as placing a heart over an *i*). That's what makes handwriting distinct and personal. In fact, experts insist that no two people write alike. Over time, the style crystallizes, showing only slight variations over the years.

Handwriting experts study writing samples to try to determine if two (or more) different documents were written by the same person and thereby to identify the known author of one sample with the unknown author of a similar one. The same odd characteristics are expected to show up across samples by the same person—even when he tries to disguise his writing.

Analysts look both at class characteristics, which derive from the general writing system learned, and at individual characteristics. It's the latter that play the most important part in forensic investigation. The best exemplars (known specimen) will contain some of the same words or phrases as the questioned document.

The primary factors for analysis are divided into four categories:

1. Form: the shape, proportion, slant, angles, lines, connections, and curves

2. Line quality: results from the type of writing instrument used, pressure exerted, flow and continuity

3. Arrangement: spacing, alignment, and formatting

4. Content: spelling, phrasing, punctuation, and grammar

While finding similarities between two documents is not a sure indicator, significant dissimilarities say they're likely to have been written by two different authors, unless there's a reason for the differences.

The goal is to collect samples that have been written within two or three years of the questioned document. Known exemplars are the primary source, but if they are not sufficient in number for a thorough examination, then the suspected author may be asked to provide more—and this has its own protocol. Handwriting samples lie outside the protection of the Fifth Amendment and therefore can be acquired without constitutional violation of privacy.

The procedure is to sit the subject at a table where there will be no distraction. The text to be written is dictated, keeping in mind the following:

- The subject shouldn't see the questioned document.

- The subject shouldn't be told how to spell certain words.

- The subject should use materials similar to those of the document.

- The dictated text should match some part of the document.

- The subject should sign the text.

- An objective witness should observe the procedure.

Besides identifying a suspect author, QD experts also attempt to recognize a forgery, the most common of which is a signature. These can be freehand or traced, as Nick points out to Sara on a forged check in "Table Stakes." Yet a forged document can also be book length . . . even multiple books.

Tracing over someone's words can generally be detected because it's difficult to follow the outline precisely. Hesitations or "forger's tremor" are noted, and erasures are easily detected. There may also be unnatural pen lifts or an unnatural evenness to the flow of writing. Even when the tracing is exact, that in itself is a giveaway, since no one who copies their own signature or document can exactly duplicate it. Freehand forgery is much harder to detect because it has a smooth flow, but the forger's own traits are bound to affect the writing. An experienced expert can point them out.

It's not only handwriting that gives away a forgery, but attempts to alter a document. The paper's surface generally shows the erasure, sandpapering, or razoring that has been applied. Any alteration made with a different color or type of ink will be detected by infrared lighting techniques.

Yet even with all the safeguards, sometimes the experts are fooled.

In the 1980s, a German publishing company was persuaded that a collection of sixty handwritten notebooks comprised the diaries of Adolf Hitler, and they paid a sum of $2.3 million. The most shocking revelation within these documents was that Hitler had wanted to resettle the Jews elsewhere, not kill them. This meant that the history books were wrong.

The story was that these papers had been smuggled out of Berlin toward the end of WWII on board an airplane that had crashed. Farmers found them and eventually they came into the hands of a Nazi document collector, Konrad Kujau. He took them to a journalist, Gerd Heidemann, who was on the staff of the newspaper *Stern*, which went ahead and serialized the diaries. However, other large papers that bought publication rights wanted the diaries authenticated. A team of international experts ended up divided, partly because they were duped into using fraudulent documents for comparison—forged by the same person who did the diaries.

It was forensics tests on the paper and ink that revealed the truth. The West German police used UV light and discovered, among other things, that the paper contained an additive that had been used only since 1954. Nor was the type of ink used available before the war. Then another test proved that the documents were written within the past year. Kujau was arrested and served three years in prison. When he died at the age of sixty-two from cancer, the one document he hadn't finished writing was his memoir, *I Was Hitler*.

Besides handwriting, an analysis of the materials used can offer important clues about origination and authenticity:

1. Paper is classified by the materials in its composition. They differ according to additives, watermarks, and surface treatments. Specialists can determine the date when a particular type of paper was introduced.

2. Modern ink can be one of our basic types: iron salts in a suspension of gallic acid, with dyes; carbon particles suspended in gum arabic; synthetic dyes with a range of polymers and acids; and synthetic dyes or pigments in a range of solvents and additives. The ink under question is tested with microspectrophotometry to determine the absorption spectrum, or thin-layer chromatography to reveal the exact composition. It's then compared with the large database of ink profiles at the U.S. Bureau of Alcohol, Tobacco and Firearms.

Also part of QD is the job of the forensic linguist. This expert comes in when a document or note is found and the author is completely unknown. This happens with ransom notes, extortion, and other types of threatening communications. Linguists examine not only the way writing is structured, but also the type of phrases and words used. They will then search text databases that contain similar language habits. The language used by an unknown author can reveal the writer's approximate age, nationality, gender, ethnicity, level of education, professional training, and ideology. Linguistic clues typically include such evidence as vocabulary—slang, professional jargon, regionalisms—spelling, grammar, syntax, and even such matters as punctuation. Other kinds of textual evidence may include borrowed or influential source material, such as books or periodicals. That's how a forensic linguist provided the probable cause for a warrant to search Unabomber Ted Kaczynski's cabin.

While questioned document examination comes under fire in the courtroom for subjective interpretation, rigorous training, certification, and other corrective measures have given the discipline more credibility. The document examiners are working toward making their methods reproducible to increase their credibility even more.

From paper trails to earthen trails, there's also a special team that finds evidence undetectable by humans: bring out the dogs.

SPECIAL TEAMS

When a rape victim is left for dead in "Too Tough to Die," a denim belt loop is found at the scene. Grissom uses dogs trained to follow a scent in order to locate where the perpetrator might have gone. He explains to Nick that dogs have a highly refined sense of smell, and a device has been invented to take advantage of this. It works with scent pads and can be used to train dogs to search for cadavers, explosives, narcotics, accelerants, and specific articles. When dogs get a "hit," they point, sit, scratch at the scene where the odor is most intense, or yelp.

One man can be credited with creating this unique device.

Longtime dog handler William Tolhurst is one of the foremost world authorities on trailing bloodhounds. He runs the Special Forces Unit for the Niagara County Sheriff's Department in New York. Hunting and trapping when he was only ten years old, he learned about scent from his dogs. Now his training devices are used in police departments around the country.

It was in 1977, after the manhunt provoked by the killing of a police officer, that Tolhurst recognized the need to preserve and control scent. Hundreds of officers responded with dogs, but they proved ineffective because the only piece of scented material they had was contaminated by the first dog handler at the scene. Tolhurst soon developed what he called a "scent sleeve," to keep a scented article away from the dogs so that multiple dogs and handlers could use it. It worked by pumping the scent into a receptacle held over the article, and when it proved effective, this told Tolhurst that scent could be portable.

By 1986, he'd further developed the Big T Trainer, where a scented item was placed in a container through which pressured air blew to deliver the scent wherever he needed it. That gave him another idea. He developed a vacuum process to collect a scent into a sterile gauze pad, which could be stored indefinitely and transported to different locations. Finally he made the device itself portable, calling it the STU100 (Scent Transfer Unit).

In New York, burglars wearing hoods broke through the wall of a building to grab a safe. Surveillance cameras caught them putting it into their van. The van was recovered with the safe but without the burglary team. Tolhurst made scent pads from the van seats and stored them. Eventually a suspect was developed from a witness descrip-

tion; the witness said that he'd been in the van's passenger seat. Tolhurst gave the pad made from that seat to a bloodhound. The dog confirmed that the suspect had indeed been in that seat and he then admitted to his part in the crime.

This invention can pick up and preserve scent even from fire and arson scenes. Scents can also be freeze-dried for long periods of time, and can be removed from water, metal fragments, and fingerprints. Tolhurst has even made scent pads off the residual scent left in the air in a building where someone broke in. The key is to give the scent to the dog and let the dog pick out the suspect.

Tolhurst calls scent "the forgotten evidence," because investigators just don't think about it. It's delicate, can't be detected well by humans, and isn't visible. However, it can be powerful, and in some cases might be the only available evidence. Scent can indicate how people moved around at a scene and where they went; it also marks one person as different from all others. Whenever someone's at a crime scene, there's always a scent.

While it's evident from these pages that there are many scientific techniques and devices available for forensic use, we haven't covered all of them, and every day new discoveries are made. Between advanced computer programs, burgeoning databases, and sophisticated machines, there may never again be a "perfect crime." Where there's a clue, there's a way to interpret it, and as Grissom says, there is always a clue.

Glossary

AAFS American Academy of Forensic Sciences, the body that certifies criminalists.

Abductive thinking A type of reasoning used in devising explanations for guiding an investigation.

Abrasion Injury to the skin that removes the epithelial layer, due to friction.

Acid phosphatase An enzyme found in high concentrations in semen, indicates recent sexual intercourse.

Accelerant A flammable substance, like gasoline or kerosene, used to create and spread a fire.

Accident Cause of death or injury from an unforeseen and unavoidable incident.

Adipocere Soaplike preservative substance that forms on corpses in damp areas.

Admissible Evidence that can be admitted for consideration by the trier(s) of fact.

AFIS Automated Fingerprint Identification System, a database for storing and making rapid comparisons of fingerprints.

Aggravating circumstances Conditions that make a crime more serious, such as knowing the risk involved that may lead to injury or death.

Algor mortis Cooling of the body after death.

Alligatoring A burn pattern in wood that indicates a hot fire.

ALS Alternative light source, used for bringing out latent fingerprints, blood, fibers, and other trace materials that are difficult to see under regular light conditions.

Antemortem Prior to death.

Anthropometry The precursor to fingerprinting, devised by Alphonse Bertillon, to take a person's key body measurements for a record of uniqueness.

Antisocial personality disorder As defined in the *DSM-IV,* it emphasizes antisocial behavior over psychopathic personality traits.

Arson Intentionally setting a fire in a way that destroys property in a criminal manner.

ASCLD American Society of Crime Lab Directors, which offers guidelines on how labs should be managed.

Atomic absorption spectroscopy A method used to analyze gunshot residue. See *spectrometry*.

Autoerotic accident A death that occurs from the hypoxia produced by masturbatory rituals.

Autoradiograph The final product in a DNA probe, also called an autorad.

Autopsy The medical examination of a body to identify cause of death.

Ballistics The science of the motion and characteristics of projectiles.

Barefoot morphology The science of reading footprints, based on well formation, pace, size, and body weight.

Behavioral evidence Forensic evidence suggestive of certain behaviors, generally used for criminal profiling.

Beyond a reasonable doubt The degree of proof that will convince the trier of facts to a near-certainty that the allegations have been established. This is the highest of the three standards of proof in a courtroom, used in all criminal trial proceedings.

Blitz attack The delivery of overpowering force.

Blood group The four ways to categorize a person, based on the antibodies and antigens present in the red blood cells. The groups are A, B, AB, and O.

Blood spatter pattern analysis Examining how blood hits a surface to determine how the event took place to spill the blood, and to assess the size and type of wound made.

Bomb A device designed for the violent release of gases for the purpose of destruction.

Brainprint The technology of determining whether a brain registers memory of an experience, such as a crime.

Buccal swab Swabs taken from the mouth for collecting epithelial cells.

Bullet track The path of a projectile as it passes through a body.

Burden of proof The necessity of proving a fact in dispute, according to the standard of proof required in a specific proceeding.

Cadaveric spasm Sudden rigidity of a group of muscles immediately following death.

Caliber The internal diameter of a gun barrel, and the bullet that it fires.

Capital offense A crime for which the death penalty may be used.

Capital punishment A death sentence imposed for a given crime. The method used varies by state.

Case linkage Finding links among cases that had seemed unrelated, such as when two men, each of whom was found murdered in a bathtub, were viewed as victims of the same killer.

Cause of death An injury or disease that produces a condition in the body that brings about death.

Chain of custody The method used to keep track of who is handling a piece of evidence, and for what purpose.

Character disorder A personality disorder that manifests in habitual maladaptive patterns of behavior.

CODIS Combined DNA Index System, the FBI database of genetic material.

Cold case Unsolved case no longer under active investigation but still open.

Comparison microscope A series of prisms and lenses that allows two views to be compared together or combined.

Competency Sufficient ability to participate in proceedings, such as to stand trial, to waive rights, and to testify.

Confession Incriminating evidence offered by the defendant in the form of a written or verbal statement. Some confessions are false or pressured, which was a motivating factor in Miranda rights.

Contact wound Occurs when a firearm is placed against the surface while fired; it produces a ragged wound.

Contusion A soft tissue hemorrhage from blunt trauma.

Coroner In some jurisdictions, the person in charge of the death investigation; might be a medical examiner or an elected official.

Corpus delicti Essential body of facts that indicate that a crime has occurred.

Crime scene reconstruction Using evidence to determine the actions involved in a crime.

Criminalistics The science of analyzing physical evidence from a crime.

Criminal procedure Legal action in which a city, county, state, or federal district prosecutes an individual for breaking a law.

Criminal profiling The use of observation of the crime scene and pattern of crimes to determine investigatively relevant characteristics of the perpetrator; it guides police in narrowing the field of suspects and devising a strategy for questioning.

Criminology The study of criminal character and legal procedure.

Daubert **standard** A recent standard used in federal and many state courts for deciding the admissibility of scientific evidence, redefining the *Frye* Standard.

Dactyloscopy The technique of developing and identifying fingerprints.

Deductive thinking The type of reasoning in which a conclusion is derived strictly from the information at hand, as stated in the premises.

Density test A floating test to see if two pieces of glass are from the same source.

Dental stone The casting material often used for footprint and tire impressions.

Deposition The pretrial statements, given under oath, by any witnesses in a proceeding.

Diminished capacity A psychological defense indicative of an inability to appreciate the nature of the crime or to control one's actions. Not used in all states.

Disarticulation Separation of bone joints.

Discovery The process through which parties in dispute find out facts about the case.

Disorganized offender Person who commits a crime haphazardly or opportunistically, using weapons at the scene and often leaving clues.

DNA profile The blueprint of a person's physical identity, as determined by his or her genes.

Drugfire A computer program for matching cartridges to those used in other crimes.

Due process Guaranteed steps in a legal proceeding.

Electron microscope A microscope that uses electron emissions; there are several different types. See also *scanning electron microscope*.

Electrophoresis See *gel electrophoresis*.

Electrostatic detection apparatus A device used to read messages on indented paper, left by the impressions of the sheet above it.

Electrothermal atomizer A device that detects art forgeries by identifying recent substances used to paint them.

Entomology The study of insect life; in forensics, it concerns bugs found at a crime scene or on a corpse that are used for determining a postmortem interval.

Enzymes Proteins that initiate specific biochemical reactions.

Equivocal death analysis See *psychological autopsy*.

Equivocal evidence Evidence that supports more than one theory, which must be interpreted with the benefit of the doubt given to the suspect.

Event memory A type of memory in which a person can recall a specific event.

Evidence Documents, statements, and all items that are included in the legal proceedings for the jury's or judge's consideration in the question of guilt or innocence.

Expert witness A person with specialized knowledge about an area, or with a special skill that is germane to the proceedings, such as hair analysis, DNA analysis, or expertise in the study of mental illness. This person's role is to assist the fact finders in understanding complicated information.

Fact finder The person (judge) or persons (jury) who weigh the evidence in a trial to determine a verdict.

Felony A serious crime for which the punishment in federal law is generally severe, including capital punishment.

Flashover The point at which heated smoke, fed by oxygen, bursts into flame.

Floater A corspe found in water, surfacing because of gas from decomposition.

Forgery An attempt to replicate an original document and pass it off as authentic.

Frye **test** A test that governs the admissibility of scientific evidence, such that evidence entered into a case must be generally accepted by the relevant scientific community.

Gas chromatography A method used to break down compounds into their component parts.

Gel eletrophoresis A method for dividing DNA for further tests through exposure to an electrical charge.

Gene A segment of DNA that codes for the production of a specific protein.

Geographic profiling Using the geographical relationship among crime scenes to infer offender characteristics and place of residence.

Graphology The art of divining traits about a person from his or her handwriting.

Grifter A person who makes a living conning people out of their valuables.

Gunshot residue (GSR) The unburned powder that follows a fired bullet; it's found on clothing and skin after a shooting, which can provide valuable evidence for reconstruction of a crime.

Hemastix A presumptive blood testing device.

High-risk victim A person continually exposed to danger, such as a prostitute.

Homicide A death caused by another person.

Homicide Investigation Tracking System (HITS) A database in Washington state for linking violent crimes through signature analysis.

Hypoxia Decrease in oxygen to the brain.

Ident The name used to refer to the Identification team, which generally does fingerprinting.

Identification memory The type of memory used to pick something out, as in a lineup.

Impression evidence Anything that leaves an impression at a crime scene that links someone to the crime; tire tracks, footprints, fingerprints, tool marks, and bite marks.

Indictment Accusation issued by a grand jury that charges an individual with criminal misconduct.

Inductive thinking A type of reasoning based on probability.

Insanity A legal term for a mental disease or defect that, if present at the time of a crime, absolves the person of responsibility.

Interrogation The art of getting suspects to talk, possibly to confess.

Intuition The flash of inspiration that can help shape an investigation.

Intent Mental state ranging from purpose to awareness of consequences.

Iodine fumes A technique for bringing up latent fingerprints.

Ion detector A device that detects the presence of accelerants in the air via an electric charge.

Jurisdiction The authority to exert power over individuals or legal matters within a defined geographic area.

Kastle-Meyer test A presumptive blood test, used to determine if blood is present.

K-9 A special evidence response team that uses dogs to trail scents, used in cases of arson, missing persons, corpses, drugs, chemicals, and others.

Laceration Splitting or tearing of skin from blunt-force trauma.

Latent fingerprints Prints left on something that aren't visible, but can be made visible with certain techniques.

Leucomalachite green A presumptive blood test, testing for the presence of blood that isn't visible.

Ligature A tie or binding, often used in bondage or to strangle someone.

Livor mortis Discoloration of the body after death, when the red blood cells separate and settle to the lowest point of gravity. Also called lividity.

Livescan Fingerprint technology that allows the fingertips to be scanned rather than rolled in ink.

Locard's exchange principle The theory that anyone entering a crime scene leaves or takes something, or both.

LCN Low copy number, a new technique for getting a DNA profile from a small amount of tissue evidence or a fingerprint.

Luminol A chemical reagent that makes invisible blood fluoresce in darkness.

Malingering Deliberate simulation of a mental illness to obtain personal gain.

Mass killer Someone who kills a lot of people at the same time.

Mass spectrometry A way to identify elements of a compound, by bombarding it with electrons; this device can identify constituent parts too small for the gas chromatograph to detect.

Medical examiner In some jurisdictions, the person who runs a death investigation; in others, the person who does autopsies for a death investigation.

Miranda warning The required statement that a police officer gives to a suspect upon arrest, informing that person of the right to remain silent (not to self-incriminate) and to have legal representation before questioning.

Misdemeanor A lesser crime than a felony, generally punished by a fine or a short sentence in jail.

Missing person Someone gone longer than twenty-four hours, or whose disappearance is suspicious, as in the case of a child or mentally incompetent person.

Mitochondrial DNA Inherited from the mother, it's found in the cell's cytoplasm rather than in the nucleus.

Mitigating circumstances Factors such as age, motivation, duress, or unstable home life that can diminish the degree of guilt in a criminal offense.

Modus Operandi (MO) An offender's method of carrying out the offense.

Multiple personality disorder (MPD) Now called dissociative identity disorder, this is a psychological condition in which people seem to have two or more distinct personas in the same body.

National Center for the Analysis of Violent Crime (NCAVC) A subdivision of the FBI's Behavioral Science Unit, which also runs the ViCAP and profiling programs.

Neutron activation analysis A technique used on trace evidence that bombards the substance with neutrons in a nuclear reactor.

Odontogram The file containing all the dental information for a person.

Odontologist The mouth expert who can identify bite mark impressions and match dental records to corpses.

Organized Offender Person committing a crime in a planned, premeditated manner, leaving few or no clues.

Palynology The study of pollen.

Pattern evidence Evidence that can be read from a specific type of pattern, such as the impression of a shoe or the forcible contact between two surfaces; includes such things as shattered glass fractures and blood spatter patterns.

Perimortem The time interval just before death.

Petechial hemorrhage Broken blood vessels in the eyes of a corpse that indicate asphyxiation, possibly by strangulation or smothering.

Phenolphthalein A substance used in presumptive blood tests.

Polygraph A machine used to determine through changes in physiological functions whether a person is lying.

Polymerase chain reaction (PCR) The method used to replicate small amounts of DNA so it can be further tested.

Postmortem After death.

Postmortem interval (PMI) The time since death, as determined by several factors.

Precipitin test The test that determines whether blood is animal or human.

Preliminary hearing A hearing held before a judge to decide whether there is sufficient evidence to go to trial.

Probe A fragment of DNA that carries the complementary code for a base sequence to help establish identity.

Prosecutor The attorney who represents the government in a criminal proceeding.

Psychological autopsy Methods used to determine state of mind of a person when a suicide is questionable.

Psychological stress evaluator A device that measures stress levels in a recorded voice.

Psychopathy Personality disorder defined by long-term antisocial behavior by a person who feels no guilt or remorse and is not inclined to stop.

Psychosis A major mental disorder in which a person's ability to think, respond, communicate, recall, and interpret reality is impaired. Psychotics show inappropriate mood, poor impulse control, and delusions. Often confused with insanity, which is a legal term, and psychopathy, which is a character disorder.

Questioned documents Any piece of writing that needs analysis for origination, authorship, or authentication.

Rape kit A collection of instruments and evidence analysis items used to process the victim of a rape; if a suspect is found, some of the items are used on him.

Red Creeper Grissom's special adhesion powder used for dusting for fingerprints.

Refractive index A ratio measurement found with a refractometer with liquid or glass to help determine its source.

Restriction fragment length polymorphisms (RFLP) The original method for getting a DNA profile, which splits the molecule and cuts it into pieces.

Rifled weapons Guns with "lands" and grooves cut into the barrels for balance and range when firing a bullet; includes rifles and handguns.

Rigor mortis The stiffening of the body after death.

Scanning electron microscope Designed to overcome the problem of magnifying substances smaller than light wavelengths; this device reflects electrons off the surface of a tiny particle, magnifying it 150,000 times.

Scent pad Used to store a scent for working with trailing dogs.

Serial crimes Any type of crime occurring in a pattern that indicates a single offender.

Serial killer Someone who kills three or more people and takes a cooling-off period in between.

Serology The analysis of body fluids like blood, semen, and saliva.

Short tandem repeats (STR) A method for getting a DNA profile after replicating it by means of PCR (polymerase chain reaction).

Signature analysis The method used to "read" crime scenes that indicate a serial offender who leaves a personal mark.

Signature crime A crime scene that bears a personality stamp of an offender, characteristic of a need for ritual or theme. These acts are not necessary to complete the offense.

Sound spectrograph The device used to make a voiceprint.

Spalling The cracking of concrete in a fire that indicates how hot it burned.

Spectrometry The detection of various wavelengths of light, which can be done with different pieces of spectrographic equipment. Some measure wavelengths emitted, some measure wavelengths absorbed.

Spree killer Someone who murders people in a frenzied succession with no cooling-off period in between.

Staging a crime scene Making a crime scene look like something other than what it is, to deflect the investigation.

Statement analysis An open-ended technique for getting a witness or suspect to describe their version of an event, in which the interrogator looks for signs of deception.

Stippling Burn marks and tiny hemorrhages left by the gunpowder that follows a bullet; also called tattooing.

Striation The linear marking on something that can be compared with another piece for a match.

Subpoena A command to appear at a certain time and place to give testimony on a certain matter.

Super Glue fuming A technique used to bring out latent fingerprints in a lab from surfaces that don't respond well to powders; its fumes adhere to the print when heated and make the print visible.

Tape lift An adhesive used to pick up trace evidence at a crime scene.

Testimonial evidence What an eyewitness says about a crime.

Thin-layer chromatography A method for separating out elements from compounds.

Trace evidence The smallest pieces of evidence at a scene, including fiber, hair, grass fragments, seeds, dust, and soil.

Trajectory The path of a fired projectile.

Trophy A personal item taken from a victim and kept by the offender as a memory aid to relive the crime, also called a souvenir.

Toxicology The section of the lab that tests tissues or products for contamination by drugs, poisons, and alcohol.

Variable number of tandem repeats (VNTRs) Polymorphic DNA regions that repeat themselves and are unique to individuals.

Verdict The decision of a judge or jury after hearing and considering the evidence.

ViCAP Violent Criminal Apprehension Program, the FBI's nationwide data information center, designed for collecting, sorting, and analyzing information about crimes.

Victimology A study of victim information to find clues about the offender's opportunity and selection process.

Voiceprint The pictorial graph made electronically of the amplitude and vibrations of the human voice.

Wick effect When a person's body fat feeds a smoldering flame and burns the person to ash without burning items in the immediate area.

References

Alter, Jonathan, "The Death Penalty on Trial," *Newsweek*, June 12, 2000.

"A Report to the American People," FBI Library, www.fbi.gov/library/
5-year/1993–98.

Baden, Michael, with Judith A. Hennessee. *Unnatural Death: Confessions
of a Medical Examiner.* New York: Ivy Books, 1989.

Berlow, Alan. "The Wrong Man," *The Atlantic Monthly*, November, 1999.

Bowers, C. Michael and Raymond Johansen, "Forensic Dentistry: An Overview of Bite Marks," in *Human and Animal Bitemark Management.*
Forensic Mailing Services, 2000.

Brenner, John C. *Forensic Science Glossary.* Boca Raton, FL: CRC Press,
1999.

Castleman, Deke. *Las Vegas.* Oakland, CA: Compass American Guides,
1999.

Clark, Wesley. "Deception Detection," *Connecticut Trooper Magazine*,
Fall, 1998.

Cleckley, Hervey. *The Mask of Sanity* (rev. ed.). St. Louis, MO: C. V.
Mosby. (1941), 1982.

"Convicted by Justice, Exonerated by Science," The National Institute of
Justice Report, 1996.

Crozier, Stacy, "Conference Helps Dentists Make Mark in Forensics," *ADA News Daily*, April 19, 1999.

Dix, Jay, and Robert Calaluce. *Guide to Forensic Pathology*. Boca Raton, FL: CRC, 1999.

Douglas, John, Ann W. Burgess, Allen G. Burgess, and Robert K. Ressler. *Crime Classification Manual*. San Francisco, CA: Jossey-Bass, 1992.

Douglas, John, and Mark Olshaker. *Mindhunter: Inside the FBI's Elite Serial Crime Unit*. New York: Scribner, 1995.

———. *The Cases That Haunt Us*. New York: Scribner, 2000.

Earley, Pete. *Super Casino*. New York: Bantam, 2000.

Ekman, Paul. *Telling Lies: Clues to Deceit in the Marketplace, Politics, and Marriage*. New York: Norton, 1992.

Evans, Colin. *The Casebook of Forensic Detection*. New York: John Wiley, 1996.

Everitt, David. *Human Monsters*. Chicago: Contemporary Books, 1993.

Fisher, Barry. *Techniques of Crime Scene Investigation*, sixth edition. Boca Raton, FL: CRC Press, 2000.

Fisher, David. *Hard Evidence: How Detectives Inside the FBI's Sci-Crime Lab Have Helped Solve America's Toughest Cases*. New York: Simon & Schuster, 1995.

Ford, Charles V. *Lies, Lies, Lies: The Psychology of Deceit*. Washington, DC: American Psychiatric Press, 1996.

Fridell, Ron. *Solving Crimes: Pioneers of Forensic Science*. New York: Grolier, 2000.

Frye v. U.S. 293 F. 1013, 34 A.L.R. 145 (DC Circuit 1923).

Gaddis, Vincent. *Mysterious Fires and Lights*. New York: Dell, 1967.

Geberth, Vernon J. *Practical Homicide Investigation*, third ed. Boca Raton, FL: CRC Press, 1996.

Goff, M. Lee. *A Fly for the Prosecution: How Insect Evidence Helps Solve Crimes*. Cambridge: Harvard University Press, 2000.

Grover Maurice Godwin, *Hunting Serial Predators*. Boca Raton, FL: CRC Press, 2000.

Hare, Robert. *Without Conscience*. New York: Pocket Books, 1993.

Hazelwood, Robert R. and Ann W. Burgess, eds. *Practical Aspects of Rape Investigation*, third edition. Boca Raton, FL: CRC Press, 2001.

Holmes, Ronald, and D. Kim Rossmo, "Geography, Profiling, and Predatory Criminals," in R. Holmes & S. Holmes, *Profiling Violent Crimes*. Thousand Oaks, CA: Sage, 1996.

Honts, C. R., D. C. Raskin, and J. C. Kircher, "Mental and Physical Countermeasures Reduce the Accuracy of Polygraphs," *Journal of Applied Psychology*, 79: pp. 252–259, 1994.

Houde, John. *Crime Lab: A Guide for Nonscientists*. Ventura, CA: Calico Press, 1999.

Inman, Keith, and Norah Rudin. *An Introduction to Forensic DNA Analysis*. Boca Raton, FL: CRC Press, 1997.

Innes, Brian. *Bodies of Evidence*. Pleasantville, NY: Reader's Digest Press, 2000.

Kapardis, Andreas. *Psychology and Law*. Cambridge, UK: Cambridge University Press, 1997.

Keppel, Robert D. *Signature Killers*. New York: Pocket Books, 1997.

———"Investigation of the Serial Offender: Linking Cases Through *Modus Operandi* and Signature," in *Serial Offenders: Current Thoughts, Recent Findings*, edited by Louis B. Schlesinger. Boca Raton, FL: CRC Press, 2000.

Kersta, Lawrence G. "Voiceprint Identification," *Nature Magazine*, Dec. 29, 1962.

Kurland, Michael. *How to Solve a Murder: The Forensic Handbook*. New York: Macmillan, 1995.

Lee, Henry C. and Howard A. Harris. *Physical Evidence in Forensic Science*. Tucson: Lawyers & Judges Publishing Company, 2000.

Loftus Elizabeth. *Eyewitness Testimony*, Cambridge: Harvard University Press, (1979) 1996.

MacDonell, Herbert L. *Bloodstain Patterns*. Corning, NY: Laboratory of Forensic Science, 1993.

Manhein, Mary H. *The Bone Lady*. New York: Penguin, 1999.

McDermott, M. and Tom Owen. "Voice Identification," on www. aftiinc.com (Applied Forensic Technologies Intl., Inc.), 2000.

McGinnis, Joe. *Fatal Vision*. New York: New American Library, 1984.

Michaud, Stephen G. and Roy Hazelwood, *The Evil That Men Do*. New York: St. Martin's Press, 1998.

———. *Dark Dreams*. New York: St. Martin's Press, 2001.

Miller, Hugh. *Proclaimed in Blood: True Crimes Solved by Forensic Scientists*. London: Headline, 1995.

Miller, Hugh: *What the Corpse Revealed: Murder and the Science of Forensic Detection*. New York: St. Martin's Press, 1998.

Newton, Michael. *The Encyclopedia of Serial Killers*. New York: Checkmark Books, 2000.

Nickell, Joe and John Fischer. *Crime Science: Methods of Forensic Detection*. Lexington, KY: The University Press of Kentucky, 1999.

Nordby, Jon. *Dead Reckoning: The Art of Forensic Detection*. Boca Raton, FL: CRC Press, 2000.

Owen, David. *Hidden Evidence: Forty True Crimes and How Forensic Science Helped Solve Them*. Buffalo: Firefly Books, 2000.

Pederson, Daniel. "Down on the Body Farm," *Newsweek*, October 23, 2000.

Randall, Brad. *Death Investigation: The Basics*. Tucson: Galen Press, 1997.

Rhine, Stanley. *Bone Voyage: A Journey in Forensic Anthropology*. Albuquerque: University of New Mexico Press, 1998.

Rossmo, D. K. "Geographic Profiling," in *Offender Profiling: Theory, Practice and Research*, edited by Janet L. Jackson and Debra Bekerian. New York: Wiley, 1999.

Rudin, Norah. "DNA Untwisted," *San Francisco Daily Journal*, April 20, 1995.

Saferstein, Richard. *Criminalistics: An Introduction to Forensic Science*, seventh edition. Englewood Cliffs: Prentice Hall, 2000.

Scheck, Barry, Peter Neufeld, and Jim Dwyer. *Actual Innocence*. New York: Random House, 2000.

Schiller, Lawrence. *American Tragedy: The Uncensored Story of What Happened Behind Closed Doors*. New York: Avon, 1996.

Staggs, Steven. *Crime Scene and Evidence Photographer's Guide*. Temecula, CA: Staggs Publishing, 1997.

Sullivan, Tim, and Peter T. Maiken. *Killer Clown: The John Wayne Gacy Murders*. New York: Pinnacle, 1983.

Taylor, Karen T. *Forensic Art and Illustration*. Boca Raton, FL: CRC Press, 2000.

Thomas, Steve. *JonBenet: Inside the Ramsey Murder Investigation*. New York: St. Martin's Press, 2000.

Turvey, Brent. *Criminal Profiling*. San Diego: Academic Press, 1999.

Venezia, Todd. "FBI debunks Spontaneous Human Combustion," APBNews, August 1, 2000.

Wilson, Keith D. *Cause of Death*. Cincinnati: Writer's Digest Press, 1992.

Wingate, Anne. *Crime Scene Investigation*. Cincinnati: Writer's Digest Press, 1992.

Wrightsman, Lawrence S., Michael Nietzel, and William Fortune. *Psychology and the Legal System*, third ed., Pacific Grove, CA: Brooks Cole Publishing, 1994.

Index

About the Author

Dr. Katherine Ramsland has a master's degree in forensic psychology from the John Jay College of Criminal Justice. She has published fifteen books, including biographies of Anne Rice and Dean Koontz. Ramsland spent a year as a research assistant to former FBI profiler John Douglas, and she currently teaches forensic psychology at DeSales University and writes for Court TV's Crime Library.